TAMING GAMING

TAMING GAMING

Guide your child to healthy video game habits

ANDY ROBERTSON

unbound

First published in 2021

Unbound

Level 1, Devonshire House, One Mayfair Place, London W1J 8AJ

www.unbound.com

All rights reserved

Text design by PDQ Digital Media Solutions LTD

A CIP record for this book is available from the British Library

ISBN 978-1-78352-892-9 (hardback)
ISBN 978-1-78352-893-6 (ebook)

Printed in Slovenia by DZS

1 3 5 7 9 8 6 4 2

Dedicated to Jo, Ellen, Thom and Ollie

CONTENTS

Foreword   ix

Author's Note   xiii

1. Why I Wrote This Book   1

2. Games Need Parenting, Not Policing   12

3. The Benefits of Video Games   33

4. The Worries Video Games Cause   47

5. How to Love a Child Who Loves Video Games   73

6. How to Love a Child Who Loves Video Games Too Much   90

7. Learning to Love Video Games   103

8. What the (Other) Experts Say   118

9. Getting Ready for Video Games   139

10. Gaming Recipes   171

Image Credits   353

A Note on the Author   355

Supporters   357

FOREWORD

I recently overheard a lively conversation about playing the online video game *Diablo*: Which characters did you choose? What level have you reached? Did your chosen tactics work out? You might think I was listening to a couple of children but in fact it was my 60-something partner and our 30-something son. They have been having this conversation now for a couple of decades, and it is deeply embedded in their relationship.

Parent–child conversations are often unequal in knowledge and power, but talking about video games allows a way of relating to each other that is egalitarian as well as committed, lively and thoughtful. Tactics can be developed collaboratively, experiences become mutual and a part of children's lives that is often closed to parents can instead be recognised and valued.

Insights such as these underpin *Taming Gaming*. The book is sympathetic to parents' struggles and worries, informed about the gaming world and strongly committed to understanding and benefiting children's lives. While it was written before COVID-19, present circumstances make the book more relevant than ever. Children's screen time has surged because their reliance on all things digital is no longer a matter of choice but one of necessity. Guidance for parents on enabling the benefits and avoiding the harms is, in consequence, more vital than ever.

Fifteen years of writing about video games, listening to children and working with families as they play games and argue about them have given Andy Robertson a wealth of experience and expertise to pour into this book. He shows convincingly how video games, like other kinds of games children play, offer fun – first and foremost – as well as opportunities to be creative, to learn, to share and collaborate with others, to face challenges, solve problems and extend their imagination and understanding, to make mistakes and recover themselves, gaining resilience, digital expertise and confidence. Video games are not only an online experience but also contribute offline – to sibling relations, relations among friends and, if you let them, a positive relationship between parent and child.

I wish I had known all this when my son was young. Echoing the book's introduction, I too remember wanting to shut the video games in a locked cupboard, even once in anger hiding the extension cord into which the computer and, it seemed, my son, were constantly plugged. I suspect many parents need encouragement to give up on the dominant (and dominating) language of controlling – even policing – the technology and, by implication, our children too.

Taming Gaming invites us instead to think in terms of actively engaging with video games in ways that are informed by evidence, balanced according to practical circumstances, and respectful of family values and children's interests. The approach is optimistic, but not naively so. The purpose is to guide parents and children living in a now-inescapably digital world, while not becoming overwhelmed by digital challenges, or forgetting about the rest of life.

Of course, there are the downsides: excessive video game time, violent and other problematic content, bullying and hostile peer exchanges, commercial exploitation and more. *Taming Gaming* attends to these with care, and points to a wealth of resources to help parents navigate the landscape of video games so as to find what is best and avoid the difficulties. While I believe it is vital for regulators and the industry to take effective action to ensure that children are both empowered and safe online, I agree with Andy

Robertson's premise that parents are a crucial influence on their children's lives, including the digital. So, a book that can inspire parents to join in the games themselves, and to develop their own gaming literacy, is very welcome.

It's time to stop panicking about technology and start prioritising what we can do with it. So much of the creative and collaborative potential of technology is under-used: we must imagine better for our children, recognising their diversity and their potential, and I love how this book guides parents step by step in doing just this, with practical tips and gaming suggestions.

Thankfully, there's no single vision of gameplay and no idealised model of family life on offer in this book, nor any 'right answer' thinking. Instead, *Taming Gaming* works to establish a new norm: that we can maximise the opportunities and minimise the risks by diversifying our understanding of video games and then making thoughtful judgements about the available options, instead of everyone opting for the same few games that everyone else plays. Families are hugely different in their interests, values and circumstances, and this can become a strength if we let it.

Many parents will like to try out the plethora of gaming recipe' suggestions in this book. And for those who want to follow up on the wealth of research and evidence that *Taming Gaming* draws upon, without ever getting bogged down in detail, the footnotes are there. I particularly appreciate the light-touch yet nuanced treatment of so-called 'gaming addiction', since this remains highly controversial to both researchers and clinical practitioners. Contrary to popular media headlines, problems of excessive use are likely to apply only to a tiny minority of children. But as I found in my own research with families, terminology contested among experts – such as addiction or screen time – are finding their way into our everyday discourse, becoming a problem in their own right by provoking family conflict, adding to parental guilt and worrying children too.

I agree with *Taming Gaming*'s recommendations to parents: learn more, join in and replace inchoate anxieties with informed choices. We don't know what the future holds. Digitally mediated outcomes for children remain unknown and may prove riskier than more traditional routes to learning and sociability. Evidence for benefits and harms continues to accumulate and must be sifted, weighed and critically discussed. In the meantime, parents have to parent. Doing so with this book in hand can only be empowering, so dive in, have fun and keep your eyes not on the 'screen time' clock but on what's good for your child.

Sonia Livingstone OBE, LSE professor and author of
Parenting for a Digital Future

AUTHOR'S NOTE

This book is the result of 15 years writing about video games for families online, in newspapers and magazines, and broadcast appearances. As with that work, it reflects my desire to offer parents practical advice and insight, rather than to critique or defend video games.

It exists in this wonderful form thanks to the hundreds of parents, carers and guardians who enthusiastically supported it, along with a range of video game regulators, academics, developers and platform-holders, not-for-profit organisations and many schools. Through their kind pre-orders, this broad coalition enabled me to spend the time I needed to gather, sift and present this crucial information that parents need. The views expressed here are my own and do not represent any particular supporter.

The conversation about video games and children has accelerated during the coronavirus pandemic. During this period I've been called on to help parents and carers keep video games healthy, with children spending more hours playing. Along with the advice you will read in this book, I created a database of video games as a quick reference for busy parents during this period. To access this database, podcasts, videos and other resources, please visit www.taminggaming.com

1. WHY I WROTE THIS BOOK

Video games promised to transport my children to magical lands, to seed their imaginations, inspire their creativity, let them compete on a world stage and tell them stories full of hope and laughter. The reality, however, was not like this. There were arguments about when to stop, family rooms full of plastic peripherals and constant pestering for the next new game before they'd done enough washing up to earn the last one.

I wanted to close the door and leave them to it. But that would admit that the games had won. I wanted to lock them in a high cupboard – the games, I mean, not the children. Besides, I was a games journalist, damn it!

For reasons I can't fully remember, I didn't get rid of the games and I didn't leave them to it. It was my job to write about these things; that was certainly part of it. I was suspicious that the technology would take over, but I didn't want to miss out on this part of their playtime, even if their games seemed juvenile, brash and boring.

A decade later, I'm glad I didn't back away. Time spent playing games with them has been as important as eating together, going for woodland walks, making dens in the garden and trips to the cinema and the beach. They didn't need my help to play the games – quite the reverse in fact – but they did need me to model a healthy relationship with them. Not just stopping well, prioritising face-to-face communication or finding a wide range of experiences to enjoy but integrating video games with the rest of our family life.

Children are expert players of video games. Digital interactive spaces are among their native habitats. They swipe to unlock before they can write, and tap, drag and scroll before they can read. They are highly literate in the language of interaction. They are instinctively drawn to video games as experiences made for them; the medium of their time.

But beyond this veneer of confidence, they are as ill-equipped to cope with these commercial, endless and powerfully connected experiences on their own as they are to handle supermarket shopping, being ill, watching adverts for toys, not eating too many sweets, football crowds, crossing roads safely, failing at tests, or the death of a grandparent.

As with these other things, children need parents and carers to show them how to navigate video games. They need advice on how to cope with losing. They need guidance on how to walk away before they throw the controller. They need grown-ups to anchor these important experiences as one part of their wider life. They need parents to integrate digital play with the real world rather than push it away as a separate, lesser alternative. They need adults to suggest more interesting or ambitious games they haven't heard of.

My children haven't come to me and asked for any of this. They bleat about games: 'Just one more go', 'It's not fair', 'There's nothing else to do', 'He's cheating', 'I've wasted my day' and 'Why can't I? Everyone else is playing it.' What they're actually asking is how to keep video games enjoyable. How to avoid getting controlled by them. How to relate their virtual worlds to the rest of life. Or maybe, even, how to avoid their gaming time increasing despite negative consequences.

VIDEO GAME ROADMAP

Video games can be played via a wide variety of technology, collectively called gaming hardware. Some are designed just to play games, while others are existing devices in the home, such as a computer, tablet or smartphone.

Game consoles, often referred to as 'consoles' or as 'platforms' on which games are played, comprise a box that plugs into your television with bespoke controllers, usually called 'gamepads'. Portable gaming devices, collectively called 'handhelds', have integral screens and controls, and run on batteries. New consoles and handhelds are released every five years or so, with each generation offering enhanced graphics, sound and controls.

Gaming computers are like any computer but with more expensive and powerful graphics cards to produce the fast-moving and highly detailed game visuals. Unlike consoles, these computers can be upgraded incrementally by installing newer parts over a number of years. Gaming computers offer the widest range of games, including ones from smaller, independent developers, although the most popular ones also appear on consoles within a year or two.

Most modern smartphones and tablet devices are also powerful enough to play complex games. These are usually called 'mobile games'. Although there is some overlap with the games on consoles and handheld devices, and you can purchase gamepads for them, the best mobile games are designed to make use of the touchscreen and tilt controls.

Game consoles have been around since the 1980s, when the Nintendo Entertainment System (NES) achieved mainstream success. In the early 1990s, this was followed by the Super NES and competition from Sega's Mega Drive and from the Amiga and Atari ST gaming computers. Around the same time, portable systems hit the market, with Nintendo's Game Boy, Sega's Game Gear and Atari's Lynx systems.

By the mid-1990s the next generation of consoles had arrived: the Nintendo 64 and Sony PlayStation. By the early 2000s the PlayStation 2 and Nintendo GameCube were launched and met with competition from Microsoft's new Xbox console. The Game Boy Advance launched and established Nintendo's portable gaming success.

In the mid-noughties Microsoft's Xbox 360 arrived, along with the PlayStation 3. This was also when Nintendo took consoles in a new direction with the Wii and its motion controller. This period also saw more powerful handheld systems, like the Nintendo DS and PlayStation Portable.

The second decade of the 2000s has brought us the Nintendo Wii U, PlayStation 4 and Xbox One. Nintendo released its 3DS portable and Sony launched its PlayStation Vita. Most recently, Sony and Microsoft offered enhanced versions of the PlayStation 4 (Pro) and Xbox One (X), respectively. Nintendo released the Switch, which could function as both a home console and portable device, and the cheaper Switch Lite that was a purely handheld version.

2020 has brought new generations of these consoles with the PlayStation 5 and Xbox Series X and Series S systems expanding the ways we play games. Along with new versions of the Nintendo Switch, they compete with gaming subscription services such as Apple Arcade and Google Play Pass on Android. Game streaming services will increase with Google's Stadia, PlayStation Now and xCloud from Xbox, which enable console-quality games to be played on low-cost and less-powerful hardware by streaming the visuals via an internet connection.

Without support and guidance, gaming can become worrying territory for parents. In the extreme, we see what the World Health Organization (WHO) designates as 'gaming disorder'. This recent addition to its disease classification only applies to a tiny proportion of children unable to stop gaming gluttony even when faced with severe negative consequences, but it's still a concerning cliff edge when your child won't stop for tea time.

Despite school-gate hand-wringing over our kids' addiction to the latest game, our tone is telling. We don't mean this in the way described by WHO. As history shows us, with any new media – comics, radio, television and even the telephone – we are predisposed to panicking that new technology will create obsessive, delinquent or violent behaviour.

By exploring the reality of the issues and science behind scary headlines – as we'll do in the following pages – I realised that the solution isn't complicated or expensive but just traditional parenting. Rather than helicoptering in when things go wrong, or snowploughing away any challenges, we need to be present and guide our children's gaming with both involvement and boundaries, as we do in the rest of their childhood. Children who play games need parenting rather than policing.

But how? Where do you start? Video games seem different and alien compared to the traditional rites of childhood: learning to read, eating vegetables, going to school, playground hierarchy, trips to the zoo and days out to the beach.

Here's the good news. The answer isn't easy, but it is simple: to raise grounded children who love playing video games, you need to play video games yourself. Sounds crazy, doesn't it? Who does that? Well, with some help and guidance, *you* can.

If you don't play games and don't want to, if you find your child's gaming worrying or frustrating, if you'd rather leave your children to it or just throw all the games away, then this book is for you. Without jargon or unrealistic suggestions, I'll explain what experts say really happens when your child plays a video game and offer simple advice for you to care for them in this crucial area of their lives. It's a positive picture of what games are, but one that also grasps the dangers we worry about: addiction, gambling, violence, strangers and unexpected costs.

The advice includes powerful tools to get breathing space from gaming when things have got out of hand and how to seek professional assistance in extreme cases, but it culminates with lots of ways to guide and engage with your child's gaming as a healthy part of family life.

The choice of recommended games in the 'Gaming Recipes' section at the back of this book has involved years of research and testing. These form a treasure trove of amazing games you'll probably not have heard of but will want to share with your child. It's the first step in a move from worrying about screen time to guiding what is happening on the screen.

As crazy as it sounds, I've selected some of these games to specifically pique your interest in the hope that you will play them yourself. This first-hand experience of video games is essential, in the same way that no amount of expert advice can replace the flavour, texture, smell and taste of wine in the mouth.

This book provides the guidance I wish I'd had when embarking on this journey with my children. I figured it out the hard way, through trial and error, trawling the internet, talking to developers, reading books and academic papers on the subject, and interviewing game-rating agencies.

I've tried all sorts of approaches with my kids. Some have worked well, and some have been utter failures. It took a long time and led me down endless rabbit holes, but I'm glad I did it because now I can make it easier for you – well, to a degree. As with all aspects of parenting, finding the right approach involves work. I'm afraid I can't tell you how much screen time is too much, or the age children can play specific video games. Anyone who says they can is usually commercially motivated, offering short-term advice that may relieve parents but let children down.

Other experts may point towards the video game industry's need to be more responsible and transparent or the need for legislation and regulation to ensure this. While it is important that the games industry continues to improve its parental controls and business transparency, and to be vigilant about helping vulnerable players, the real requirement for ensuring healthy consumption isn't more protective laws but parents' own gaming literacy. A deep, first-hand understanding of video games will unlock your powerful presence in this area of your child's life. What you need are resources that enable you to move beyond limits and bans to understand and experience the real benefits and pitfalls of games.

Gaming literacy in the family can powerfully move children from being enraptured by blockbuster video games and back under the guidance of parents and carers. This is what will curb potential runaway game obsessions and make gaming more like its media stablemates, films and books.

Best of all, by developing this literacy you get to share the fun with your child as you play together. You can enjoy games with them, guiding their passion and discovering a deeply useful context in which to prepare them to thrive in their digital future.

WHO PLAYS VIDEO GAMES

With a book aimed at parents of children who love playing video games, it's easy to forget that people of all ages regularly enjoy playing. The Entertainment Software Association (ESA) data for 2018 showed that 65 per cent of Americans played games, with 46 per cent of these players being female. The average age for US gamers is 34 for women and 32 for men. The picture is similar in the UK: figures from games analysts Newzoo show that in 2018 40 per cent of men and 32 per cent of women played video games.

The breadth of video games caters for this wide demographic, but contrary to the general perception, only a small percentage of them are too violent for children. Of the 4,034 physical and downloadable console games assigned ratings in the USA by the Entertainment Software Rating Board (ESRB) in 2019:

- 45 per cent were rated EVERYONE
- 14 per cent were rated EVERYONE 10+
- 28 per cent were rated TEEN
- 13 per cent were rated MATURE 17+

Numbers are similar for Europe, where data from Pan European Game Information (PEGI) showed that of the 1,755 games rated in 2019:

- 26 per cent were rated PEGI 3
- 21 per cent were rated PEGI 7
- 23 per cent were rated PEGI 12
- 19 per cent were rated PEGI 16
- 12 per cent were rated PEGI 18

If all this isn't news to you, then skip on to the Gaming Recipes at the back of the book for hundreds of new games to play with your children. If you're less convinced, or even a little suspicious, the following chapters will expand on this perspective. They cover ideas I've tried with hundreds of families. Mums who didn't want video games taking over. Dads concerned about the effect of watching violence. Carers worried about a potential addiction. It's been a privilege to help equip them to do what they do best in this area of childhood: to parent and care for children.

Some cases stand out. There's the mother who was worried about losing her son, Harry, to video games. After talking, I suggested she try playing one of the games in the back of this book, *That Dragon, Cancer*. The next morning I woke up to this email:

> *I played it last night. Hadn't realised how long it would be so had to pause it as it was getting on for 1 a.m.! What a very unfamiliar feeling to be playing a video game into the night! Beautiful animation and graphics. I loved the music and of course, the story – very poignant.*
>
> *It's opened up all kinds of possibilities in my mind with Harry, which feels good. I slipped it into the conversation this morning and his whole demeanour shifted. I really have felt like he was disappearing in front of me with the video game issue as the driver, but I absolutely feel that this is the way to go.*

Stories like this are why I wrote this book: to empower parents and carers with video game literacy and the confidence to guide their children in this new, inevitable and normal part of childhood.

2. GAMES NEED PARENTING, NOT POLICING

'If you're worried about video games' effects on children, why not just keep them out of the house?' . . . 'You wouldn't leave your child with a bottle of vodka in their room, so why a video game?' . . . 'It's simple, read the age ratings and just say no!' . . . 'Just limit them to an hour a day if they've done their homework and chores.' . . . 'Say no to the brats.' . . . 'Don't let games rewire your child's brain.'

I've heard this advice in many contexts: waiting at the school gate; from the ITV *Good Morning Britain* couch; at dinner parties; in radio interviews; on Facebook support groups. Strong parents of younger children see games as something to control, like you would an addictive substance. Worried parents of teenagers bemoan not instigating stronger screen discipline in younger years.

These kinds of answers sound good: taking back control; limiting screen time; monitoring behaviour against bad habits; not welcoming a technological monster into the home. But the short-term respite fails to help parents develop a sustainable strategy. More importantly, it fails to help children develop a healthy relationship with the digital world. It is advice and thinking that stem from a misunderstanding of what video games are, and the role they play in a child's life. A combination of worrying headlines about extreme gaming and intentionally addictive design along with books suggesting that games permanently change children's brains make it seem obvious that we must guard against these experiences.

It's a pattern we see each time a new form of mass entertainment is created, particularly one embraced primarily by children. Rather than being a normal, somewhat inevitable facet of childhood, video games are seen as a special case compared to other media. It's assumed that we need special measures to resolve parents' impotence in the face of such a powerful force. They become a problem to solve rather than a pastime needing parental guidance.

Harold Schechter, a professor of literature at Queens College in New York City, highlights the phenomenon of this response to new media in his book *Savage Pastimes*.* 'Very quickly, high-minded reformers begin to denounce [the new medium] as a sign of social decay . . . a corrupter of the young'. Tellingly, Schechter highlights that the panic stops not when the medium has been brought under control in some way, but when newer, more exciting technology means the 'onetime media menace comes to be looked at nostalgically as a harmless, old-fashioned form of play. In retrospect, moreover, it is clear that – for all the hysteria of the moment – none of the dire predictions came true.'

It's helpful to acknowledge that in the future parents and carers will look back nostalgically at online video games and ask why children don't play like that any more, in light of some new scary technology.

---

* Harold Schechter, *Savage Pastimes*, St Martin's Press, New York, 2005.

This isn't to say we shouldn't pay attention to the media our children are consuming. In fact, we should pay closer attention so we can better understand what's really happening beyond any moral panic. But this needs to go beyond simplistic limits over screen time or prohibitions around violence and spending.

GAMING INVENTORY PART 1: THE CONTENT

An important step towards healthy family gaming is getting an accurate understanding of the kind of media games are. Creating a gaming inventory is a structured way to start mapping, navigating and guiding this part of your child's life. This will chart each game's content, the wider context in which its played and the craft required to play it. It won't change things immediately but it's the background we need to frame more in-depth conversations later on.

Get a notebook and write your child's name on the front. Then, one to a page, write the name of three or four of their favourite video games out of the ones they've played over the last couple of years. Under each game write an answer to each of the following questions, which focus on the content of the games. Some of these things you may know, but others you will need to talk to your child about.

- What sort of game is it?
- Is it a new game or one that's been around for a long time?
- How much money have they spent on it?
- How did they find the game in the first place?
- Is there a back story to the game?
- What is their role in the game?
- What is the game rating?
- Do they know why the game got its age rating?

Whether or not a moral concern is warranted, the real danger is that this puts parents off engaging in that area of their children's lives. The more we stigmatise video games as being only addictive, powerful and coercive, the more this self-perpetuating cycle continues. Blanket advice to quit, ban and limit video games further removes them from normal family life.

This pushes video games out of our sphere of parental influence and leaves children to game without our guidance, interest or appreciation. Inevitably, games then compete with, and draw children away from, other family activities. Perhaps worst of all, this muddled approach makes it hard for parents to identify the real cause of problems that children might exhibit while playing.

Don't worry, though; there is another way to deal with this that doesn't alienate children or demonise video games. It probably still sounds absurd to suggest that busy parents spend time playing video games. But this will sound less crazy as we get a better understanding of what games are and why children play them. We need to understand the *content* video games offer, the *craft* players need to play them, the *context* in which they are played – and how they relate to other parts of childhood.

The Surprising Content of Video Games

The breadth of topics and themes addressed by video games is much broader than we might at first realise, as a flick through the Gaming Recipes at the back of this book will demonstrate.

We all know about *FIFA*'s football challenge, *Call of Duty*'s wartime power fantasies and *Minecraft*'s block-building survival. But less well known are games like *Journey*, which embodies the importance of companionship; *Concrete Genie*, which offers hope beyond bullying; *Florence*, which uncovers the beautiful fragility of relationships; or even *Hellblade: Senua's Sacrifice*, which offers a first-hand understanding of psychosis.

Writing and speaking about new video games for newspapers, websites and broadcasters every day for the last ten years has made it abundantly clear to me that there are games about pretty much every topic. Some of these are a new way for children to engage with important subjects while others offer adults a fresh perspective on the world in which they live. Games address these themes in ways that books, films and television can't.

When a child steps into the shoes of a shop owner in *Toca Life: Town*, their imagination is sparked in a different way from when they play with toy tills in the living room or read books about shopping trips. When they play *A Fold Apart*, they get a first-hand experience of what it's like living far away from someone you love. Or, playing *Portal*, they get an

embodied understanding of how the physics of momentum work unlike any learning they might do in the classroom.

The breadth of this content and the unique experience of encountering themes in this way explains why children love to play video games so much. But more than this, it cracks open the door to a world in which games can be a positive part of family life, and even of interest to adults.

This final point is the hardest to communicate: that games may offer content of interest to parents and carers themselves. We assume games are too hard, juvenile, costly, frivolous or time consuming to grant them time in our adult lives. The reality is that there are accessible, mature, affordable and short games with content that provides a unique way to engage with topics as diverse as bereavement, environmentalism, relationships, homelessness, childhood memories and even adoption.

Clearly, this breadth of content needs to be handled responsibly, as not all topics are suitable for all ages. Understanding and experiencing gaming content for ourselves enables us to make informed choices about which games our children should play. It also gives us first-hand enjoyment of this new medium so we can consider which themes and topics may be beneficial and appropriate for our children, either on their own or in shared play with us.

The Craft Required to Play Video Games

Another defining aspect of games is the level of craft and skill required to play them. Contrary to popular opinion, video games are hard work. As Ian Bogost, professor of interactive computing at the Georgia Institute of Technology, writes in *How to Talk About Videogames*, 'You don't play a game to experience an idea so much as you do so in an attempt to get a broken machine to work again.'[*]

Steven Johnson, in his book *Everything Bad is Good for You*, highlights our blind spot about the benefits of this video game work when he says, 'We urge parents to instil a general love of reading in their children without worrying as much about *what* they're reading – because we believe there is a laudable cognitive benefit that comes from the act of reading alone, irrespective of the content.'[†]

For Johnson, there is a similar intrinsic benefit in playing games that's easy to miss. The complexity of modern games requires players to tackle grown-up tasks and balance complex systems on multiple levels. Taking this online extends the work further as players must deal with other people and evolving environments.

---

[*] Ian Bogost, *How to Talk About Videogames*, University of Minnesota Press, Minneapolis, 2015.
[†] Steven Johnson, *Everything Bad Is Good for You*, Penguin, London, 2006.

It is achievements from this mental labour – like the satisfaction of learning field-craft for nature photography, musicianship for playing an instrument, or the nuanced grammar required to speak a new language – as much as the content of a game, that keep players coming back for more.

'We hear a lot about the content of games: the carnage and drive-by killings and adolescent fantasies. But we rarely hear accurate descriptions about what it actually *feels like* to spend time in these virtual worlds.' This, Johnson says, 'makes it difficult to discuss the meaning of games in a coherent way'.

The two, perhaps competing, ideas – that video game content covers diverse, interesting and unusual themes while at the same time requiring hard work to operate – offer insight into why children enjoy the games they play. It's a combination of fascination with the content and the effort required to access it.

While it's good to want children to play games with interesting and engaging content, this insight enables us to see that even seemingly mundane or repetitive games can be fertile ground for building important and rewarding skills and traits.

The Wider Context of Video Games

The effort required to access video game content is hard to decipher as an outside observer. Whether it's shooting, fighting, racing or endlessly jumping, gaming interactions can seem inane or negative. However, James Paul Gee, a literacy researcher who has looked deeply into video games and education, writes in *What Video Games Have to Teach Us About Learning and Literacy* that 'video games do not have effects good or bad all by themselves . . . Technologies have effects only as they are situated in different contexts'.*

When a child starts playing a video game – particularly a large, commercially successful one – they encounter a new world: the game itself and how to get good at playing it; the dialogue, jargon and etiquette of other players; the mythology and lore of the game that has evolved over the years; the videos and websites about this particular game and celebrity professional players.

Video games that are played with other people, either in the same room or online via an internet connection, extend this context further. These games offer a chance for community and friendships to develop as players meet online, collaborate, compete and communicate with typed messages or with headsets and microphones. This is extended further still with conferences and exhibitions where the community finds tangible expression.

---

* James Paul Gee, *What Video Games Have to Teach Us About Learning and Literacy*, Palgrave Macmillan, New York, 2007.

It's this 'affinity group', as Gee calls it, that defines how players interpret what is happening on the screen. This community context of gaming is as much an influence on how long children spend playing as moreish game design. Agreeing fair and healthy boundaries includes consideration of this wider world of the game. Finding games with appropriate content for your child also involves helping them engage with, understand and interpret its wider context.

Discovering this opened my eyes to why video games were so important to my children. It was not only the experience itself but the wider activities and communities. I could appreciate the hours they spent researching the physics of momentum and collision to improve their *Rocket League* play. I could understand their fits of laughter watching fan-created *Red vs Blue* animations, made using

the *Halo* characters. I was no longer worried that my daughter's notebook full of diagrams and plans about her next *Minecraft* castle was a sign of obsession.

My role in this area of their life changed. It was no longer to stop them playing for too many hours, or getting too obsessed, but to help them capitalise on, understand and evaluate games in this wider context.

GAMING INVENTORY PART 2: THE CONTEXT

We can now deepen our understanding of the world of gaming our child enjoys by expanding the details for each of the games in our gaming inventory. This will create new ways to talk about games with our children and spark conversations that go beyond disagreements over when to stop.

Get out the game inventory notebook you started earlier. Previously, we listed things about the game content. This time we'll answer questions that focus on the playing context of that game for your child.

- Who do they play the game with?
- Is the game online or offline?
- Do they have favourite websites for learning about the game?
- Do they watch videos of other players, and who are their favourites?
- How do they communicate with others in the game?
- Have they joined communities or chat groups outside the game?
- How harsh or supporting is the community around a particular game?
- Are there conventions featuring the game they'd like to go to?
- Are there any fiction or non-fiction books about the game they'd like to read?

Video Games in Childhood

Along with the content, craft and context of our children's gaming, the final piece of the puzzle is understanding how games relate to other important things in their lives.

Jordan Shapiro is a professor who works on global policy and education. In his book *The New Childhood* he suggests that creating a sense of belonging for children is no longer just about mealtimes, displaying important family pictures or having grandparents' furniture around the home. We must also 'make an intentional effort to inject an ethical education into emerging technology contexts'.* Developing digital family traditions and sharing important moments both online and offline helps children navigate a blended online-offline world as they mature.

Games offer an opportunity to practise these skills in safe, innovative ways. As Andrew Przybylski highlighted in the Oxford Internet Institute London Lecture 'Screen Time – Myths, Misconceptions and Making Sense of it All', 'Screens, games and social media are the royal road into the internal and behavioural lives of young people today. They are an opportunity to be out ahead of your young person.'[†]

'All behaviour is communication,' writes parenting psychotherapist Phillipa Perry in her *The Book You Wish Your Parents Had Read*. 'Your job is to decipher your child's behaviour. Rather than dividing our children up into "good" bits and "bad" bits, there are questions you need to ask. What is their behaviour trying to say? Can we help them communicate in a more convenient way? What are they telling us with their bodies, with their noises, and with whatever words they choose to us?'[‡] What are they telling us with their video game playing?

Rather than limiting their digital world in an effort to squeeze out the new in favour of how our childhoods used to be, we can root and tether video games as part of family life so children learn to navigate their connected world healthily and robustly. Shapiro writes, 'We must teach [children] the values, rules, and etiquette necessary to referee a fair fight between scale and intimacy, to maintain an honor code and reinforce the chivalrous ethics of participation.'

---

* Jordan Shapiro, *The New Childhood: Raising Kids to Survive in a Digitally Connected World*, Hodder & Stoughton, London, 2019.

† Oxford Internet Institute, University of Oxford, 'Professor Andrew Przybylski delivers the OII London Lecture', 25 October 2019, available at www.youtube.com/watch?v=CsDxg2sTG20

‡ Philippa Perry, *The Book You Wish Your Parents Had Read: (And Your Children Will be Glad That You Did)*, Penguin, London, 2019.

Achieving this is as simple as watching and playing games together so they become one of the things the family does. This is a good way to create a healthy balance for video games in our children's lives as it naturally brings them under the same considerations and comparisons as other things we enjoy doing. This may lead to a reduction of play time, but equally, it may escalate the activity in new, more positive and ambitious directions.

TRY GAMING FOR YOURSELF

The challenge that's easiest to skip in this book is that of playing games yourself. Not just playing games with your children because they enjoy them but playing games on your own. Like any new medium, first-hand knowledge is second to none. If you do one thing after reading this book, I hope it's to try some games for yourself.

Flip to the Gaming Recipes section and browse the categories. Perhaps you want to 'Solve a Mystery', 'Inhabit Another World', 'Face Tough Decisions', 'Laugh at Silliness' or 'Walk in Someone Else's Shoes'. If those don't appeal or sound too confusing, pick one from the 'Games for Non-Gaming Grown-ups' section. They are all short, quite easy, accessible, grown-up and affordable.

A particularly good idea is to choose a game you can get for a device you already own. The instructions in the Gaming Recipes will provide everything you need to know to get started, including what system the game is on, how long it will take to play as well as highlighting some reasons other parents, carers and families have enjoyed it. You can also google the game name and the phrase 'Game play no commentary' to search for a video of the game without anyone speaking over the top of it.

This process can take a while if you haven't played modern games, but this is important time, well spent, in the care of your child. Give yourself space and time to have the best chance of engaging with your chosen game. Don't worry if you feel like you're getting it wrong or don't know what to do. Start with the easiest difficulty level from the menu. Over the space of an hour or so with the game you'll be led through the early tutorial stages. If it still hasn't clicked, don't feel bad about choosing a different game.

Parenting, Not Policing

Understanding the wide range of content that games have to offer, the craft they require to play, the context they are played in and how this is positioned alongside other aspects of childhood has enabled me to discover this world of video games that my children enjoy.

This world is not what I imagined it to be. And my reaction is mirrored in other parents and carers I've worked with. Whether from an understandably narrow view of what games are – perhaps because video games have changed so much since we played them growing up ourselves – or simply because of how our children imaginatively interact with them in unexpected ways, we need fresh ways to make sense of this new gaming world.

To take stock of what we've learned so far, here are seven important truths that shine fresh light on the nature of video games for children:

1. Video games are the medium of our time

   Along with existing media, video games form the cultural air that children breathe. With films, they are the theme of many playground games. Like television used to be, they are the bulk of what children watch. Like telephone use of old, they are the first place children learn to interact with people in another place. Like books, they tell important stories that are shared the next day at school. Like music collections, they represent identity and affiliations, and form tribes.

2. Video games require a new literacy

   Although they are familiar-looking, how we operate, understand and interpret video games is something we have to learn, similar to the skill and knowledge required to read books or watch films. But unlike books and films, there's not yet a common understanding of what video games are or what they do. This means there's a gap between many parents and their children that makes it hard to talk meaningfully about the games they play.

3. Video games are hard work

   Playing games ourselves builds understanding and literacy, but also reveals that games require considerable effort to play. As well as acquiring quick reflexes and fast reaction times, players must learn to manage complex systems, persevere in spite of failure, adapt their approach and in many ways treat the game systematically, like work. This mastery and craft is rewarded not only with success and recognition but with being able to access new ways to play.

4. Video games are cultural compositions rather than inanimate substances

The experience of playing a game is closer to enjoying books, films, music and theatre than it is to rollercoaster rides, caffeinated drinks or sugary snacks. This means that keeping them out of a child's life has more ramifications than deciding they won't eat sweets. Without experiencing video games in some way, they won't have access to this new form of sharing stories and socialising with their peers; it can be hard for them to interpret and understand many of the conversations friends are having around them.

5. Video games are a normal part of life

They may seem confusing and new to us but to children video games are an entirely normal part of life. Whether we resist or embrace video games, we need to do so in a way that accounts for them as an ongoing and permanent presence in the world they're growing up in.

6. Video games are not completely understood

Although they have technically been around since the 1970s, this new form of mass media only began entering the home in large numbers in the late 1990s. Unlike studies on how television has affected multiple generations who have grown up watching it, video games haven't been with us long enough for anyone to conclusively analyse their effects on our children. Equally, we are only scratching the surface of their potential.

7. Video games are big business

The meteoric success of video games is a testament to how well they fit the times in which we live. They make more money than films and music combined. It's therefore important to equip children to understand this industry. Like making a point of highlighting the music, sound effects and smiles in toy adverts, playing games with your child creates a context for a similar discussion about how games advertise products and make money.

Let's return to those common suggestions from the start of the chapter. 'If you're worried about video games' effects on children, why not just keep them out of the house?' We can now see that this is a misunderstanding both of what video games are and the place they hold in a child's life.

Video games are not a problem that needs solving any more than learning to share with siblings, the first day at school, teenage heartbreak or leaving home for university. What's needed, as with these other aspects of growing up, is guidance and support so that children grow through all of these challenges in preparation for the reality of their future lives. In fact, overly protecting them from these hardships or dangers can stunt their future maturity in these areas.

Those common suggestions and headlines often taunt us with what ifs about video games. What if video games become uncontrollable? What if we lose our child to them? What if they grow into addicted adults? What if they become violent at school? Perry has good advice for parents who are worried that children won't grow out of strange eating or sleeping habits, which is also helpful on their latest odd video game obsession: 'Believe me,' she

writes, 'almost everything with children is a phase. So it's fine to go with what works in the present, however odd it seems.'*

The family is a unique and powerful space for this work. It's 'the one anchor we can't pull up', as Shapiro puts it. Rather than minimising and keeping games at a distance, having them as part of family life not only makes them more enjoyable but creates conversations and critiques that equip children with the skills they need to make healthy decisions about the games they play and the affiliations, commitment and behaviour that go with that.

You can probably tell where this is heading – back to my crazy suggestion: to care for a child who loves video games we need to not only understand the games but play them ourselves and with our children.

This takes our video game literacy from theory into first-hand experience. It changes your role from protecting to parenting when it comes to your child's gaming. Like other areas of childhood, we don't need to overly worry when things go wrong. That's one of the points of the family home. It's where children experiment, push boundaries and learn from mistakes as well as successes.

It's not easy. In fact, in the short term it feels like much harder work than simply forcing video games into submission. But every bit of this parenting work – all the heartache, each argument, every time you start again, the questions you listen to, each misunderstanding clarified and disagreement resolved – is making a difference to your child's future. And as parents and carers, we can accommodate and hold this tension with a longer view in mind.

---

* Philippa Perry, *The Book You Wish Your Parents Had Read (and Your Children Will be Glad That You Did)*, Penguin Random House, Great Britain, 2019.

This isn't about changing your family values but empowering you to implement them effectively. To use the terminology helpfully outlined in Sonia Livingstone's *Parenting for a Digital Future*, parents' and carers' approach to games can be 'embracing, balancing or resisting'.* Each of these perspectives is completely valid. Equally, each of them benefits from parents playing video games with children and on their own.

BETTER QUESTIONS TO ASK

We have children with us for a limited time. When they leave, we want them to be able to make good decisions without us. Rather than worrying about how much screen time your child is racking up, there are better questions to ask them about their gaming:

Can they acknowledge how games affect their emotions?

Can they structure their game time to maximise their enjoyment?

Do they know when they've had enough?

Do they treat other players with respect?

Can they enjoy the game even if it doesn't go well for them?

Are they developing an appetite for a wide range of experiences?

Can they make informed decisions about expense and value?

Can they discuss the games they play with detailed and thought-through ideas?

Can they happily compromise gaming time for family commitments?

Do they share their gaming achievements and progress with you?

Are they enthusiastic about playing games together as a family?

Is their gaming integrated with a varied mix of other activities?

---

* Sonia Livingstone and Alicia Blum-Ross, *Parenting for a Digital Future*, Oxford University Press, New York, 2020.

Instilling this attitude and understanding into our children positions video games as a new form of media that is becoming a normal part of life. It equips children to benefit from their gaming time and be ready to thrive in digital aspects of their future.

INDUSTRY RESOURCE:

DISCOVERING REAL CAREERS IN VIDEO GAMES

Digital Schoolhouse is a not-for-profit programme delivered by the UK games industry trade body Ukie (The Association for UK Interactive Entertainment), which enables UK primary schools to experience free creative computing workshops from the foundation's local Schoolhouse.

The project has attracted both financial support and expertise from the games industry. Nintendo UK is the programme's lead partner, with other sponsors including PlayStation, SEGA, Warwickshire County Council and Ubisoft as well as support from the Department of Digital, Culture, Media and Sport (DCMS). This not only adds weight to the programme but opens doors into real future careers in an industry that needs a wide range of talented individuals.

Digital Schoolhouse's expert network of certified Schoolhouses and lead teachers deliver playful computing workshops to local primary schools across the UK. Underpinned by evidence-based research and combined with ground-breaking careers education, the programme successfully bridges the gap between academia and industry, to ensure pupils are aptly equipped for the future digital economy.

More recently this has included annual e-sports tournaments for older children in UK schools and colleges. Students aged 12–18 years can participate as players or fulfil professional roles crafted by the video games industry, for educational purposes. They manage the event itself, photograph the action, organise production logistics, referee, commentate on live match streams, manage team community, logos and branding and even deal with most of the paperwork themselves.

Whether it's the Digital Schoolhouse programme or something similar, finding a way to inspire and cheer on children towards a career in video games not only opens a door to their future, but creates a healthy understanding of the industry today.

3. THE BENEFITS OF VIDEO GAMES

Understanding the role that video games have in a child's life not only clears space for parents and carers to guide them towards healthy habits but uncovers the benefits that video games have to offer.

Children aren't stupid. They don't play video games just because they're exciting, easy to access and what their friends are doing. They play because of a range of benefits that, being children, they can't fully articulate.

Listening to how my kids (now 11, 14 and 16 years old) talk about video games is like a foreign language. Even when they were younger I didn't understand everything they said, but the bits I did understand were often surprising and fascinating.

They rarely talk about how thrilling games are or how amazing they look. Instead, they tell me how good it is to escape the day for a while and find some order. They light up, discussing the excitement of thinking deeply about new strategies and then being able to perfect them. Their friends come up in these chats in the same way they do when describing the latest playground game. They talk about support and advice they get from more experienced players. And when I still look confused, they take me by the hand and show me video clips of their victories, web pages they're using to research strategies, and other players they watch online.

I love these conversations. They are a rare opportunity to hear the inner workings of my children's hearts and minds. Not just what they are getting from the games they play, but how these experiences sit within the rest of their life.

Playing games with our children moves the conversation beyond them explaining their games to us as an outsider, to the easy candour of a shared experience. Taking the step of playing together while you talk brings a further understanding as guards are dropped and more is revealed about why your child loves this game.

This creates a powerful context for children to benefit from the games they play. By being interested and present in our children's gaming, we can stitch these experiences – the thinking, conversations and interactions that come with them, the 'infinity group' as Gee calls it – into family life.

In the past, game-positive voices have suggested benefits from gaming such as transferable skills and cognitive advancement. But there is mixed evidence for whether hard skills like hand–eye coordination, problem-solving or quick reactions transfer to other parts of life. What's more, looking to these secondary aspects of video gaming to justify the time spent on it misunderstands what video games really have to offer – like justifying the time spent gazing at a beautiful painting based on what it teaches you about history, or enthusing about a novel because of the words you learned.

The real benefit of video games is found in the innate nature of the games themselves. Games are a new media that we are only just starting to understand. But as we scratch the surface of what video games are, as I discuss in more depth in Chapter 6, we start to get a better picture of what these benefits look like.

Games create an endless variety of spaces to play in. They can be deeply social or intricately complex, they can challenge you with competition or collaboration, let you escape yourself, confront you with questionable decisions you've made, frustrate your best efforts or even soothe you into relaxation and calm. Sometimes they can do many of these things all at once. 'Games are where I can unfold,' is how my daughter describes it.

Then there are the benefits that arise as 'collateral learning', as Johnson puts it, from the hard work required to succeed. 'Games force you to decide, to choose, to prioritize. All the intellectual benefits of gaming derive from this fundamental virtue, because learning how to think is ultimately about learning to make the right decisions: weighing evidence, analyzing situations, consulting your long-term goals, and then deciding.'

My children's school homework books display a diagram of a compass. It's split into four areas: wisdom, community, compassion and courage. For wisdom it lists planning, making links, being methodical and questioning. For community it lists collaboration, humility, forgiveness and reflective learning. In courage it lists possibilities, perseverance, considered risks and integrity. In compassion it lists generosity, reflection, self-control and thankfulness.

GAMING INVENTORY PART 3: THE CRAFT

The benefits that a child gets from playing a video game come in part from the effort they are putting into it. With this in mind it's a good time to revisit our gaming inventory and think about the work children are putting into their gaming.

Having mapped the content and context of the games they play, we can now add questions that address the play-craft, skills and character they are developing while playing.

- How long have they been playing it for in total?
- What time of day and days of the week do they play?
- Do they spend time practising or training?
- Have there been times when they kept losing, and how did they improve?
- What do they do if they get stuck in the game?
- Do they have a proudest moment in the game?
- What are their goals for the game over the next week?

Talking about one game inevitably leads to talking about another. You can then expand your list of games by working back through more or all of the games they have played over the years. Although this may sound laborious, it's something most children relish and provides a wealth of information about their gaming tastes.

Your gaming inventory should now be a good map of your child's gaming. This not only helps you understand their tastes but highlights the types of games they shy away from and areas where you can encourage them to expand their repertoire. You can also start to appreciate areas where they have worked to improve and achieved success in games.

I recently realised that many, if not all, of these things are what I see my children develop or practise in the video games they play. In this way, games produce results which we usually presume can only be achieved in our homes, schools, libraries, sports centres, community halls, churches, synagogues and mosques. Games nurture children's character as much as their motor skills.

Over the years, in my work with parents of avid gamers, I've kept a list of the benefits they start to see from the games their children play. This list has grown quite long, and of course isn't exhaustive, but I hope it sparks something for you about the previously hidden benefits of your child's gaming:

- Character Benefits
  - **Independence** from finding their expertise and aptitude in a game. In games like *Stardew Valley* children can build a thriving farm against the odds, achieving hard-won success on their own.
  - **Compassion** from playing game characters with different socio-economic opportunities or situational challenges. Playing games like *My Child Lebensborn* and *Bury Me, My Love*, children can develop gratitude for their advantages and appreciation of life beyond their own town, city or country.
  - **Civility** towards other players by resolving disagreements and considering other perspectives. Games like *Concrete Genie* depict the impact of bullying and how to deal with people who do not offer them respect.
  - **Generosity** towards other players in how they communicate, share resources in a game and teach

newcomers in online games how to progress. Games like *Roblox* and *Fortnite* create the opportunity to share with other players on the same team.

- Social Benefits
  - **Social maturity** from experiencing how people and groups communicate in games. Competitive games like *Rocket League* enable children to experiment with social interactions and consider the impact on other players.
  - **Communication** from having to accurately share information and instructions in limited time. Games like *Keep Talking and Nobody Explodes* and *Spaceteam* teach children how to make themselves heard, as well as the importance of listening to other players.
  - **Altruism** through participating in multiplayer games where outcomes benefit other players or the community rather than the individual. Games like *Eco* and *One Hour One Life* provide a unique way to take responsibility for building something that other players benefit from.

- **Belonging** from feeling important and valued in a game world and its wider community. In games like *Go Vacation* children can contribute to a treasure hunt and playground-style games that don't rely on physical prowess.

- Well-being Benefits
  - **Resilience** from continuing to try after failing and from tackling problems that require many hours to develop the skills to solve them. Games like *Kingdom: Two Crowns* and *Subnautica* offer achievable challenges that seem impossible when first encountered.
  - **Peace** from escaping the busyness and pressures of life by spending time in the calm, holding, more controllable environments of video games. Games like *Terraria*, *Stardew Valley* and *The Legend of Zelda: Breath of the Wild* offer a soothing, predictable space in which to spend time and escape the day.

- ○ **Self-awareness** from encountering elegiac stories in games as an involved participant rather than a remote observer. Games like *Florence*, *ABZÛ* and *Brothers: A Tale of Two Sons* are a gentle way for children to learn about their own emotional responses to challenging situations as well as appreciating how other people may feel.
- ○ **Spirituality** from interactions with large narratives or engulfing spaces that engage the emotions and encourages a sense of mystery. Games like *Gris*, *Flower*, *Proteus* and *Passage* are mysterious experiences that invite children to linger in beautiful and intriguing spaces with themes of nature, hope and love.

- Intuition Benefits
  - ○ **Trusting instincts** from solving problems that require conceptual leaps or learning to make decisions without having all the information beforehand. In games like *Kingdom: Two Crowns*, *Reigns* and *Life is Strange*, players

learn to trust their instincts through experimentation in game worlds that are built to encourage risk-taking and hunch-following.

○ **Deep thinking** about specific topics and scenarios that video games address, including social, ethical or environmental issues. Games like *A Fold Apart*, *Eco* and *Papo & Yo* invite children to ponder particular narratives as they explore video game worlds in a way that enables them to sustain and develop their ideas.

○ **Embodied learning** from experiencing scientific theories and principles first-hand in a video game. Games like *Portal*, *Zelda: Breath of the Wild* and *Monument Valley* enable children to learn about physics by experiencing how gravity, heat, cold and perspective work in extreme situations. Games such as *Fantasia*, *Fru*, *Fruit Ninja*, *JoustMania* and *Just Dance* invite children to move and interact with their bodies without ability barriers.

○ **Rooted sense of place** through travelling to real and imagined cities, trekking off the beaten path or jetting off to distant worlds. Games like *Feather*, *The Endless Forest*, *ABZÛ* and *80 Days* enable children to spend time as virtual tourists in places that create fresh perspectives on where they live.

• Intellectual Benefits

○ **Weighing up evidence** of how a game works and what you need to do to progress. Games like *Reigns* offer minimal instruction and thereby force players to weigh previous actions and on-screen clues to determine the likely result of potential city expansions.

- ○ **Creativity** is discovered when children open the door to fantasy and everyday scenarios otherwise out of reach. Games like *Toca Life: Town*, *Roblox: Work at a Pizza Place*, *Tearaway Unfolded* and *Fable* spark intelligent creativity, while *Dreams* and *Super Mario Maker* enable children to create their own worlds.
- ○ **Pursuing long-term goals** without getting overly sidetracked by non-critical actions and quests. Games like *Heaven's Vault* offer multiple ways to progress, so players must stick to their goals to determine how to respond to characters and which course of action to take.
- ○ **Systems analysis** of multiple interrelated variables under specific pressured situations requires clear thinking and reasoning within a limited timescale. Games like *Rocket League* require the player to predict competitor trajectory, levels of boost and the position of the ball to execute a strategy to attack or defend.

But beyond these individual qualities that games offer children, it's when encountering them as a whole that they really reveal their full potential. Like books, films and theatre, there's something magical about them that only happens with the sum of their parts.

Games are beneficial because they offer a new way to look at the world. The novelist Jeanette Winterson could have been writing about video games in her book *Art Objects*: 'We need to look at the experience of the piece. The riskiness of art, the reason why it affects us, is not the riskiness of its subject matter, it is the risk of a new way of seeing, a new way of thinking. It does this by overturning the habits and conventions of previous generations.'*

Video games at their best are like this. Wild, unpredictable, fragile and risky. They are the medium of our time, which we have yet to fully embrace. As Winterson describes art, they are the emotional and psychic resonance of our world, 'a living, breathing, winding movement that flows out of the past and into the future while making its unique present'.

Being blindsided by the overwhelming emotion of losing your adoptee in *My Child Lebensborn*, being frustrated by your lack of deduction in *Return of the Obra Dinn*, finding something true about your own daughter in Ellie from *The Last of Us* or watching in horror as your lovingly planned subway fails in *Mini Metro* – games are not always what we expect or want them to be. But, as with poetry, music and paintings, when we take time to play video games we are, as Winterson puts it, 'clearing a space for new stories about ourselves'.

We discover not only new ways to laugh, compete and giggle with our kids, but new ways to see the world. From tiny puzzles to grandiose landscapes, the spaces that video games create invite us to investigate and overhear stories in completely new ways. I'm getting better at noticing how we learn from video games. But by playing together, the real benefit is what we learn about ourselves and our children.

I know that capitalising on these benefits may seem a world away from your son or daughter who just wants to shoot things in the head online rather than do their homework. But it's not as hard as you might imagine. If you've read this far you are already taking big steps in the right direction.

---

* Jeanette Winterson, *Art Objects: Essays on Ecstasy and Effrontery*, Vintage, London, 1996.

INDUSTRY RESOURCE:

GAME INFORMATION FOR PARENTS

Along with books like this, there are many great tools and resources that can help parents understand the benefits of gaming. For a number of years I've been the editor of askaboutgames.com, developing resources that offer information about games and offer a window into other families' gameplay. Learning how other families play games is an important way to expand your knowledge and consider how their approach might work for you.

The not-for-profit website is funded by the games industry via Ukie (The Association for UK Interactive Entertainment), the industry trade body for the UK's games and interactive entertainment, and the VSC (Video Standards Council) Rating Board, which administer the PEGI ratings in the UK. It's a place for parents and carers to ask questions about video game age ratings, how to play games safely and responsibly, and to find tips on how to get the most out of the games they enjoy with their children. This includes stories about games that other families have enjoyed, detailed video guides to the most popular games, and weekly age-rated gaming charts to highlight what's currently trending. It also offers explanations of the PEGI ratings, parental controls and online gaming.

One of my favourite features of the site is the option to 'Ask A Question', where you can send all manner of queries to on-hand gaming experts for a rapid response. These range from finding a good game to play with a particular age of child, to why a particular game has a certain rating, or even how grandparents can get involved in children's gaming.

There is also a link to the VSC Rating Board website and app, which provides the full examiner's report behind each video game rating. This is particularly useful as you can search for games by both genre and age rating to find titles well matched to your family.

4. THE WORRIES VIDEO GAMES CAUSE

If video games invite children to new worlds that build character, sociability, well-being, intuition and intelligence then why do we read so many scary stories about them creating violent behaviour, being addictive, encouraging gambling or enabling unwanted interactions with strangers?

Along with any benefits, we need to face the challenges of video games honestly. The messy reality of family gaming is a long way from the pristine surfaces and sparkling smiles of hired talent in family gaming adverts. Left to their own devices, children tend towards playing for too long, getting frustrated, not stopping for mealtimes and arguing with siblings.

In the past, games were short, offline and expensive. This made them self-limiting. Many new games are infinite, online and free, and consequently have lower barriers to repeat-plays and more ways to cultivate avid players than other media do.

Add to this the World Health Organization's (WHO) inclusion of 'gaming disorder' to their disease classifications, scary headlines about the effects of violent video games on children's behaviour, in-game purchases that offer gambling-like transactions, and anonymous strangers in online game worlds, and it's not surprising that video games are a hot topic for parents.

As the title of this book suggests, video games can sometimes be problematic in the lives of children. As with many things they eagerly enjoy – sweets, football, television, sticker collecting and shopping, to name a few – we need to steer them in the right direction so that their hobby works with family life rather than against it.

However, because video games are a new medium, we don't have the same level of understanding or first-hand experience to enable us to play this role as we do in other areas. Sifting through the conflicting newspaper articles and reports, school warnings and children's charities' advice is time-consuming and confusing. Along with developing our literacy about what games are, digging into the details of our worries about gaming is essential if we are to offer children consistent guidance rather than knee-jerk reactions or short-term solutions.

Addiction

Addiction is a worrying word for parents and carers of children who play a lot of video games. Children are absorbed by the gaming screen, twitching and grimacing as they play and often unaware of the world around them. They can find it hard to stop when asked to come to the table for mealtimes, do homework or go to bed. They appear to be obsessive and compulsive about their gaming.

This worry is compounded by experts such as Susan Greenfield in her book *Mind Change*, in which she states that video games can damage children's brains and lock them into powerful addictions.[*] These addictions are then often treated like drug or alcohol habits that require children to quit gaming for ever, with games not being let back in the house.

However, as Pete Etchells points out in his book *Lost in a Good Game*, 'As far as research is concerned there is no clear picture of how many people are likely to be affected, what the characteristics of those people are,' and, crucially, 'whether playing video games is the *causal* reason behind any negative issues in their lives.'[†] This isn't to say there's nothing to worry about, but simply that the science around

---

[*] Susan Greenfield, *Mind Change: How Digital Technologies Are Leaving Their Mark on Our Brains*, Ebury Publishing, London, 2015.

[†] Pete Etchells, *Lost in a Good Game: Why We Play Video Games and What They Can Do For Us*, Icon Books, London, 2019.

gaming is still in its infancy and shouldn't solely drive our fears or approach to parenting children who love playing video games.

This is why WHO's criteria for 'Gaming disorder' under its 'Disorders due to addictive behaviours' are controversial and seen by some as premature. If taken seriously, it nonetheless reserves addiction language for a tiny set of children displaying clear, stark and severe symptoms.

WHO states that gaming disorder is characterised by a pattern of persistent or recurrent gaming behaviour manifested by:

1. Impaired control over gaming frequency, intensity, duration and termination
2. Increased priority given to gaming to the extent that gaming takes precedence over other life interests and daily activities
3. Continuation or escalation of gaming despite the occurrence of negative consequences[*]

Furthermore, this behaviour pattern is expected to be of sufficient severity to result in significant impairment in personal, family, social, educational, occupational or other important areas of functioning. It is also expected to be continuous or episodic and recurrent, normally over a period of at least 12 months in order for a diagnosis to be assigned, although the required duration may be shortened if all diagnostic requirements are met and symptoms are severe.

---

[*] '6C51 Gaming disorder', ICD-11 for Mortality and Morbidity Statistics, September 2020, available at icd.who.int/browse11/l-m/en#/http%3a%2f%2fid.who.int%2ficd%2fentity%2f 1448597234

As you can see, the criteria requires extreme symptoms for someone to fall into this diagnosis. This is not to deny that gaming disorder can occur, nor diminish its seriousness, but to ensure we take care to reserve these diagnoses for the cases that need it.

Where the addiction does exist in this clinical sense, it's still very different from addictions to substances, such as drugs, tobacco or alcohol. WHO classifies gaming disorder under 'Disorders due to addictive behaviours' rather than 'Disorders due to substance use'. Dopamine is often referenced as the hormone generated by addictive activity such as taking drugs. It is also generated when we do anything we find enjoyable, including playing video games. But, as Patrick M Markey and Christopher J Ferguson state in their book *Moral Combat*, 'The quantity of dopamine released while [playing a video game] is much closer to that triggered by eating a slice of pepperoni pizza than by consuming methamphetamine.'*

However, seeing the definition for gaming disorder enables parents to take balanced and effective action if their children are gaming to the detriment of other areas of life. Rather than detoxing, quitting, boot camps or expensive private treatment programmes, children need their parents to engage and guide their gaming.

If you are worried that your child may be exhibiting addictive behaviour, see it as a parenting problem rather than a medical one. Take the same steps as you do when other things in your child's life get out of balance.

As I discuss in Chapter 5, come alongside them and play together so you can help them understand where gaming is beneficial and

---

* Patrick M Markey and Christopher J Ferguson, *Moral Combat*, BenBella Books Inc., Dallas, 2017.

where it is out of hand. Listen carefully for signs of them feeling disconnected from other parts of life and areas of pain for which video games are being used as a salve. It can be worrying, but in most cases that I've been involved with, parents can help children re-find balance in their gaming without medical assistance.

SHARE YOUR CHILD'S GAMING WHILE THEY ARE YOUNG
Engage with your child about gaming sooner rather than later. Taking an interest as they discover games when they are young helps them set up healthy habits for later life. This not only positions you as a person of influence and authority in this area but situates gaming as something the family does together.

It takes time and effort to engage in this way, and at first it may be something you are reluctant to invest in. However, like reading simple children's books together, it's time well spent if it means you are equipping them to develop a lifelong healthy relationship with video games.

Working with the gaming inventory you have created and playing games together enables you to carefully consider whether a child is avidly playing because they are benefiting in some way or whether they are mindlessly repeating unhelpful play patterns. This avoids treating gaming like a harmful substance and enables you to implement longer-term plans that resituate gaming as something the family enjoys together. This gently guides children to think more critically for themselves about the time they spend playing.

If, in spite of your interest, involvement and boundary-setting for a number of months, the gaming falls into WHO gaming disorder criteria, professional assistance is important. However, just googling 'gaming disorder' or 'gaming addiction' will return websites and organisations looking to attract business from worried parents.

There are a growing number of these 'specialist' gaming addiction services that are expensive and lack a breadth of clinical expertise.

AGREE AUTOMATIC TIME LIMITS
Setting stricter limits on gaming time can create valuable space to see clearly what's going on. All modern game consoles enable you to set up daily limits for your children in ways they can't circumnavigate. Still, this is best done in conversation with your child, with you agreeing together on appropriate game time – and you should see it as a short-term tool rather than a long-term solution.

It's important that you find help that provides both holistic and empirically valid treatments. The first action to take is to see your doctor, who can give appropriate medical advice. This may be to identify gaming disorder as stipulated by WHO, but it may equally identify other pre-existing issues as the cause of the effects you see in your child's gaming.

Violence

Video games often involve violent virtual content. The exuberance and excitement of shooting or fighting have been fertile territory for big-budget games, not dissimilar in approach to blockbuster films. Add to this the competitive and interactive satisfaction of hitting a target with a gun and you can see why some video games have been drawn to taking this approach.

While graphic novels have become synonymous with superheroes, video games face the danger of being seen as only about shooting. 'I don't read graphic novels,' I'll say, 'because I'm not into superheroes.' Which is kind of ridiculous when they could be about anything, and when they offer an artistic and mature way to tell stories. In the same way, those 'not into shooting' can regard video games in general as 'not for them'.

As you can see in the Gaming Recipes later in the book, in truth video games are a broad medium being created by all kinds of people in all manner of settings with an unending array of topics, themes and narratives. Many of these games are non-violent, not because they want to make a point but because violence is unnecessary in the interactions they create.

However, the Gaming Recipes also include games that intentionally use violence to communicate a particular theme. *Limbo*'s protagonist comes to all sorts of violent ends, for example, but this is to create the dark, fairy-tale aesthetic which makes the game intriguing and moving for adult players. As the ratings suggest, this violence still needs to be taken seriously for younger players, but parents will be best placed to judge what's appropriate.

There is considerable back and forth in the scientific community over the impact of video game violence on children, both in terms of effects on behaviour and how they view the world. When Susan Greenfield's *Mind Change* was published in 2015, it sounded an alarm about the effect of technology and games on children, quoting from over 500 papers to pull out overarching trends that point to how our minds are physically adapting to technology. Writing specifically about video games, Greenfield suggested that we are repeatedly rehearsing and becoming susceptible to 'low-grade aggression, short attention span and a reckless obsession with the here and now'.

However, when this view is tested in focused research, a more complex picture emerges. Take, for example, the preregistered (or peer-reviewed) study of video game violence and its effects by Andrew K. Przybylski and Netta Weinstein of the Oxford Internet Institute (OII).* 'The idea that violent video games drive real-world aggression is a popular one, but it hasn't tested very well over time,' says Przybylski, who is Director of Research at the OII. 'Despite the interest in the topic by parents and policy-makers, the research has not demonstrated that there is cause for concern.'

'Our findings suggest that researcher biases might have influenced previous studies on this topic, and have distorted our understanding of the effects of video games,' says Weinstein. An important step taken in this study, but often absent in previous work, is preregistration, where researchers publicly register their hypothesis, methods and analysis technique prior to beginning the research to ensure it is balanced and unbiased.

---

* Andrew K. Przybylski and Netta Weinstein, 'Violent video game engagement is not associated with adolescents' aggressive behaviour: evidence from a registered report', *Royal Society Open Science*, Royal Society Publishing, 2019.

What studies often prove is correlation rather than causation. An example Przybylski often uses is the correlated rise of ice cream sales and violence in cities. To claim causation from this correlation would obviously seem ridiculous, but this is what many studies on violent video games have strayed close to suggesting. In such cases, other factors causing the correlation are often missed – in Przybylski's example, rising temperatures lead to more ice cream sales but also to more young men being out on the streets in the evenings.

The panic over violent video games is sometimes escalated on the basis that today's sophisticated technology is more immersive and realistic. However, as Howard Schechter writes, 'Popular works that seem utterly innocent to us – the product of more innocent times – were, in their own day, condemned for precisely the same reasons that today's mass media scapegoats are: for creating illusions of violence so intense and convincing that impressionable young minds were bound to be corrupted by them.'*

Steven Johnson highlights how the effects of incumbent media on the brain are undetectable. But, he says, 'the effects of the new media become apparent because you have something to measure them against'. Rather than young minds being moulded towards violent tendencies, the pattern he sees is that of 'the mind adapting to adaptation', as a younger generation is 'more comfortable with the process of probing a new form of media, learning its idiosyncrasies and its distortions, its symbolic architecture and its rules of engagement'.

---

* Harold Schechter, *Savage Pastimes*, St Martin's Press, New York, 2005.

This isn't to suggest that there is no issue with violent content in video games. Rather, we need to pay close attention to the realities of the situation – how these things have played out historically, how new media often seem unhelpfully disruptive, and how children may be using this new technology to imaginatively deal with issues they face – so we can provide healthy and consistent guidance.

This loosening of assumptions around video game violence and progress towards better understanding creates a context in which parents and carers can take positive action rather than start to panic. Most will want to clearly distinguish which violent games are designed only for adults to play and ensure appropriate boundaries are set up. Some will choose to avoid violent games entirely until children are older. Others may play together with their children to enable them to better process any violence. Either way, having open and healthy conversations about violence in games ensures we can help children process it.

Hearing my son gleefully talking about headshots and kills in *Fortnite* caused me to suggest that he watch the film *Saving Private Ryan* with me to get a fuller understanding of the reality of those kinds of battles. He was 12 at the time and the film has a 15 rating. While not everyone agreed with my approach, it enabled us to talk about violence in general and specifically in games and films.

This kind of processing, along with playing a wider range of video games, enables children to think through this violence. Far from perpetuating violence, in this way video games can help children build an ethical understanding, sensitivity and appropriate responses to the reality of violence in the world.

USE PARENTAL SETTINGS TO AUTOMATICALLY APPLY AGE RATINGS
If you are worried about violence in the games your children are playing, look up the Pan European Game Information (PEGI) ratings in Europe or the Entertainment Software Rating Board (ESRB) ratings in America. These disclose the level of violence with age limits on game boxes and in online stores.

For physical or boxed games, more detailed information can be looked up on the PEGI and ESRB apps or the associated websites. Along with the age ratings themselves, these provide the examiners' reports, which go into great detail about the level of violence.

You can limit access to games of particular age ratings via family settings and parental control settings on all modern consoles. This feature has been available since 2006 on the Wii, Xbox 360 and PlayStation 3, and has evolved and expanded over the years.

Setting up these limits today is easier than ever, and well supported with detailed instructions on each console-maker's website. It's as simple as creating a child or teen account that is linked to the parent's account and then picking the appropriate age limit for your child. Once set, children have to request permission to access older-rated games, which parents can choose to accept or deny.

Of course, these ratings are a helpful tool rather than replacement of the important role parents and carers play in guiding media consumption. PEGI 7 rated games, for example, have content appropriate for any child aged seven years or older, but parents and carers should still guide online interactions, in-app purchases and how long children play.

On the Xbox you also get a weekly email report that outlines which games your child is playing and how long they've played them for. On Nintendo Switch the Parental Controls app provides a similar report. This not only provides useful information on the age rating of games they are playing, but is also a good way to understand your child's play pattern to add to your gaming inventory.

Unexpected Costs

In the past video games have struggled to maintain profits from young audiences. The industry has pursued a variety of business models, from targeted family games on the Wii to movie tie-ins and selling toys that unlock in-game characters and levels as in *Skylanders*. This area of the market is still changing at a rapid pace.

In recent years, publishers have started offering games for free in an effort to generate a large number of players who are then incentivised to make small purchases of in-game items. For example, *Fortnite* is free to play but makes lots of money from players purchasing outfits, dances and other things. This lowers the barrier to entry, enabling a game to create a buzz in the playground and build a large audience before introducing the hurdle of payment.

There are different forms of this approach. Some developers apply the model to existing styles of video games. This enables the game to be tried for free, with the developer's knowledge that players will likely spend some money in the future to access particular items or features.

Less positive are games that have been shaped by a business model to the extent that they exist solely to incentivise purchases in order for the player to progress. At worst, these become pay-to-win challenges, where the more you pay, the better you do. Or, less aggressively, games may allow you to upgrade characters more quickly if you pay money or watch advertisement videos within the app. For example, *Zombies vs Ninja* is a game on iOS and Android where you tap to kill increasingly large hordes of zombies. It's free to download but you are quickly prompted to make purchases of up to £99.99 to gain new weapons. In addition to the in-game store, many of the buttons prompt players to watch advertisement videos to access weapons and keys.

In-game purchases come in different forms. Sometimes you know the exact item you are getting in advance. Sometimes, like collecting football stickers, you have a chance of getting items of differing rarity. These paid games of chance, often called 'loot boxes', have been accused of marketing gambling to children. Some countries, such as Belgium, have legislated against these kinds of in-app purchases.

In the UK, the Gambling Commission does not generally see these chance-based, in-app purchases as gambling if the items have no monetary value outside the game. Recent government reports have suggested that this definition be changed to include 'loot boxes'. The Gambling Commission's spokesperson clarified this for me: 'We are concerned with the growth in examples where the line between video gaming and gambling is becoming increasingly blurred, and where we are clear that a product has passed the line into gambling and is posing a risk to players, we will take action.'

This action takes the form of criminal prosecution against websites that enable children to gamble in-game items then cash them out for real money. In 2017 the Gambling Commission successfully prosecuted the unofficial FUT Galaxy website for providing in-game FIFA-item gambling to children.

With or without real-world monetary value, parents watching a child opening a 'loot box', 'pack' or 'box' in a game will see the similarity to other games of chance. The ability to make large purchases of in-game currency for these items (as much as £79.99 at one click) should also be cause for caution. If the console, smartphone or tablet your child uses is linked to your account, they may be able to make a payment without additional passwords.

It's therefore important to set up passwords and restrictions for these purchases via systems' parental and credit controls. This enables you to turn off in-game spending or grant only a certain amount of spending each week. The tools and passwords are simple to set up and ensure parents are in control. They also provide a context for useful conversations with children to help them understand and consider value before making a purchase.

'Digital media has mostly become an instrument to facilitate niche consumption,' writes Jordan Shapiro.* In his view, this means that 'children need adult mentorship that teaches them

---

* Jordan Shapiro, *The New Childhood: Raising Kids to Survive in a Digitally Connected World*, Hodder & Stoughton, London, 2019.

not to surrender blindly to ritualised digital actions. They need to recognize that software is almost always designed with an agenda.'

Conversations around different ways to purchase video games, and experimentation with doing this, are a good way to help children build this understanding. Part of this learning process is allowing children to make mistakes, while keeping these within reasonable bounds. For example, I had a long-running battle with my son, who was desperate to purchase a motorbike in the *Jailbreak Roblox* game for £12. I asked him to show me what it would look like, and whether it would really make a big difference in the game. 'Think of what else you could use the money for,' I said. He was still sure he wanted to spend his pocket money. I eventually let him, expecting the novelty to quickly wear off and serve as a lesson in the value of virtual items. However, he enjoyed the vehicle for many weeks and was more than happy with the value he got from it.

It initially felt like a failure in parenting. But, actually, the point wasn't about controlling how my son spent his money. Rather than winning an argument, the real benefit here were the conversations about the transaction and my engagement in this part of his gaming world. He'd had to engage critically with me about his decision and was able to defend his choice. Whether or not this had turned out to be good value, the process would help him make informed decisions in the future.

This kind of involvement in the purchasing and payment transaction that happens in games that children play, along with setting up passwords for purchases, helps parents not only avoid money being spent unintentionally but get a better understanding of how children find value in these games and how the games themselves make money.

**SPENDING BOUNDARIES HELP KIDS UNDERSTAND
DIGITAL CURRENCY**

As with any big business, be that films, fast food, football clubs, sweets or toys, parents and carers have a role to play in educating children about how video games make money. Like spending pocket money on collecting football stickers, letting your child experiment with small in-game purchases enables them to understand how this process works and to make informed choices about getting good value.

In the same way that you wouldn't hand a child your smartphone logged in to Amazon and let them click around, it's important that you set up game devices with appropriate accounts and passwords. Here are the ways to keep gaming costs and purchases predictable:

1. Set up a master account that only you have the password for.

2. Specify an email address you regularly check, as this will notify you of purchases.

3. Set up individual child accounts for each child.

4. Specify purchasing limits on each child account that require you to enter a password to agree transactions.

5. Add periodic credit for them to spend or use book-token-style top-up gifts.

Talk to your children about how they spend money on the games they play. Check through the payment history on your console or smartphone with them so they can see and talk about how much they are spending and whether this has been good value for them.

The questions I ask my children about their video game spending include:

- How did they discover the item they want to buy?

- Do they think their purchase is good value?

- What else could they have spent the money on?

- Will the item make a difference to how they play the game?

- Are they still playing with previous purchases?

- How much do they think they'll spend over the next year?

Online Strangers

The video games I played growing up were offline. If I wanted to play against someone else, I would have to take my console and large, heavy television to their house and fiddle with the network settings before we could play. It was exciting, but the complexity meant it was something for special occasions.

Today, children can play against hundreds of other people all over the world at the press of a button. This is exciting and beneficial for youngsters, not only in terms of the scope of experiences they can have, but also through the wide range of cultures and social settings of other players and in ongoing connections with more local friends.

The old divide between games and social media doesn't exist like it used to. For children, video games *are* their social media, and their social media is increasingly like a game. Based on the Office of Communications (Ofcom) report 'Children and parents: media use and attitudes', most children will interact with an online stranger for the first time in a video game rather than through social media. The report also states that 37 per cent of 3–4-year-olds take part in online gaming, while only 1 per cent of them have social media profiles.[*]

The frequency and reach of these online interactions should bring with them informed caution. Children interacting with others online don't necessarily know who they are talking to. Even when they play online with known friends, there is the possibility for antisocial behaviour – directed from and towards your child.

---

[*] Ofcom, 'Children and parents: Media use and attitudes report 2018', available at www.ofcom.org.uk/research-and-data/media-literacy-research/childrens/children-and-parents-media-use-and-attitudes-report-2018

Online video games are similar to playgrounds. Like a child's willingness to play with other children they don't know, it can be joyful to watch these games unfold. However, it's important to realise that these playgrounds are harder to fence off from strangers. We can't see who is entering through the gate as we can in real life, and if your child is playing on a tablet in another room, or wearing a gaming headset, we can't hear what's being said. This means that, particularly for young children, rather than sitting to one side, chatting with other parents and sipping a coffee as we do in real-world playgrounds, we need to be involved in the play and give specified limits for what they can and can't do with the technology.

The parental and family settings of the device your child uses to play online need to be set up appropriately. From chatting via

messages to speaking on a headset or sharing images and videos, there is a wide range of ways for players to communicate with each other. The settings on your device let you specify which of these means of communication are allowed and enable you to restrict more open interactions to just those friends they know in real life.

Fixing these settings with your child not only enables you to agree to the boundaries together but can also help you understand how each setting impacts the play. It's important that this conversation includes what to do when things go wrong and something upsets your child or makes them feel uncomfortable. Online games generally offer advice to parents and provide clear reporting routes for unacceptable behaviour.

As we do when children are learning to use swings and roundabouts, being present as they start gaming online enables you to support their play and hone these settings for them over time. It also creates a context of understanding and a celebration of their gaming achievements that ensures an open dialogue as they get older and play more complex games. This is much easier if we can keep games in family spaces. Although this is hard to maintain with tablets and portable gaming devices, ensuring the main console and biggest screens are downstairs is a good way to keep online interactions more visible.

If your child uses headphones to communicate with other players in games, get them to have the sound on the TV as well from time to time so you can hear what's going on. It's also a good idea to install the related smartphone app for the console and, with your child's permission, log in to their account so you can see the gaming messages they get. Also be aware of other social media apps, such as Discord, that they may use to communicate with other players.

SETTING UP THE ONLINE PLAYGROUND

As adults, we don't always relish taking children to the playground or days out to theme parks. There's a lot of effort involved in getting them dressed for the day's weather, travelling to the park, encouraging them to play, soothing tears when they fall over and remembering to pack enough lunch. We do it because we know children enjoy it and benefit from the experience, and once we are there it's lovely to see them run off and play.

Getting online gaming right for your child can be just as much hard work but is equally rewarding.

Setting these things up with your child present creates a context for important conversations about appropriate online behaviour and what to do if someone or something upsets them. These are the key tasks you need to undertake before your child runs off to play online:

- Set up a separate game account for your child to have their own settings and boundaries.

- Specify on your child's account the interactions they can engage with.

- Specify the content they can share and view from other users.

- Specify whether they can play with people from different consoles.

- Specify whether they can add friends to their list themselves or if this is something you do for them.

One common way to limit chatter from players you don't know is to make an online group of your child's friends in the console lobby area before starting the game. Then in the game they can mute other players and only communicate with people they know.

Worrying Better

Technology companies, governments and parents often point the finger at each other for not doing more to ensure these experiences are handled responsibly and healthily. The reality is that this is a shared responsibility.

While government legislation and self-regulation need to continue to improve, and industry must be more open with player data and enhance parental controls, we as parents need to capitalise on the tools and laws already in place: PEGI and ESRB age ratings; automatic limits based on these age ratings; detailed reports on how long children are playing for; automatic ways to set daily time limits, spending boundaries and restrictions to online interactions.

Along with this, it's important to debunk misrepresented and misreported science. The fears evoked from such articles can drive reactionary bans and limits where parents further distance themselves from this area of their child's life. If we are going to worry about video games, let's worry about the right things and in a way that engages us with our children.

As Andrew Przybylski said in his lecture, 'We need to abandon the idea of screen time because it's sucking all of the oxygen out of the room for more meaningful questions. We need to be able to ask more meaningful questions to have the faintest hope of turning this around.'

Andy Phippen, Professor of Digital Rights at Bournemouth University, and research scientist Maggie Brennan suggest the direction for these questions in their book *Child Protection and Safeguarding Technologies*. They say the UN Convention on the Rights of the Child 'should be any policy maker's go-to for the development of new resources, technologies, policy, or legislation.'*

They suggest that we move from worrying about whether content is either safe or harmful and instead focus on the things

---

* Andy Phippen and Maggie Brennan, *Child Protection and Safeguarding Technologies*, Routledge, London, 2019.

that young people say upset them: people's online behaviour, real news stories, online bullying and rudeness. They distil this into how young people say they want parents and carers to help: 'Listen, don't judge, and understand.'

Rather than worrying about screen time, violence, spending and online strangers in a way that distances us, let's worry instead whether we are *listening* well to our children's gaming, let's worry if we are too quickly *judging* why they are playing so much, let's worry if we are accurately *understanding* the role games are playing in their lives.

Avoid letting video games become an area of your child's life that you're not involved in. Make use of the comprehensive tools on consoles and gaming devices to set boundaries and gain deeper understanding of risks. Actively watch children play and talk to them about their games, play with them and, best of all, find games to play yourself.

Treat video games like other areas of childhood. There are dangers in most things that children benefit from – riding a bike, baking a cake, going to a theme park, playing in the sea, climbing trees – but that shouldn't eclipse their value.

My son used to be terrible at crossing the road. He wouldn't properly check both ways. He'd choose to cross between parked cars. He'd get distracted by friends on the other side. He was a government safety advert waiting to happen. I'm making light of it, but it was actually pretty scary. We instigated a rule that he wasn't allowed to cross on his own unless he was holding either my wife's hand or mine. But, of course, this road-crossing ban only got us so far. We spent time with him crossing together so he could learn how to do this safely. One day we wouldn't be there to hold his hand. Worse, he would be with friends and other distractions.

We could have decided to never let him cross a road on his own by making sure he saw roads as being too dangerous to approach. That is technically possible, but my son wouldn't have thanked us when he saw his friends happily navigating busy carriageways. We could have limited his road time to a few minutes a day, but that would have been just as bonkers. He could still get into plenty of trouble in a few minutes.

Like roads, video games are an unavoidable, normal and important part of the world our children are growing up in. They can both take them to all sorts of wonderful new places, provided they have the right guidance; but like any powerful and beneficial aspect of life, there are dangers.

As children grow older and move from road-crossing to becoming road users, it's tempting to build and police roadblocks to limit their travel and make things safer. In extreme cases, we might even think about closing this gaming road altogether.

What they really need, though, is parents and carers to join them on their journey, whether it's just an enjoyable leisure activity, a way to extend playground friendships, to gain a sense of connection missing in other parts of life or maybe to cope with stress or deal with anxiety. On the road together – playing with them – we have a really good chance of finding out what's going on.

INDUSTRY RESOURCE:

BEYOND E-SAFETY TO DIGITAL CIVILITY

Most of the video games that are popular with young children offer parents information, tools and initiatives to help them guide the play in healthy directions. *Roblox* is an example you are likely to be familiar with if you have children aged between 5 and 12 years old.

Roblox is a way for young game developers to create and share games with a huge audience. Children love playing its range of games that follow popular playground trends. Like made-up games during morning break at school, *Roblox* games change and evolve as children play online together, and its developers quickly respond to feedback.

Along with settings to limit interactions and specify which of the *Roblox* games your child can access, it has an innovative 'Digital Civility' initiative. With a specific section on the website,* and a parent-focused social media presence with regular content, the programme moves beyond e-safety to help children foster the skills to create positive online experiences for themselves – not just on the *Roblox* platform, but also on others.

Laura Higgins, who heads up Digital Civility, told me, 'Because *Roblox* is rapidly growing into one of the most popular places for kids and teens to hang out and play online, we have a duty to make sure that when they use our platform they can explore their creativity freely and safely. Rewarding camaraderie and empathy creates an opportunity to empower and educate kids with the digital character that they need to thrive.

'Online gaming communities are often labelled as toxic. Our players don't always behave perfectly, but that's because they are young, not because they are toxic. We have an opportunity to engage with young people in a unique way, and I hope that by listening to them and giving them a voice, we can help shape their positive behaviours both online and offline.'

---

* 'Digital Well-Being', Roblox, available at corp.roblox.com/digital-well-being

5. HOW TO LOVE A CHILD WHO LOVES VIDEO GAMES

Some children love video games more than other forms of play. The common thinking is that they were susceptible to the tricks of a powerful industry with coercive technology. They got distracted from healthier hobbies. I too want my children to have a varied childhood: building dens, individual and team sports, writing and painting, amateur dramatics, ultimate Frisbee, playing an instrument, fossil hunting, travelling the world, camping . . . The list could go on for ever. But this doesn't mean I shouldn't nurture other things they love, such as video games.

I know that encouraging a child to play video games sounds like a plan to make sure they eat more sweets. But this is about quality, not quantity. Just as we are ambitious for their reading, diet, exercise, education and even film watching, we can be equally ambitious for our children's gaming to be more than a sugar rush that makes them crazy.

Seeing the families I work with discover the potential of video games and cherishing them as a part of family life – perhaps even as important as mealtimes – is what drove me to write this book. Enabling parents to stop worrying and start guiding gaming in healthy directions is rewarding work because it changes something perceived as negative and scary into something positive and healthy. I want children who love video games to be able to pursue that passion with the transforming ambition, encouragement and cheering-on that parents and guardians uniquely provide.

Caring for a child who loves playing video games includes setting boundaries and helping them balance gaming with other parts of life. But this is not the essence of our care in the long term. Gaming limits are a good short-term framework to enable our involvement, but it's our presence, attention and wisdom, rather than our monitoring and pestering, that deliver the real benefits.

Our rush to limit screen time doesn't match our approach in other areas. We don't limit a child's eating time just because they only like one type of food. Instead we worry about what's on their plate and come up with ever more ingenious ways of getting them to eat vegetables. The primary issue isn't how long our children spend at the screen, but the quality, texture, content and context of their activity.

Like the effort spent planning, shopping for, cooking and scheduling meals, understanding and guiding gaming takes time and forethought. We need inspiration from recipe books for mealtimes, and I hope that this book can play a similar role in broadening your family's game time. The parents, carers and children I've worked with have found the rewards well worth the effort.

There's no way to fake this work – discovering for ourselves what games feel like to play, playing games with our children, asking questions about the games they play and listening to their answers.

Kids are brilliant at spotting adults pretending to know or be interested about something. If I'd never eaten vegetables, there is no way I'd have got my kids to eat them. In fact, I made a point of eating them in front of my children when they were younger. I'd demonstrate – complete with yum-yum sounds – that I understand what vegetables are like. If we never play games ourselves, it's very hard to genuinely guide the children we love in this area of life.

Playing Video Games Ourselves

To care for a child who loves playing video games we need to have played them ourselves. It's not what parents and carers want to hear, I know that. It sounds like a pain in the rear. But there's no better way to tame the video games in your family. Grasp this nettle now, particularly if your children are younger, and the flow of games through your home and their lives will be transformed for ever.

The nature of games, as a new medium distinct from films and books, means that they can't be fully understood without experiencing them. If a child was avidly watching cartoons and you'd never seen a cartoon, the best expert advice in the world, or the best scientific reports, couldn't replace the value of watching some cartoons yourself. You need to experience the emotions they evoke, how they tell stories, handle violence and make you laugh. Cartoons have a different texture and feel to other media. Describing them only gets you so far.

Playing a video game yourself may seem like an impossible and undesirable task. Being a parent or carer is busy enough without another thing to add to the list. Then there's the level of skill required; how long you need to invest; putting up with the perceived juvenile nature of it all; the embarrassment of being really bad at it; the incessant bright flashing screen and shrill sounds; or the assumption that your child doesn't want you impinging on their gaming world.

It is hard. But it is important.

With the right advice – the Gaming Recipes at the back of this book, for instance – you can discover games that are mature, easy to play, address themes that interest you and don't take hours to finish. Games that will reframe what you think of the media beyond *Mario Kart*, *Fortnite* or *Minecraft*. Games that, as I discuss in chapter 7, offer a unique way to experience narratives with emotional involvement, offer fresh perspectives on old subjects, create a context to slow down and relax or enjoy ordering a disordered world.

Yes, that's right. You, an adult. A busy parent. You, with a list of all the books you want to read and films to watch. You, who are resolutely never going to play video games. There are games that you will enjoy and benefit from playing.

Playing video games yourself can be your secret weapon. Although often it's not a weapon at all. It's a secret interactive drama, virtual paintbrush, compass, deck of cards, time machine, backpack, soap opera, hidden camera, blossoming garden, spaceship, instrument, blank canvas or love story.

That's the mission of this book: to offer a concrete and tangible route to tame the gaming in your family by putting games in your hands that you will want to play. Not just because they are valuable or engaging but because experiencing them will transform video game fears and concerns into opportunities and understanding.

Playing Video Games With Our Children

Playing games with your children is easier than playing games on your own. Although parents and carers worry about intruding into their child's gaming world, or embarrassment at not being able to play very well, children are usually enthusiastic when parents take an interest in the games they are playing.

If you aren't confident or proficient enough to play yourself, sitting with a child and observing what's going on is a good way to start. Ask questions about what you see. Applaud successes and commiserate with failures. Ask them to show you other games they enjoy, to broaden your understanding.

The parents and carers I work with are often surprised at how transformative their involvement can be. One high-profile example is parent and broadcaster Nihal Arthanayake, who I spoke to a couple of times on his BBC 5 Live show. 'I took your advice on board, so I sit with my son when he plays *Fortnite* . . . I have to say that he derives more joy from that experience of being able to share it with me than sitting on his own and doing it . . . It was an entry into a conversation in his world.'

Establishing this as a long-term sharing of their interest, rather than helicoptering in to check nothing untoward is happening or snowploughing away any dangers, is important. By taking the time to play regularly – no matter how proficient you are – you get to see how video games develop and evolve over weeks and months.

Over the years, playing games together has become part of my family's rhythm, like mealtimes and film nights. If we have a day with nothing planned someone will suggest playing a game together. The simple bow-and-arrow combat of *Tower Fall* or the race to balance a stack of blocks in *Tricky Towers* have us all howling with delight or pain as we win or lose. Or we play a deeper game like *My Child Lebensborn* on our separate devices and then compare our progress over dinner.

It felt strange at first, putting time and effort into video games that I had previously tried to minimise. But I'm now glad that I did. I've worked through the fisticuff adventures of *Uncharted* with my daughter, gone toe-to-toe for hours with one of my sons in *Wii Sports Resort*'s table tennis and explored the mysterious underwater worlds of *Subnautica* with the other. They love escaping into these imaginary worlds with me, and we've had some of our most enjoyable conversations while doing it. Sometimes we'll chat as we play. On other occasions, we share an experience in a game that makes us put the controller down and talk about what just happened.

It's the kind of sharing we do with books and films, but games are particularly good at crossing the generation gap because, as Steven Johnson puts it, they blur the distinction between children's and adults' roles. 'The kids are forced to think like grown-ups: analyzing complex social networks, managing resources, tracking subtle narrative intertwinings, recognizing long-term patterns. The grown-ups, in turn, get to learn from the kids: decoding each new technological wave, parsing the interfaces, and discovering the intellectual rewards of play. Parents should see this as an opportunity, not a crisis. Smart culture is no longer something you force your kids to ingest, like green vegetables. It's something you share.'

This sharing is much more than passive approval. Your presence in your child's gaming world fundamentally changes it in powerful and ongoing ways. With you there, children inevitably start seeing it through the eyes of the family. They wake up to the need to evaluate what it is they are playing and become active participants rather than sleeping consumers. Instead of limiting gaming, in the hope that children will learn good habits in a rote manner, playing together actively involves them in forming what James Paul Gee calls an 'appreciative system' of the norms that guides their participation.

This is an opportunity for parents to nurture conscious reflection and critique of video games. How do they compare next to other things the family spends its time on? How do games stack up socially, culturally and personally? How do we feel after playing them? Do children like the things they do in the games they play? How harsh or supporting is a particular gaming community? The questions I suggest in each gaming inventory are designed to start this process.

This may lead to children stopping playing some games, withdrawing from certain player communities or making more informed decisions about the money they spend on gaming. But equally, it may cause them to spend more time playing to hone skills, develop more structured play patterns or discover new games with more ambitious challenges.

PLAYING GAMES TOGETHER IS EASIER THAN YOU THINK

Some games are easier than others to play. Ask your child which of their games would be good to start with. Most games have difficulty settings, which I suggest you set to 'Easy', or the equivalent, to begin with. Games that have cooperative modes, where two people work together, are good to start on as your child can help you. Game systems also offer assistance with controls, like the Xbox One's excellent Copilot mode, which grants the expert player dual controls, like when you are learning to drive and the instructor has their own brake.

Look through the Gaming Recipes section together to find new games to play. Maybe you want to solve a mystery, explore a new world, step into unusual relationships or be a quipping B-movie hero. Maybe you want to compete or join forces to win.

Children may be resistant at first, suspecting that these are worthy or educational games – why else would you be suggesting them, right? But with a bit of perseverance, and because the Gaming Recipes are all great games, they will warm to the idea. The joy of discovering these experiences together is a powerful way to guide how games are played in your home.

Take your time and don't expect to become proficient in a single session. If you get stuck, you can google the title of the game and the area where you're having trouble. YouTube can offer videos of other people playing at your level. Don't see this need to research as failure; it's what your child will do if they are stuck and it helps you to understand the wider community and world of a particular game.

Talking About Video Games

Playing video games isn't something many parents and carers relish in its own right – not at first, anyway. But then we don't do the food shop because it's how we want to spend our evening. We don't read *The Gruffalo* for the hundredth time because we love the repetition. These things are necessary for healthy meal-, story- and playtimes. They are an important way to care for our children.

This commitment to play, both alone and with our children, creates a new context for video games. It's a simple thing, but it significantly changes how we relate to our children's gaming and to the games themselves. Rather than something that is enjoyed in a separate affinity group, gaming becomes another normal part of our family rhythm.

You'll notice when this happens because the video game talk in your home changes. The questions you ask are different, and children's responses start to make more sense. Rather than helicoptering in to pester them to stop, play less or check the ratings, you are able to ask about their progress, victories, emotions and the new stories they are enjoying in their games.

This leads to questions that deepen, rather than close down, the gaming discussion. Your interest and shared play make children more willing to talk about their hobby. This open context makes it more likely for them to tell you if something upsets them in a game they are playing. Or, conversely, you are more likely to discover when they have achieved something outstanding, or advanced further than they thought possible.

Video games can then become a proper topic for your family, rather than something that has to be kept in its place. Guidance about how long, how often and where the family play video games is then a very different proposition.

This more open conversation about video games situates them as a normal part of life. This clears space to move beyond children wanting ever more screen time and adults increasingly worrying or limiting this. Instead, talk can turn to understanding what they are working at and enjoying in the games they are playing. This will inevitably include discussing annoyances and stresses as well as highlights.

Together, you can move the conversation on from short-term worries to long-term opportunities. This family context is where children can become more than just passive consumers of the games they play and of the communities they are part of: they can evaluate how a game incentivises players to spend money; consider how toxic, ethical or civic-minded a community is; or even find a desire to discover games that aren't the latest fad.

••• ASK BETTER QUESTIONS

Getting out of the habit of the usual interactions around video games can take time if you have older children. However, by playing games yourself and with your children you can turn this corner. Here are some questions that families I've worked with have found helpful, and they've often been surprised at their children's answers:

How do you get around in your game world?

Do you play in teams?

Are you getting better at it?

What are you working on in the game at the moment?

What are the other players like?

How do you develop your character?

Can you show me the best thing you've done in the game?

What do you think it's about?

How does it feel to play?

Do you think I'd be any good at it?

How about we play some together?

My son was having trouble playing *Rocket League*, a highly skilled game of football played with agile, rocket-powered cars. It sounds bizarre, I know, but bear with me. He played for 14 hours a week but was increasingly frustrated and angry during play, and sullen when he had to stop. It was distracting him from schoolwork and casting a shadow over his weekend.

I wanted to understand what was going on so I asked if I could watch him play. He enthusiastically agreed, but also wanted to play it together sometimes as well. As we did this, I started to see how difficult the game was and how proficient he was at it. I was genuinely impressed.

I got him a book on sports psychology to help him find a more positive attitude. This helped us identify that my limiting him to hour-long play sessions meant he didn't have time to warm up before he competed. He came up with a solution where he'd play for longer sessions, using the first hour to practise and warm up before heading into the ranked matches. He would play less in the week and get his homework done promptly to have time for these longer weekend trials.

My role was no longer policing his behaviour but guiding him to healthy play. Rather than pestering him to stop, limiting his time or saying no to the next game he wanted, I could deepen his thinking about what he was playing, encourage him to be more ambitious in his gaming choices and know himself better as a gamer.

He came running down to my garden office the other day, beaming. 'I'm Champ Two, Dad. Champ Two!' he blurted out before he was even in the room. A few months previously I'd have smiled and maybe offered an obligatory 'Well done.' But having played together I knew this meant he was in the top 2 per cent of players worldwide. I could congratulate and celebrate with him on how he'd finally got there after weeks of hard work. We went out for ice cream to celebrate.

Connection like this can only happen as you play together. Like the deeper conversations that happen when you sit down as a family to eat, being part of your child's gaming world is possible because of the effort and preparation invested to create these gaming mealtimes.

It's Not About Changing Your Values

We are used to advice about video games being polarised as either for or against this new media. This can lead to the assumption that game-positive voices are pressuring you to change your family values. However, rather than defend or critique video games, my aim is to equip parents and carers to guide children in healthy directions.

The first-hand understanding of video games I'm suggesting doesn't assume or require any particular stance towards screen-based technology. I don't want you to change your parenting style, just to help you to implement it more effectively. I don't want to convince you to embrace video games, but to engage with them to better understand them and your child's interests.

I've worked with families who are robustly resistant to screens, technology and shooting-play. By the end of my time with them, they are often still committed to their values, but with a better understanding of the technology and how to work with it.

What changes is that video games are no longer seen as the enemy but as a potential ally in preparing children for the outside world.

To use the terminology helpfully outlined in *Parenting for a Digital Future*, parents and carers' approaches to games can be described as 'embracing', 'balancing' or 'resisting'. Of course, each of these is a completely valid approach. But whether you rush to *embrace* the latest gaming experiences, want to *balance* risks and opportunities or *resist* the march of video games into your child's life, you can most effectively establish these values when you have experienced games for yourself and played them with your child. Understanding video games enables you to implement your values in an informed and nuanced way.

If you want to *embrace* games, you can choose the specific experiences that fit best with the maturity, age and interests of your child. If you want a more *balanced* approach, understanding games helps you pick specific ones where the benefits are worth the time and effort. If you want to *resist* too much gaming, you can make informed decisions about what children are missing out on, as well as better understanding the games you want to protect them from.

I should come clean on this issue of values. Most people assume that because I write about video games I wholeheartedly embrace them. However, I'd characterise my personal approach as being in the *balanced* category. We have a high number of games pass through our home, but I'm picky about which ones can stick. When I find a game I love, I often play it through multiple times, but I spend more time doing the crossword than holding a controller.

Whatever our values, caring for a child who loves video games is about creating a healthy context that escapes the extremes of authoritarian or permissive perspectives. Developing our own

video game literacy enables us to earn the trust of an authoritative relationship. We can offer children guidance tailored to the world they are growing up in because we have a growing understanding of the video games they want to play.

This moves us away from ineffective worrying or sentimental nostalgia to offering holistic, worldly-wise care. At our own pace and in our own way, we can ensure our children develop a healthy relationship with this new medium. Within the committed boundaries of our parenting style, we can start to integrate digital interaction into everyday life.

This not only keeps gaming healthy but has significant value for our children's digital future. Increasingly their friendships, work, leisure and community will flow between the virtual and physical world. Coming from a home where this back and forth is practised – with both successes and failures – equips them to thrive in that future.

If you have a child who loves video games, consider yourself fortunate. This is an excellent opportunity to learn together about the value of digital experiences and how to healthily situate them in everyday life.

INDUSTRY RESOURCE:

iNET GUARDIAN'S GOOD TOOLS FOR HEALTHY CONVERSATIONS

There are many services and tools you can subscribe to for additional information and for help with managing online gaming in the home. While some tools, like Circle, focus on limits and monitoring, iNet Guardian is a family-owned example that helps parents to guide children towards healthy gaming through engagement. By downloading and installing its software on your devices, you can use the parent dashboard to understand how your family uses technology.

It was founded by the parents of two young boys who wanted to 'develop easy-to-use tools to help parents and carers to manage their children's online world'. Because it's by parents for parents, rather than coming from someone with a background in policing or teaching children, it has a greater focus on enabling parents and carers to have informed and practical discussions with their children, leading to a safer and more enjoyable online experience.

When it comes to online safety, the more children understand the reasons to stay safe, the easier it is to incorporate online safety into their everyday lives. 'We feel that our responsibility as providers of parental guidance software and services is not only to offer the tools but also to provide parents and carers with up-to-date information about trends in their children's online world,' says iNet Guardian's co-founder Paul Ford. 'As with all aspects of parenting, it's about parental guidance rather than parental control.'

The benefits of services and tools like iNet Guardian is that they can apply the same criteria to multiple devices via the internet. This can prevent children cruising from one device to the next once their time has run out. Instead, they can have a conversation with parents about what they want to do next.

6. HOW TO LOVE A CHILD WHO LOVES VIDEO GAMES TOO MUCH

Everything we've discussed so far is all well and good, but doesn't there come a time when enough is enough – or, rather, too much is too much? Engaging with video games, having healthy conversations about them and guiding your child's play sounds good on paper. But what about children at the extreme end of the spectrum, where common sense and balance has become impossible in the face of obsession?

However small the percentage of children with a clinically diagnosable problem with video games at the level WHO describes, surely there are still limits to the touchy-feely approach for parents of gaming-obsessed offspring? With new games holding children's attention for longer and longer, doesn't there come a time for detox camps, quitting all video games, hiding power cables or unplugging the Wi-Fi?

Johann Hari, an author and journalist specialising in addiction and depression, challenges the abstinence assumption common in drug addiction treatment: that the most pressing concern should be to remove the object of obsession from the life of an addict.

In his book *Chasing the Scream*, he suggests that drug addiction is due not only to how chemical substances operate on the brain but to the environment of the addict. He tells a story of an experiment on rats. When in an empty cage with two bottles of water, one mixed with heroin and one without, they quickly preferred the drugged water and killed themselves. By changing the environment so it was full of everything rats love – good food, company, reproduction and entertainment – none of them overdosed.[*]

'For a hundred years now we've been singing war songs about addicts; I think all along we should have been singing love songs to them,' he said in his TED talk, 'because the opposite of addiction is not sobriety; the opposite of addiction is connection.'[†]

It's a shocking statement, 'the opposite of addiction is connection'. It goes against assumed common knowledge. Rather than focusing on removing the thing that is apparently driving detrimental behaviour, we should focus on creating an environment where the person can re-establish connections with other people, work, society, the future and themselves.

Of course, rat behaviour doesn't necessarily equate with human behaviour, and video games aren't chemically addictive. Also, as Hari acknowledges, we need to be careful not to encourage enabling relationships that may lead to addiction relapse. But

---

[*] Johann Hari, *Chasing the Scream*, Bloomsbury Circus, London, 2015.
[†] Johann Hari, 'Everything you think you know about addiction is wrong', available at www.ted.com/talks/johann_hari_everything_you_think_you_know_about_addiction_is_wrong

still, he makes a powerful point about the danger of hammering an addict with pressure to stop, before or without addressing their need for connection.

Gabor Maté, a physician with 20 years of experience in family practice and palliative care for addiction, underlines the futility of forceful parenting in his book *In the Realm of Hungry Ghosts: Close Encounters with Addiction*. 'While it is natural for the loved ones of an addict to wish to reform him, it cannot be done . . . The person attached to his addiction will respond to an attempt to separate him from his habit as a lover would someone who disparages his beloved: with hostility.'[*]

In the book *Video Game Influences on Aggression, Cognition, and Attention*, Rune K. L. Nielsen and Daniel Kardefelt-Winther highlight other reasons not to rush to ban or limit technology. 'In a day and age where video games form an important part of

---

[*] Gabor Maté, *In the Realm of Hungry Ghosts: Close Encounters with Addiction*, Vermilion, London, 2018.

children's lives, the message that video gaming is addictive can have unintended consequences. Indeed, scholars warn that immersion and engagement with video games is frequently misinterpreted as addiction which might be used as an excuse to restrict access and undermine children's rights.' Overstating the risks can lead parents to rush to apply restrictions that 'might be ineffective or even harmful for children, limiting their opportunities to benefit from digital technology'.*

Similarly, UNICEF highlights the point in its 2017 *Children in a Digital World* report:

> *Applying clinical concepts to children's everyday behaviour does not help support them in developing healthy screen time habits . . . And conflating the screen time debate with addiction can even be harmful. For example, in some countries, the idea of addiction to technology has been used to justify the incarceration of children in treatment camps despite a lack of evidence for the efficacy of such approaches.*[†]

How we love children who appear to be addicted to video games requires particular care. Not only in terms of how we apply clinical concepts to their behaviour but how we interpret the cause and effect of their excessive gaming. On both of these levels, simply pressuring children to stop gaming may do more harm than good.

Hari expands his theory beyond addictive substances, in his book

* Rune K. L. Nielsen and Daniel Kardefelt-Winther, 'Helping Parents Make Sense of Video Game Addiction', *Video Game Influences on Aggression, Cognition, and Attention*, Springer, Switzerland, 2018, pp. 59–69.
† Brian Keeley (ed.), *Children in a Digital World*, available at www.unicef.org/publications/files/SOWC_2017_ENG_WEB.pdf

Lost Connections.[*] Too quickly treating any addictive behaviour means we can miss the underlying issues. He reframes clinical depression and anxiety as symptoms of our environment, not just our biology. They are the smoke that we need to understand and pay attention to, rather than just get rid of, so we can see and address the fire.

Unlike chemical substances or physical gratification, gaming is not an easy way to deal with disconnection. Playing video games, as professor of interactive computing Ian Bogost describes it, requires considerable effort. They are 'rusty machinery we operate despite themselves', he writes in his book *How to Talk About Videogames.*[†] Contrary to appearances, video games are hard work and require great effort to play.

A child who is using games to deal with other issues in their life has put in considerable energy to get what they need from them. They have taken a risk on a new and imaginative way to cope. They have taken their place in what Johnson describes as 'a generation that welcomes the challenge of new technologies, that embraces new genres'.

It's something underlined in the recent study by Pekka Mertala and Mikko Meriläinen that found that 'children are not mere passive consumers of digital games but are agentic meaning-makers who are capable of critically evaluating digital games when a safe and supportive space and the appropriate medium are provided'.[‡]

Particularly at the extreme end of this group, seeing excessive gaming as possibly being brave action by children in response to life's harsh challenges makes it clear that we shouldn't remove this

---

[*] Johann Hari, *Lost Connections*, Bloomsbury Publishing, London, 2018.
[†] Ian Bogost, *How to Talk About Videogames*, University of Minnesota Press, Minneapolis, 2015.
[‡] Pekka Mertala and Mikko Meriläinen, 'The Best Game in the World: Exploring Young Children's Digital Game-related Meaning-making via Design Activity', Global Studies of Childhood, available at https://journals.sagepub.com/eprint/BKI25RJBYXHJJGMXPV7R/full

remarkably innovative coping strategy without first ensuring they have a connected way forward.

Maté states that 'the precursor to addiction is dislocation . . . the loss of psychological, social and economic integration into family and culture; a sense of exclusion, isolation and powerlessness.' If playing video games too much is a response to this scenario we have a responsibility to understand how the games are helping or hindering our children so we can then guide them to maximise the former and minimise the latter. We can start to undo what Maté describes as the child's perception of not being 'seen, understood, empathized with and "gotten" on the emotional level.'

Unlike chemical addictions, we can share the video games at the centre of children's obsessive behaviour. We can see first-hand what it is about a particular game that they enjoy, and perhaps even need, as a solution to other things happening in their world.

What's more, unlike addictive substances, video games can offer some of the types of reconnection Hari suggests in his *Lost Connections* book. As we saw in the chapter 'The Benefits of Video Games', they can be a place for positive social and psychological benefits. They can create deep connections with other people. They offer space to pursue ambitious, long-term creative projects at a comfortable pace. They enable us to imagine the possibility of different values and think deeply and critically about how that might work. They take players who would never consider meditation into a state of meditative flow where they escape anxiety and reconnect with themselves.

This enables us to ask different questions of children at the excessive end of the gaming spectrum. Taking a lead from Maté, we can move from asking 'Why the addiction?' to 'Why the pain?'

Rather than 'Why can't you just stop?', 'What's so important about your game?', 'Can't you see you're obsessed?', we can ask, 'What happened to you before you started playing so much?', 'What are you getting from the game that you can't get elsewhere?', 'Why is the effort and work you spend on your games worth it?'

This is what it means to love children who play video games to the extremes described by the WHO's definition of gaming disorder: paying attention to them, not as broken or tricked by technology, but as individuals responding to their environment in a way that enables them to survive. Rather than putting more pressure on them to curb their behaviour or detox from their obsessive relationship with the screen, we can support them to understand and refine the place video games holds in their lives.

HOBBIES FOR GAMERS

As well as engaging with the video games our children are playing, it's useful to spend time developing alternative activities. Like the use of limits and restrictions, this can create space for them and us to reflect on their gaming as well as introducing new things to do.

Along with the sorts of things you can uncover by googling – learning a musical instrument or language, drawing and painting, making dens, collecting, getting a pet – the following activities have a particular synergy with people literate with video games, either because they create a similar experience or because they draw on similar skills and abilities.

Miniature wargames

Games like Warhammer 40,000 or Warhammer Age of Sigmar involve creating a battle scenario played on a table with minature figures, counters and scenery. Movement and shooting are calculated with dice rolls, measuring tape and the rule book. The boxes of figures can be quite pricey but offer good value as they not only create a social tabletop game but also encourage players to spend many hours patiently painting figures. There are also many free clubs in Games Workshop or similar stores where players can compete.

Board and card games

Beyond the familiar games of *Monopoly* and *Cluedo*, there is a whole world of new board games that cross over to the video game audience. Particular favourites in my family include the geographical tactics of *Carcassonne*, the jewel collecting of *Splendor*, the card-collecting hilarity of *Exploding Kittens* and the strategic Greek villa-building of *Santorini*. You can find these and many others in your local toy store or online.

Cubing

The competitive nature of solving a Rubik's cube as fast as you can is the initial draw here. But as this hobby develops there is a wide community to engage with, including advice and tips on YouTube and lots of algorithm solutions to learn. Add this to the physical technique of manipulating the cube, and the wide range of cubes that can be purchased, and this is a hobby with a long life – provided you can put up with the infernal click-clacking everywhere you go.

Geocaching

Using an app on your smartphone, you go on a treasure hunt to find physical boxes hidden by the geocaching community and enter your name in a logbook. There are hundreds of thousands of boxes hidden all over the world. Kids enjoy the combination of technology and exploration, and there's a real thrill in finding these hidden in your local area. You can also hide your own boxes and add them to the website for others to find.

Gaming books

The majority of popular video games have associated fiction and non-fiction books that can be a good route into other activities. There are also books that extend the backstory of a particular game world and its characters, or offer players tips for the next time they play. Then there are game-like choose-your-own-adventure books that offer an interactive experience.

Running

Along with all sorts of sporting activities, running is particularly easy to get into because you can start from whatever fitness level you have. You might want to find a 'Couch to 5k' programme online or join a local weekly run via the parkrun.org.uk website. There are also some great apps that combine gaming with running. These range from *Zombies, Run!*, the interactive zombie radio play that incentivises you to run faster, to *Run an Empire*, where you capture territory by running round it in the real world.

Flying things

Learning how to create different types of paper aeroplanes from scratch or making your own kites are fun hobbies that can go in interesting directions. There's a competitive element to the paper-folding that also leads to origami. Interestingly, the *Tearaway* games on PlayStation reward players with papercraft objects to print and make. The kite-flying can also lead in competitive directions or towards kiteboarding for more exuberant fun.

Survival skills

Developing outdoor survival skills often connects well with children who have enjoyed games with a similar theme. This can be as simple as route planning, building fires or wild camping for the night. Orienteering with a mapping app, using your phone as a compass or reading the night sky with a star chart app can also add some technological interest.

Depending on the underlying issues uncovered by our engagement with our children, we may still need to help them limit or abstain from video games for a period of time. Using the tools and settings on gaming devices can play a vital role in helping them find ways to create connections that don't require technology or screens.

Doing this consistently, with understanding and compassion, but also with strength, patience and resilience during inevitable and sometimes extreme push-back enables us to establish breathing space when things have got out of hand. This reveals if their inability to stop playing comes from loving the game too much or from something deeper. Now, though, we can do this as loving allies, rather than opponents, of our children and of the games they are using to ease their pain.

This avoids the risk of what Phippen and Brennan term 'over-blocking' children's access to video games, which blunts their ability

to learn both the benefits and pitfalls of technology. Remembering what they found that children ask of us – 'listen, don't judge, and understand' – we can avoid being dismissive and treat them with the respect and authenticity that lead to safe, ongoing support. Rather than win our disagreements over whether gaming is good or bad, we can provide guidance that goes beyond simply 'kicking the can down the road', as Phippen and Brennan warn.

'Addictions arise from thwarted love, from our thwarted ability to love children the way they need to be loved, from our thwarted ability to love ourselves and one another in the ways we all need,' writes Maté. 'Opening our hearts is the path to healing addiction – opening our compassion for the pain within ourselves, and the pain all around us.'

Where this exceeds our ability to cope, it's important to get advice from a doctor and other medical professionals. This should be from those trained in holistic and empirically valid treatments rather than commercial game-addiction clinics or detox camps, which often have no evidence base behind them. Rather than googling 'gaming addiction', start by visiting your doctor, who can direct you to an appropriate service to identify what can be a range of complex problems NHS England describe as including 'compulsive behaviours, development disorders and difficulties earlier in

childhood that underlie addiction'. For more urgent help contact your GP or call Samaritans (116 123 in the UK).*

My hope is that with your growing gaming literacy and the game suggestions in this book, even when the behaviour and worries are extreme you can join your child in their innovative way of finding connection from the games they play; not to blindly endorse their gaming pastime, or to allow antisocial or disruptive behaviour, but to help them understand their gaming more fully and how it impacts on their life, both positively and negatively.

You can help them distinguish between the times they're playing because they want to and when they are playing because they can't stop. You can guide them towards a wider diet of gaming experiences that can better serve their mental well-being. You can appropriately use automatic restrictions to create space for the growth of this understanding. You can help them articulate what they get from the games they play. And, most importantly, you can discover what else is going on in their lives that excessive gaming is soothing.

---

* NHS England, 'Country's top mental health nurse warns video games pushing young people into "under the radar" gambling', 18 January 2020, available at www.england.nhs. uk/2020/01/countrys-top-mental-health-nurse-warns-video-games-pushing-young-people-into-under-the-radar-gambling

7. LEARNING TO LOVE VIDEO GAMES

Not everyone loves video games. Not everyone has to. But if your child loves video games, it helps if you at least like them, even if it's just a little bit.

'I don't play video games and I'm never going to' is a common response I get from parents and carers. This usually gets validating nods. After all, games are for children, right? Why would a busy parent waste time on them, even if they wanted to?

What's happening here is what always happens when new media emerge. Parents aren't to blame for their video game blind spot. All they need to turn this around is to encounter a video game that has been made for someone like them. *Fortnite* or *Minecraft*, great as they are for young players, aren't going to do the trick, but there are some amazing examples in the back of this book that will.

More than advice, tips or strategies, the discovery of video games you want to play yourself can supercharge your care of children who love games. I've enjoyed many games as much as my favourite books and films. *The Last of Us* moved me deeply with its intimate look at the reluctance of fathers and daughters to admit they need each other. *Limbo* drew back the curtain on the powerlessness of childhood in a way that still shapes how I talk and listen to my children. Losing myself in the

landscape of *Shadow of the Colossus* has been as profoundly calming of my anxiety as listening to my favourite albums. The camaraderie of soaring with temporary companions in *Journey* before walking hand-in-hand into the bright, cold blizzard has been as spiritual as any church service I've attended.

Sharing these experiences is difficult, though. We all know how to acquire books or access films. We all know what books and films are, how they work and what they might do to us when we read or watch them. We have an established way of talking about them, and welcome expert introductions from chat show hosts and newspaper journalists. But we have no such shared understanding, language or route to discovery for video games.

This lack of gaming literacy is what stands in the way of parents making informed choices and guiding their children's gaming as they do other areas of life. Like learning a new language, we can start with expert tuition and advice, but it only really blossoms when we step into another country and surround ourselves with fluent speakers.

BAFTA HIGHLIGHTS CULTURALLY IMPORTANT VIDEO GAMES

A great way to appreciate the cultural importance and new developments in video games is the BAFTA Games Awards. Since 1998 these have been presented annually to recognise, honour and reward outstanding creative achievement in games. In 2006, the BAFTA Games Awards gained a higher profile as BAFTA announced its decision 'to give video games equal status with film and television'.

Awards like this are also an excellent way for parents to discover brilliant games to play. The Family category highlights games that will work really well for parents and children. The Game Beyond Entertainment category is also of interest, as this highlights more unusual games with an emphasis on storytelling that addresses topics parents may find appealing.

But like children starting to read for the first time, these first interactions with games are fragile. If they are too baffling it may seem that video games are simply not for you. Maybe you've tried playing games before and found the experience confusing or frustrating? Perhaps the video games you've tried were aimed only at children? Maybe you were put off by the complexity of the game's strategy, the confusing flashing screen or the number of buttons on the controller?

Those things are all understandable, inevitable even, without the right advice. But set aside the technological hurdles and none of this is as complicated or expensive as you might expect. First, let's try some different ways of looking at video games. The metaphors I use below – of games as cathedrals to explore, mountains to climb, paintings to lose yourself in, and so on – are my way of tempting parents and carers to give video games a try for themselves.

More Like Cathedrals Than Playing Fields

Viewed from a distance or at an angle from across the room, we only see the flickering flat surface of video games. Position yourself over your child's shoulder or next to them, though, and they become a window to another place. Linger there for more than a few minutes and this view becomes a door through which the player enters another world that responds to their interactions.

These virtual worlds are spaces where players can do things and be someone they can't in their normal life. This might be the simple satisfaction of completing rows in *Candy Crush*, taking charge of pizza delivery in an ad-hoc restaurant team in *Roblox*'s *Work at a Pizza Place*, or exploring the weather-worn landscapes and day–night changing tundra in *The Legend of Zelda: Breath of the Wild*.

This may sound similar to how books and films offer windows into imaginary or historical worlds, but games don't focus your view with directorial control of the camera, insist you listen to particular dialogue or progress at a certain pace. Instead, they invite you to step into the space they create.

This is more complex than the well-known rules of the flat playing field. The football pitch, rugby ground and tennis court are marked out for simple and well-understood competitions. Playing a video game is more like walking into an ancient cathedral, pristine shopping mall, quiet library or moody auditorium. These spaces invite different interactions and use of imagination depending on the way they look, sound and feel.

And unlike playing fields (apart from games that simulate sports), the rules of video games aren't always marked down or apparent; they can take time to understand. When we first enter a space like this it can be confusing, but over time, and by returning to it periodically, it can become a valued part of our lives.

Remembering this is helpful when we first encounter video games. Allowing ourselves to get a little lost, get it wrong, miss things or go the wrong way is a natural part of being somewhere new. It takes time to understand how these new spaces work, how other people behave in them and how we want to engage with this ourselves.

This sense of initial confusion, exploration and trial-and-error is part of what players love about video games. As much as for the completing, solving or winning, games are enjoyed for the spaces they create. Worlds where the usual rules don't apply.

VIDEO-GAME-ENRICHED CATHEDRAL SERVICE

I was invited to test the theory that games create culturally rich spaces in a similar way to old buildings by Exeter Cathedral. With the clergy I created a series of Sunday communion services involving a video game. We chose games that matched the theme of each service (*ABZÛ*'s underwater depths and the story of Jonah, *Journey*'s wilderness and the story of the Exile and *Flower*'s flock of petals and the story of creation) and projected them onto a large screen at the front. The congregation took turns to engage in these games by passing the controller round as the other elements of the service continued – singing, Bible reading, prayer and sharing bread and wine.

As could be seen when the service was featured on the BBC's Stories of Us series, the combination of the ancient and the modern was jarring at first to some of the older congregation who had not played a game like this before. However, by the end of the service many of them said that the game offered new ways of worshipping that fitted surprisingly well with the other elements. For example, as the communion cup was raised in one service whoever had the controller inadvertently triggered a group of blood-red flowers to bloom on the screen. It was as if it had been planned, but of course this was just a natural consequence of the cultural quality of the game and its use in this way.

For children, this is the chance to be heroes, regardless of playground hierarchy, or physical or psychological challenges. They can engage in social interactions at their own pace. They can escape worries or fears and establish the calm they need to think clearly while they play. For adults, games can be like stepping into a museum packed with cultural artefacts or a cathedral with stained-glass windows and soaring architecture. These spaces offer a chance to spend time somewhere that is designed for us to discover, participate in and interpret for ourselves.

More Like Mountains Than Machines

On the face of it, video games are machines. Under the visual veneer, they are frantically responding to our tapping, pressing and pushing of screens, buttons and sticks. They're working like the clappers to present us with a game world to enjoy.

But they are strange machines. The printing press, the factory and the car are considered worthwhile for what they enable us to achieve or what they produce. Shortcomings and costs are balanced by the benefits of production. As a result, it's tempting to see video games as a new way to achieve things. Gaming is sometimes justified for its entertainment, transferable hard skills or how it can incentivise players to behave in a certain way and learn things. But this mixes up the noise of the engine with the ability to travel somewhere.

The algorithms that drive video games – whether it's the hero's journey of *Tearaway Unfolded,* the jumping ascent of *Celeste* or the hunting in *Horizon Zero Dawn* – aren't primarily designed to produce a tangible benefit or have a particular function. Video games aren't designed to enable you to produce something. They are more like mountains, created to be climbed.

'We think they are appliances, mere tools that exist to entertain or distract,' writes Ian Bogost in his book *How to Talk About Videogames*.* But, with their looming presence, 'they insert themselves into our lives, weaving within and between our daily practices, both structuring and disrupting them. They induce feelings just as art or music or fiction might do.'

'We play games because they are there to be played. Because we want to feel what it's like to play them,' continues Bogost. Like the challenge of climbing great snow-capped peaks or running a coast path, it's hard work to play a game. There's the discomfort of concentrating on something solely for its own sake; the commitment of taking time out of our busy lives to persevere with it; the irritation that the game is reluctant to submit to the plans we have for it.

We play video games such as *Animal Crossing, Subnautica* or *Hollow Knight* not for any particular benefit but because they are immovable, mountainous challenges. We climb them even though failure is likely. Even at their summit, there are endless other mountains to climb.

But as Jesper Juul puts it in *The Art of Failure*, 'Failure connects us personally to the events in the game; it proves *we matter*, that the world does not simply continue regardless of our actions.'† Video games exist for us but at the same time are oblivious to what we need them to do.

For young players standing at the foothills of a new video game, there's an invitation to climb further than they have gone before and commit to something bigger than they can imagine. For adults, video

---

* Ian Bogost, *How to Talk About Videogames*, University of Minnesota Press, Minneapolis, 2015.
† Jesper Juul, *The Art of Failure: An Essay on the Pain of Playing Video Games*, MIT Press, Massachusetts, 2016.

games offer an almost insurmountable challenge. They can be a place of reflection and deep thinking, provided we are willing to count the cost of the climb. Reaching the peak isn't just about making it to the top, but what we had to find inside ourselves to get there.

More Like Paintings Than Films

Video games let us progress at our own pace. We control our path through their worlds with the movement of our character, how quickly we solve puzzles and which interactions we choose.

In this way, although many games increasingly look like movies or animations, they are experienced more like paintings. It may sound strange to compare an endlessly moving, interactive space to finite brushstrokes, but whether we are playing *Flower*, *Fe* or *Alan Wake*, the encounter is strikingly similar when you experience it.

Gazing at a painting draws us in until nothing else exists in the

room for us. Our eyes move over the canvas at our own pace, noticing some details while missing others. We explore the scene in seemingly random order. What we see mingles with memory and brings to mind all manner of other images. As Jeanette Winterson puts it, 'There is a constant exchange of emotion between us . . . the artist I need never meet, the painting in its own right, and me, the one who loves it . . . The picture on my wall, art object and art process, is a living line of movement, a wave of colour that repercusses in my body'.

This is what games do. Like a painting, they create space to meditate and think deeply about what we are seeing. Whether it's the lifelike tundra of *The Witcher 3: Wild Hunt,* the stylised darkness of *Limbo* or the children's storybook pages of *Florence,* game worlds bring to mind other real-world places, people and times of life, so that the real and virtual intermingle in our mind.

In a game, though, the canvas moves and responds to our presence. There is an unexpected reversal as we become co-creators of the world we are exploring. It is as if the painting isn't complete until we see it, and now that we do, it becomes visibly malleable and porous to our ideas. The experience is a combination of appreciating the brushstrokes that create the space while at the same time being granted the exhilarating permission to move the paint around.

For young players, like the fascinating and absorbing experience created by good galleries and museums, video games are a chance to see the world differently, with space and time to think deeply about what that means. For busy adults, their interactive worlds trick us into dropping our guard and lingering in their electronic brushstrokes.

More Like Poems Than Novels

Although some video games include a lot of dialogue and narration, playing them is more like reading poetry than novels. They intentionally break the rules of storytelling, just as poems break the rules of grammar.

Rather than tell stories directly, or in an accepted order, we overhear narrative from passers-by, or deduce it from how the world responds to us. The way a button behaves in *Firewatch*, or how a puzzle is solved (or unsolvable) in *Uncharted: Drake's Fortune*, offers as much of a story as the things characters say to us and to each other.

Like poems for our fingertips, we must feel our way forward with interactions. At times all we can do is continue headlong into confusion. We worry that we've missed crucial information or are unable to interpret what's happening. Games like *Hellblade: Senua's Sacrifice* or *What Remains of Edith Finch* don't make things easy for us. Like a poem, they continue with impenetrable confidence regardless of whether we can keep up, insisting that everything will make sense by the end.

Both games and poetry can seem as though they're not meant for us; poems aren't for children, and games aren't for adults. Only they are. Whether it's age, class, literacy, culture or technology, there are hurdles to overcome before we can access either of these precious resources, but there are substantial benefits to people of all ages and from all backgrounds once we do.

There's no easy way round this, apart from starting to read poems and play games. Discovering the pleasure of either can happen in a moment and last a lifetime. We can be minding our own business when we pick up a controller and then, out of the blue, encounter

something that changes our perspective forever. Video games like *That Dragon, Cancer* or *Papers, Please* come to us – as Jeanette Winterson describes as the role of fiction in her book *Art Objects: Essays on Ecstasy and Effrontery* – with exhilarating force from outside our familiar experience, 'clearing a space for new stories about ourselves'.*

Games offer children a way into something they can't fully understand or explain. For adults, video games offer unusual, experiential perspectives on familiar topics that get under the skin in unexpected ways.

More Like Walks Than Races

Video games create participatory spaces where we spend time with virtual characters. Like family walks, their worlds and dramas are an excuse to talk, move and orienteer together. We set out with just the thought of adventure and discovery but return home with a greater connection to the people we've travelled with.

Whether it's the puzzles in *Heaven's Vault*, coming-of-age drama *Knights and Bikes* or *Affordable Space Adventures'* intrepid

---

* Jeanette Winterson, *Art Objects: Essays on Ecstasy and Effrontery*, Vintage, London, 1995.

exploration, games invite our participation as friends, guardians, brothers, sisters, mothers, fathers, aunties and uncles (to name a few), rather than mandatory competitors. And, like walks, our interactive options are limited. Locomotion is predetermined, and our route can't stray too far if we're to get home again. We can do certain things and can't do others. We linger at the back or rush on ahead. We fall into the steady rhythm of play and find ourselves talking and listening rather than racing.

In many ways, video games shouldn't work. The heavy-handed narrative of *Detroit: Become Human*, awkward characters in *The Legend of Zelda: Breath of the Wild*, rudimentary anthropomorphic shapes in *Thomas Was Alone*, and inability of two characters to touch each other convincingly in *Uncharted: Drake's Fortune* should undermine any emotional quality game developers try to create.

But because these peculiar and uncanny visuals represent people we travel the virtual world with, they actually affect us deeply. Heading out the door to walk virtual streets with video game characters creates a connection with them (as well as the people we are playing with). Together we stand shoulder to shoulder in shoot-outs, hunt down missing artefacts, travel vast distances and even come close to death. So when they permanently die or admit to character flaws, it feels as though these things are happening to people we know. And in many ways they are.

Like those family walks, games create a calm space to learn about people and relationships without particularly worrying about where we are going or keeping up with others on the same outing. For children reluctant to put on wellies, such games are a chance to walk in someone else's shoes. For adults, they take us to a new horizon with space to discover fresh perspectives when we get there.

HOW TO READ A VIDEO GAME

Today's video games look increasingly like the real world, but the spaces they conjure have been specially built for you to understand, move through and interpret. Even when you're exploring a mountain, a cave, a park or a desert in a video game, it has been created with design principles similar to that used in public buildings like museums and libraries. As your literacy and understanding of video games grows, you'll start to 'read' them as you would any new space, picking up on clues that help you understand what to do.

Here are some techniques that game designers often use to help you navigate their games:

Lights Flashing lights, or brightly lit areas, in video games often indicate the way to proceed, or the location of key items you need to collect.

Maps and signs Video games often provide a map for their game world, either from the start or picked up soon after the beginning. This and any signage in the game world are important reference points.

Cookie trails Some games will give you a visible trail of arrows or crumbs to follow to the next destination or person on your mission.

Colour Games often tell players that a particular colour signifies an object you can climb up or over. These coloured surfaces are usually in contrast to the rest of the world.

Texture The precise appearance of walls and buildings often indicates whether you can scale them or interact with them some other way. The ground is often signed with track marks or worn paths to direct your travel.

Sound Games use sound to direct players towards certain areas or objects. Wearing headphones can help you benefit from the directional nature of video game noises, where volume increases as you approach the required location or item.

Collectables Many games include items to collect. These work not only as a challenge for the player but can lead you in a certain direction, like a trail of cookies, and indicate which areas you have been to.

Destinations Games often use large buildings or structures as destinations when their visibility in the distance helps orient your direction of travel.

There Are Video Games for You

Video games aren't substitutes for cathedrals, paintings, poems, mountains and family walks, but these features of the real world bring us closer to understanding what video games are like to play.

I know this sounds far-fetched when you just want your daughter or son to go outside more often and get muddy, but this perspective on games helps us see them for what they are: a normal part of life. Along with the Gaming Recipes in the back of this book, I hope it gives you some new ways to see how video games may be of interest to you. Picking up a video game and playing it yourself is parenting dynamite that empowers you to tease apart legitimate concerns and unfounded fears.

Best of all, playing video games yourself makes it impossible for your child to see gaming as separate from the rest of the family. It anchors gaming alongside other family habits and traditions so that your child learns how to integrate digital experiences with everyday life. It transforms vague concerns into a clear understanding of what might be driving gaming excess in your children.

Perhaps most importantly, playing games yourself enables you to partake in this new media and benefit from it directly. Maybe you'll discover characters, stories and worlds that change you. Maybe you'll find a new route to well-being. Maybe you'll experience first-hand emotional insight into complex topics. Maybe you'll get really good at using toy cars to get footballs into goals. It's got to be worth finding out, right?

8. WHAT THE (OTHER) EXPERTS SAY

My advice on children's video game playing comes from my own experience as a parent. While I've kept things focused on equipping you to guide your children in your own way, inevitably I'll have my blind spots. After all, my children aren't like your children.

During my research for this book, and in my work as a video game journalist, I've had the privilege of learning from other parents and carers: friends, fellow journalists, game developers, child welfare professionals, and academics. I asked each of them to tell me the one thing they wished parents understood better about video games. Here's what they said.

··· Simon Parkin, journalist for the *New Yorker* and author of *Death by Video Game*

Parents often baulk both at the sight of their child playing an online game and at the head-mic wobbling in front of the mouth, the ears encased, worryingly, by headphones. It can give the appearance of being closed off to the world (and, of course, brings the spectre of stranger-danger somehow into the home).

However, online games have increasingly become an extension of the school playground, a place where a child can choose with whom he or she plays, and what they do together. Online games can be places that open a child's imagination and expand their horizons. They can be places of joy, delight and cooperation, just so long as they are set within thoughtful boundaries and, even more importantly, honoured by parental interest.

I'd recommend *Nidhogg*. It is a sword-fighting game that is simple enough for younger children to play, brief enough to play in fifteen-minute bursts, and intense enough to keep everyone laughing or screaming.

Anne Longfield OBE, Children's Commissioner for England

I'd like parents to know that not having a games console doesn't mean your child isn't a big gamer. So much gaming is now done on smartphones, and girls, in particular, may choose not to game on a console or PC but do so on their phone.

Talking to children reveals that gaming is important to them in ways that aren't always obvious to parents. They invest hundreds of hours in creating their online gaming worlds. If their creations are damaged by other players – whether intentionally or not – they will understandably be upset. They can also play for a long time because of a commitment and pressure to support other players in their team.

Games in and of themselves aren't bad for children. Don't ignore or dismiss it if your child is really interested in them. Get involved by playing with them and watching them play. Taking an interest in this way enables you to support them when things go wrong and celebrate their successes. As with online and social media, it also means that they will listen to you and you can set healthy parameters.

••• Keza MacDonald, video games editor at the *Guardian*

Playing video games can be as social, creative and fulfilling a passion as any other – it all depends on what you play and how you play it. Like TV, film or whatever else, there's junky fun entertainment and enriching, high-quality entertainment, and most people play a mix of both. Although games are social spaces where children hang out with friends, the visual is that they're sitting alone in front of a screen. It's important to remember that, in reality, they're often chatting with pals and having adventures together.

Screen time is just time. Don't worry about how long they play, but the quality of the experience. With younger children, we curate TV and toys; it's important to curate games too. Don't feel guilty if they don't stick to strict time limits, but engage with them while they play and do what you can to ensure they're playing something age-appropriate and imagination-sparking.

Like movies, not all games are equal. *Candy Crush* is fun, but it's disposable junk like *The Care Bears Movie*. Nintendo games are more like a Pixar film that sparks imagination and emotions. Then there are indie games like *Starbound*, which are less well known but great. Understanding this is the first step to guiding children to a balanced gaming diet. You don't have to cut out the junk entirely, but it shouldn't be all they play.

When my son was two, he loved *Toca Kitchen* on the iPad. It's a game where you select and prepare food for various characters to eat. Unlike other kids' games, it's open-ended so you can play it how you want, like you would a real toy kitchen. While I dutifully created culinary masterpieces for our guests in the game, my son just delighted in feeding them disgusting food – lemons, onions, raw sausages. He loved it.

··· Ben Anderson, Mental Health First Aid instructor

Parents should have more confidence in their children. Young people should be listened to and respected in fields where they are fast becoming experts, or already are. In spite of commercial pressures, young people are driving these industries. They are deciding what sinks and what becomes the next big thing. We need to support and respect their knowledge and power rather than look to hold it back.

In my work on the front line within schools and youth organisations, I find young people need help to develop the hard skills needed to navigate through this new digital landscape in a safe and responsible manner. In helping here, we need to be super-careful not to alienate or push children away. We want them to trust our support in the future so when they encounter potentially dangerous or difficult situations there is a communication channel to get our support in a non-judgmental manner.

I love playing *FIFA* with my 15-year-old nephew. Our relationship while gaming is one without barriers, where we are equal, and one where he feels he can talk to me about anything. Although it's my job to know about this stuff, he still teaches me something new about gaming, youth culture and the dynamics of young people when we play.

··· James Paul Gee, Mary Lou Fulton Presidential Professor of Literacy Studies at Arizona State University

Parents of young children should know that video games are technology devoted to problem-solving. Unlike school, though, games are good at getting children to want to spend time (and even pocket money) for the chance of learning how to beat the next problem.

In the twenty-first century, we need the benefits games offer. This might be how they enable the player to embody and experience complex systems to fuel passion and persistence. This might be playfulness that leads to innovation and design-thinking. Or this might be collaborations, in which groups are smarter than the smartest person in the group.

Like books and other media, they work best when they are part of interactive discussions with parents about what the children think and are learning. Games create a context for this, where real understanding leads to problem-solving and not just test-passing.

Children should teach their parents about their games and gameplay. Parents should ensure that, just as with books, children connect their interactions with games to the world and other media, as well as to good social relationships around the games.

Flower is a great example of a playful game in the form of an interactive poem infused with emotion. *Portal* is an excellent, fun and funny game for deep problem-solving involving physics in a compelling story. It can be played collaboratively, so parent and child can solve problems together.

••• Matthew Taylor, founder of Wholesome Games

Games don't have to be categorized by technical terms that describe how you play them: 'first-person shooter', 'racing', 'platforming'. Many games are better described by how you feel playing them. On the Wholesome Games Twitter feed (@_wholesomegames) I hunt down games that are cosy and welcoming, and create a safe space for players to express themselves without fear of failure. These games have found an audience because of our desire – no matter our age – to have a safe, comfortable place to retreat from the pressures of the world. If only for a moment or two.

This trend started with *Animal Crossing*. It's a game about living life at your own pace. You're free to fish, decorate your home, to garden, make improvements to the town, or interact with your animal neighbours, however and whenever you see fit. This lack of pressure was unique when the game launched in 2002 and has inspired developers who grew up at that time to create similar-feeling games like *Ooblets*, *Mineko's Night Market* and *Snacko*.

There are so many wholesome experiences now. *Among Trees* offers a colourful and peaceful survival simulator teeming with life. Build a cabin, explore the forest, grow plants and eat the food you forage. *Spiritfarer* reminds us that games can tackle heavy topics with a deft touch: build a boat to explore the world, then befriend and care for spirits before finally releasing them into the afterlife. In *Untitled Goose Game* you get to soothe frustrations by playing the bad guy (bad goose?) as you steal hats, honk a lot and generally ruin everyone's day. In *Way to the Woods*, you help a deer and fawn journey through an abandoned world to get home.

··· Dr Jo Twist OBE, CEO of The Association for UK Interactive Entertainment (Ukie) and chair of the BAFTA Games Committee

Something not always obvious to parents and carers is that games are one of the most powerful forms of expression, storytelling and art of the twenty-first century. There is no substitute for playing games with children and young people to understand why they are – in their many diverse forms – such compelling places to spend time.

They are also a thriving industry with many career opportunities. Playing and making games requires and develops many unique skills that no other medium can provide. These skills, such as teamwork, collaboration, problem-solving, resilience and communication, are what future jobs will require and employers look for.

Initiatives such as the BAFTA Young Game Designers competition show how the next generation is using games to make sense of the world around them, tackle serious topics such as loss and climate change, and to better understand their place in the world.

··· Stuart Dredge, freelance journalist for the *Guardian*

For parents who didn't play a lot of games growing up, I'd love them to get some hands-on time with some of the most creative, original, playful games from the past and present. It's the memory of the games I loved growing up that influences my parenting in this area. It steers me away from ever being tempted to generalise about games being good or bad.

First-hand knowledge of the good stuff helps me understand what's bad. So, as an extension of that, I wish all parents knew that gaming isn't just *Fortnite*, *Rocket League* and *Minecraft* – there's a whole world of wonderful stuff out there, and a lot of it is ripe for parents and children to explore together.

I'd recommend *Stardew Valley*. This is good not just because farming and dungeon-exploring is a fun combination but also because it has some genuinely touching human stories to uncover as you get to know its characters. It's a game about empathy and friendship as much as turnip-planting.

... Greg Toppo, author of *The Game Believes in You* and senior editor at Inside Higher Ed.

It would help parents to know they haven't the slightest notion of what's really happening in their kids' heads when they are playing video games. What's happening is often exactly the opposite of what it looks like. What looks like escapist fun is actually deep concentration. What looks like instant gratification is, in fact, delayed gratification in clever disguise. What looks like a twenty-first-century, flashy, high-tech way to keep kids entertained is, in fact, a tool that taps into an ancient way to process, explore and understand the world.

I'd like understanding, not suspicion or an arms' length inclination, to inform parents' attitudes to gaming. This understanding of kids' gaming habits can only come from playing the games themselves.

I'd recommend the *Alto's Adventure* snowboarding game. Beautiful design, intuitive controls, lovely graphics and music. It's meditative, reflective, low-stakes gaming at its best – and a great example of payoff for persistence. The game's 'Zen Mode', which automatically restarts your snowboarder at the spot where you fell, is just dreamy.

... Keith Stuart, author of *A Boy Made of Blocks* and *Days of Wonder*

I'd like parents to understand that playing video games is a creative endeavour. It's not just about mastering reflex actions and hand-eye coordination – the imagination that goes into this kind of play is considerable.

Since my son was diagnosed on the autism spectrum, I've learned how important and valuable games can be to autistic children (and adults). While the real world is unpredictable and confusing, video games are built around systems and mechanics that can be learned and anticipated, and you can't come to physical harm when you get something wrong.

My son spent hours driving the roadways of *Burnout Paradise* and building weird little castles in *Minecraft*, bending the rule-sets to his own interests, but always understanding the parameters. Gamers on the autism spectrum tell me they've learned about social interactions from role-playing games such as *The Witcher* and *Dragon Age*; some have learned about managing a home and relationships through *The Sims*.

When *Pokémon Go* was launched I heard from several parents of autistic children who were delighted that this game had encouraged their sons and daughters to go out to the park and meet other kids – the game gave them an excuse, a distraction and a motivation to be social and to be outdoors.

These are not trivial things – these are life-changing moments. Wherever I go to talk about video games, whether it's an NSPCC conference or a literary festival, parents tell me stories about how a video game helped their autistic child – this hasn't happened once or twice; it happens every time.

··· Iain Simons, director of the National Videogame Museum

I'd like parents to know that gaming isn't a single thing. It's really tempting (and wholly understandable) to think that video games are just *Mario*, just *Sonic*, just *Minecraft*, just *Pokémon*, just *Fortnite*. As a parent, I know that the full spectrum of video games and what they can be isn't easily available to parents and carers, as very few publications are talking directly to us.

While it's very likely that your kids know more than you do about how to operate video games, don't necessarily assume that they have an encyclopaedic knowledge or curiosity about the possibilities and potential of what games are. Lean in a little, and you can start to unearth a whole load of exciting, weird, fun and different games to explore with them.

I'd suggest playing *Hidden in Plain Sight*. This is a game that has given my family lots of fun. One member of the family has to identify the other ones as they try and blend into a crowd of other characters. It's a simple, beautifully distilled concept that hasn't had nearly enough attention.

James Batchelor, compiler of Non-Violent Game of the Day

It's important for parents to know that while some games are centred around violence, games – like any other entertainment media – can cover a wide variety of subjects. Indeed, *Pong* – the very first commercial game – was non-violent, offering a slimmed-down version of tennis.

After the Sandy Hook shooting in America, online players declared a gaming ceasefire, dedicating one day to playing games without any kind of violence. This inspired me to create Non-Violent Game of the Day (@NVGOTD) on Twitter. It offers a brief summary of a game that is devoid of killing or other graphic scenes. There's no *Call of Duty*, *Fortnite* or *Grand Theft Auto*, of course. But there are also no *Mario* games because of how Mario stomps the Goombas under his boot. *Wii Sports* isn't there either because the boxing involves pummelling cartoon versions of your family in the face. I had to rule out even *Minecraft* since, between all that building, you have to fend off weird cactus zombies.

Looking through this lens, you start to see the full breadth and sheer potential of video games as a medium. The touching love story of *Florence* or the heartbreaking tale of *That Dragon, Cancer*. The space-faring archaeology of *Heaven's Vault* or the exploration of *Outer Wilds*. The meticulous authenticity of *Flight Simulator*, *Train Simulator* and even *Farming Simulator*, or even the utter daftness of the pigeon-dating simulator *Hatoful Boyfriend*. There truly is so much more to video games than guns and gore.

··· Andy Phippen, professor of digital rights at Bournemouth University

Gaming can be an incredibly positive thing for young people to be involved in – it gives them an interest, a possible future career, and it opens them up to worlds where they meet people and interact with like-minded individuals.

Of course, there are concerns needing care, but we shouldn't let this distract us from the fact that in the vast majority of instances, young people's experiences in gaming are positive and supporting. I once spoke to an amazing autistic young person who talked about how he could be a *hero* in games, whereas in reality he was timid and scared of the world around him. He felt he could be himself in games, whereas in the 'real world' he was always afraid.

Many children tell me how gaming has a positive impact on their well-being – they're having fun, they're hanging out with friends, they're being entertained. Talk to children about the games they are playing and why they enjoy them; they might even get you playing too!

I'd suggest *PaRappa the Rapper*, recently reissued for PS4. It's an amazing rhythm–music game with innovative design and interactivity. Take on bullies with some decidedly un-gangsta rap and button-tapping. It's light-hearted, silly and charming from start to finish, and burst out of an era where everything else was sports or shoot-em-ups.

··· Valerie Vacante, founder and managing partner, Collabsco

As parents and caregivers we can forget that, although we had fewer screens and less technology, toys and games ignited our imaginations when we were kids. As new technologies have evolved, so have the ways children interact with the physical and digital world. But it's not something we need to be afraid of. Play is still play.

My work at Collabsco explores how children live in a more connected world filled with voice assistants, artificial intelligence, robots, augmented reality, virtual reality, location-based entertainment and plenty more. This creates new play opportunities for children to discover purposeful, connected play experiences that blur the lines between the physical and digital world. Parents and children who learn how to navigate this intersection together can discover new ways to play.

In my home, I love how the physical nature of connected play leads to different skills and appeals to different personalities. Whether it's coding robotic battles, painting the world in augmented reality, having a voice assistant as a gaming copilot or bringing action figures to life through light and sound, these things merge physical and digital experiences through connected play.

David Surman, artist, and a curator at the Game Masters exhibition

Games are an international, global art form. Games make explicit something that is true of all art more generally: that the player is directly involved in creating their own experience. We make our own meaning through the way we play; it's not just the character but we who are doing things.

Game-makers have created an international and universal artistic language of gameplay that crosses all geographic borders. I can pick up and play a game like *Botanicula* by Czech game-makers Amanita Design and not need to know a word of Czech – and that's very powerful.

I'd suggest families try playing *The Last Guardian*. Very few games have the ability to communicate sensitivity and psychological complexity like those of designer Fumito Ueda. Like his previous works *Ico* and *Shadow of the Colossus*, *The Last Guardian* is a work of art exploring the relationship between human and non-human beings.

Then there's the easy-to-overlook *Sonic the Hedgehog 2*. It is a committed and triumphant work of highly accessible game art. The shimmering, beautiful graphics and lightning-speed gameplay conjure a world of unabashed energy and optimism. Sega regularly rereleases its landmark titles, so the game is easy to find, and new players will find it remarkably untarnished by age. *Sonic 2* is true game art.

Pete Etchells, author of *Lost in a Good Game* and professor of psychology and science communication at Bath Spa University

There's an assumption about video games that kids could be doing something much better, or more wholesome, with their time. I don't really know where this view comes from. Video games offer us unparalleled ways to explore what it means to be human, allow us to travel to far-off fantasy vistas from the comfort of our own homes, and can connect us and bring us closer together. We just need to use them in the right way.

Rather than see them as something scary, the best thing parents can do is to get involved with games with their kids. Playing together gives us a better handle on what constitutes an appropriate, positive gaming experience. Of course, that doesn't mean that playing video games alone is always a bad thing. Games can enable us to explore emotions and feelings such as sadness and grief in a relatively safe space.

When I was 14, my father died from motor neurone disease. In the aftermath of his death, the only way that I was able to process and come to terms with what had happened was by playing video games; by having something else to focus on for a little while, I was able to give my brain the time and space that it needed to work through what had just happened.

When I come back as an adult to those games I played at the time – games like *GoldenEye 007* and *The Legend of Zelda: Ocarina of Time* – there's a newfound depth in them, in that they remind me of my dad and what he meant to me. Games, in that sense, allow us to find out a little bit about who we are, and what's important to us.

··· Andrew Przybylski, associate professor, senior research fellow and director of research at the Oxford Internet Institute

When we treat games like they are something special or different we give them a power they don't have. They are just another part of childhood. What we know about parenting hasn't changed because of games. In fact, they may be a good medium for our time, teaching confidence, connection and freedom of choices. When I do the science, the fears about violence or addiction are unwarranted.

This works in the other directions too. Games don't have special powers to endow players with the transferable skills or the hand-eye coordination cognitive nonsense often called upon to justify them. There really isn't the science to support this. Games are social, fun and relaxing – that's where we are more likely to find benefits.

Finally, there's an assumption that it can be near impossible to stop playing some games. But games are hard; people bounce off them all the time. There's effort and motivation required by players to continue playing for long periods. Studies looking at games from a clinical angle show that engagement in problematic gaming suggests they're used as a coping mechanism related to underlying problems such as anxiety or depression.

Super Mario Maker has become part of my young children's playtime. It's wonderful to see emergent gameplay as they enter this social world with each other and with online creators. It's part sharing the *Mario* games I grew up with and part Microsoft Paint. There's a really neat element of 'Look what I drew', and a lot of laughing at trying to play the absurd levels they've built.

··· Sonia Livingstone OBE, LSE professor and author of *Parenting for a Digital Future*

I wish parents realised that multiplayer games often have their own aesthetics, social norms and narrative structure. This means you can't just glance over a child's shoulder to grasp what the game is all about, and nor can you reasonably ask your child to suddenly stop playing without first figuring out what's happening in the game and where a natural break might occur.

These are good things to ask your child about as a way of understanding the game. For instance, what do they like or dislike about the look of the game; how long did it take them to figure out the way to behave in the game; and how do they guess what's going to happen next? In other words, let's ask children questions that aren't all about risk, or invite them to be thoughtful in discussing games with us.

I'd recommend *Monument Valley*. I interviewed a parent who had suggested this to her young sons because it is visually pleasing, intriguing and fun to play. Importantly, it has a distinct and alternative artistic aesthetic which, being a creative family, she wished to foster in her children.

··· Jordan Shapiro, author of *The New Childhood*

Many parents worry about digital play due to nostalgia: we remember our own childhoods and therefore we think that this is how childhood is supposed to look. But childhood experiences are always situated in a historical context. There were no sandboxes before the nineteenth century; also no playgrounds, no family dinners and barely any toys. Childhood is always changing and therefore family life is always changing. That means we need to adjust our expectations to take the current technological and economic conventions into consideration.

It's as simple as getting more involved in your children's connected lives: play video games together so that your kids learn to integrate your values into their digital lives.

Think about it this way: when children are very little, we take them to a playground or a park. We show them how to use the equipment safely and responsibly. We teach them how to interact with the other children: no hitting, no biting, be kind, share. We constantly intervene when they make mistakes. And we do this for many years. In fact, we don't let them play unsupervised until we are confident that they can be trusted to navigate the complexities of social play.

But when it comes to the digital landscape, we just let them go, almost entirely unsupervised. Then we're surprised that gaming doesn't look the way we'd like it to look. It's because we haven't taught them how to do it.

In my house, family time often involves multiplayer video games. *Mario Kart* is a favourite still. *Cuphead* and *Overcooked* are great for their frantic co-op modes. Sometimes we'll even have a round-robin *Mortal Kombat* fighting tournament. When we play together, I'm able to model mature etiquette, responsibility, gamesmanship, digital citizenship and safety.

⋯ Siobhan Reddy, studio director at Media Molecule

Play is play. Whether this is with friends in a video game or in the playground or up a tree, social interactions and imaginative spaces get children's brains fired up for fun wherever they find them. What I really love, though, is that moment when children realise they can change and create games themselves.

With our PlayStation game *Dreams*, and a little practice, anyone can make that thing their imagination desires. This is so much more interesting than it sounds. Not only does it give creators a powerful voice, but it brings together all manner of skills and disciplines. Games are the intersection of so many roles: musicians, animators, coders, community management, systems people, interaction experts, illustrators, 3D artists, producers.

Like learning an instrument to play in an orchestra, game-making stretches individuals to hone talents and collaborate in multidisciplinary teams. Unlike learning the piano or violin, though, it's not something society fully appreciates yet.

I look forward to the day when we are as ambitious for children who are making video games as for those learning an instrument or a second language. Encouraging them to stick to what they've started to create, or follow through on an idea they've had, could well open a door to a future career – not just in the games industry but all manner of other professions.

With or without us, it's happening already. Young people are picking up game-making tools and surprising the world with what they create. Game-making teams, like bands, come together around a creative philosophy and make something completely new. In their hands games are wild and raw, and it's almost impossible to predict where they will go next. For parents and carers it's a huge opportunity to support children in becoming literate in digital arts and excelling in an important part of their future lives.

··· Bex Lewis, senior lecturer in digital marketing at Manchester Metropolitan University and author of *Raising Children in a Digital Age*

There's so much pressure in contemporary life on children to achieve, both in school and in extra-curricular activities. Video games are another space where this can happen, as children compete with each other to be the best or earn the latest outfits to wear when they play.

There is space, however, for activities in children's lives that don't have to lead to such obvious achievements. Research has shown that playing online games just for enjoyment, or spending time playing games with a parent or other family members, can positively impact a child's mental health.

Those who play games for an average of two hours (no more) per day have been shown to have a wider circle of friends, do more physical activity, and do more homework than others. The message I would emphasise is that it's about balance and finding games to enjoy together as social, rather than competitive, family time.

Wonka's World of Candy is my current favourite three-in-a-row game. It draws upon the Gene Wilder film to slowly create a beautifully colourful factory. *Harry Potter: Wizards Unite* is from the people who made *Pokémon Go*, which I've enjoyed. The thing I really love about these games is that they encourage players to get out and about, walk long distances, engage with cultural spaces and create opportunities to play with friends.

9. GETTING READY FOR VIDEO GAMES

Getting the technology set up to access the games in this book – and automatically keep things safe and sensible – isn't complicated or expensive, although, yes, I know it can seem like it when you encounter it for the first time.

Because they are new, video games can seem unlike other paraphernalia of family life. The boxes, cables, controllers, cartridges, discs and screens can be intimidating and alien. But as Iain Simons and James Newman say in *A History of Videogames*, we need to remember they are just things, like other things our children play with – buckets and spades, a grocer's set, a bike, crayons, a trainset. 'For sure, video games are about graphics and sound, they are made of zeros and ones, data and code . . . But most importantly, let's not forget that they are things (and they're covered in fingerprints).'[*]

In the same way that my children used to mark their favourite toys by scrawling their names on them, their game systems look a state by the time they'd had them a year: covered in stickers and fingerprints, with floppy hinges from overuse and being inadvertently dropped. Official styluses were soon lost, and replaced with pen lids. Controllers' sticks became droopy, and their buttons always looked like they needed a good clean.

My children are older now, so they keep things (a little) tidier. Their gaming is more about pro-controllers, gaming bean bags, branded headsets and limited-edition consoles. The premise is the

---

[*] Iain Simons and James Newman, *A History of Videogames*, Carlton Books, London, 2018.

same, though: they treat video games like any other thing in their lives. Sometimes they get the latest technology – on birthdays or at Christmas – but often they make do with what they already have or find what they need second-hand.

Getting ready for video games in your family doesn't mean spending loads of money on pristine plastic monoliths glowing in the corner of the living room. Second-hand or handed-down consoles and games are a great way to get started. Just as important is the time you spend researching and choosing what games and systems you will play on. Add to this an afternoon setting things up before your kids start playing and you are on the road to an affordable, safe, enjoyable new hobby.

Use What You've Got

You already have many devices in your home that can play video games. Before you think about getting a console or dedicated gaming computer, it's worth knowing that most smartphones and tablets are good for games too. Smart TVs or streaming boxes like Apple TV or Amazon Fire TV also offer a range of video games.

For older smartphones and TVs the range of games on offer will be more limited, but they can still be a lot of fun, and younger children won't mind what they're playing games on. Older children may baulk at the idea of not having the latest kit, but starting like this means you're more likely to discover games that aren't just the latest fad.

Use the Gaming Recipes at the back of this book (and at www.taminggaming.com) to find some really good games for your children to play on the devices you already own. Download the games onto your own device as well as theirs, so you get a first-hand understanding of what they are doing. This means you not only dip into the experience but see how it develops over time along with any notifications or incentives to play.

Unlike games consoles or handheld devices, generic hardware like tablets, smartphones, smart TVs or streaming boxes don't come with dedicated controllers. Many games embrace this and are beautifully designed for touchscreens. Purchasing a Bluetooth gamepad provides a controller with buttons and joysticks that makes playing a wider range of games – even on older smartphones, tablets or TVs – easier. It's also worth noting that many tablets and smartphones support wireless PlayStation and Xbox gamepads that friends or family may be able to lend you.

INDUSTRY RESOURCE:

FINDING GOOD, CONCISE, ACCESSIBLE ADVICE MATTERS

One of the challenges of gaining video game literacy is knowing where to go for advice and information. There are many organisations to choose from. Internet Matters is a non-profit organisation I've worked with for a number of years that provides information to empower parents and carers to keep children safe in the digital world. With support from the likes of BT, Sky, TalkTalk, Virgin, Google and the BBC, as well as many other organisations, it creates clear and topical information. Other organisations cover some of the same ground, but Internet Matters stands out for the clarity and design of its pages.

Along with the website and its guides at internetmatters.org, the organisation also works collaboratively with industry, the government and schools to reach UK families with its tools, tips and resources to help children benefit from connected technology smartly and safely. Its recent work on video games and families stands out. Not only is it fascinating, and a little relieving, to read what other families make of their children's gaming, but it has led to fresh information on video games and an encouragement for families to play games together.

'With the majority of children playing online games, it has become part and parcel of growing up in the digital age,' says Carolyn Bunting, CEO of Internet Matters. 'Through our research we recognise that empowering parents with the right advice about online gaming, and encouraging them to get involved, can help them be better placed to make sure children benefit from their experience.'

Starting with technology you already have is a good way to test the water and develop good habits. But still, before handing a child a smartphone or tablet to use for gaming, it's important that you set it up so they can use it safely and without any surprises.

These devices each offer detailed ways to set boundaries and control what your child can and can't do. The key areas to consider are whether you have a credit card or account set up on your device with which your child could spend money; whether they can play online with other people; and what gaming content they can access.

A few minutes in the 'Restrictions', 'Parental Controls' or 'Family Settings' menus on your device will enable you to specify whether your child can download or purchase apps and how (or if) they can communicate with other players. Ensure any credit cards on the system are linked to an email address that you regularly check so you can see any notifications of online transactions. You can also set age limits to avoid inappropriate apps being used. Finally, you should apply a password to these settings before your child starts playing.

LIMITS SHOULD CREATE CONVERSATIONS

As well as setting up automatic restrictions, have a conversation with your child about what you are happy for them to do and not to do. Should they check before downloading a free game? What information is appropriate to share online? What should they do if they come across something that makes them uncomfortable or scared? Do they understand buying games and how in-game purchases work?

Setting up a small amount of pocket-money credit on the device not only lets them experiment with how games make money but helps them understand the value of virtual currency and relate it to the real world. This can be done by purchasing cards in high street stores that offer currency in the same way that book tokens do.

Choosing a Console or Handheld

As children get older they will likely ask for games that friends are talking about in the playground. There is no rush to get the latest titles or gaming consoles, and before you do it's good to consider which games are must-haves and which are optional. This will inform which game hardware you decide to purchase. An Xbox,

PlayStation or Nintendo game console is a good way to keep this simple, as they come with everything you need in one package.

While games such as *FIFA, Fortnite, Rocket League* and *Minecraft* are available on all consoles, other games are often exclusive to only one. For example, *Mario* games are found only on Nintendo systems (although simpler *Mario* games are now also available on smartphones). On consoles, *Roblox* is currently only on the Xbox, although also on PC, smartphones and tablets. *Ratchet & Clank* games are only on PlayStation.

Although equivalent games are found on pretty much all devices, these are usually not as high-quality as the original versions. For example, while you can find platform (running and jumping) games on any console, children usually want to play the *Mario* version only available on Nintendo systems. This is partly due to strong branding and marketing, but also because the original games are well designed, with bigger budgets and development prowess.

While dedicated portable gaming systems now compete with the rise of children's access to powerful smartphones and tablets, they can be good starter systems. The Nintendo DS is a portable system that can

be found cheaply second-hand and has thousands of affordable games to play with your child. The Nintendo 3DS is a newer version of this, with a more physically robust 2DS model aimed specifically at young players. The PlayStation Vita is now discontinued but it's available second-hand and is another great first system. With a couple of DS or 3DS systems you can also try multiplayer games, many of which can be played with a single cartridge via the game share feature.

Such older portable systems make an affordable way to get started. The games are a little simpler for parents and children to learn together, but they still offer great experiences that develop a gaming literacy which is useful as a family's gaming matures. They also only need minimal set-up because most games are offline and the system includes an integral screen.

The Nintendo Switch comprises both portable and home console options in one system. It can be docked to play on a TV, but also provides its own screen to be played as a portable system. The Nintendo Switch Lite is a version of this system focused just on portable play. It can play the Switch games but you can't plug it into a big screen like the main Nintendo Switch, which means it's less flexible to share in a family, but it does cost a little less.

Another novel way to access video games is through the classic consoles, rereleased in miniature form. The C64 Mini, Nintendo Classic Mini, SEGA Mega Drive Mini and PlayStation Classic, amongst others, come with controllers and lots of games built in. You can't purchase additional games for these systems, but they are a simple and affordable way to revisit classics and try out gaming as a family.

Whether you choose tablets, smartphones, portable or console gaming, the decision should be led by investigating which games you and your family would like to play and which systems you can play them on. Children will have their own opinions on this, and the Gaming Recipe section should also help you decide.

PERIPHERAL COSTS

When comparing costs of different consoles and portable systems, it's worth including additional controllers in your calculations. This is important as it ensures that the local multiplayer games I suggest later in the book can be enjoyed together.

Most consoles come with one controller, although the Nintendo Switch comes with detachable controllers for two players. Adding enough controllers to let everybody in the family play can nearly double the cost of these systems. You can reduce this cost by opting for controllers made by other manufacturers rather than the official ones that come with the system.

Other gaming system costs to consider are that the Xbox One requires batteries or charger packs for its controllers. Additional controllers for the Nintendo Switch are more expensive because they come in pairs that support an additional two players.

The Gaming Recipes each specify what technology you need to play a particular game, and plenty of games I'm suggesting can be played on older consoles and on smartphones or computers.

Second-Hand Bargains

Before choosing a console, it's worth asking friends and family whether you could borrow one to try it out. Failing that, you can purchase second-hand consoles and older smartphones at a discount price (and often with a shop warranty for peace of mind).

A second-hand Nintendo Wii U, Xbox 360 or PlayStation 3 grant access to some amazing and varied games. The best games on a system often come at the end of its life, so opting for the generation before the current one enables you to capitalise on this. Older games also have the added benefit for families of focusing more on playing together in the same room rather than online.

You can also find earlier revisions of the current console generation selling cheaper second-hand. These play the same games but are usually physically larger and have fewer extended features. A second-hand early version of PlayStation 4 or Xbox One is another affordable way to start playing video games.

Second-hand games are also good value, particularly for yearly franchises where the old version is a fraction of the price. You might pay £50 for the latest version of *FIFA* when last year's game can be picked up for as little as £10. As long as your child doesn't want to play online against friends, or need the player names and stats to be bang up to date, last year's games are both cheap and viable.

Many of the games I suggest in the back of the book are available on older systems and can easily be found second-hand. Particular bargains can be found when a system falls out of vogue with gamers. The Wii U is a good example here. It's an excellent system for families that can be found at a fraction of the cost of new Nintendo hardware.

It's worth noting that many newer devices will also play the previous generation of games that can be purchased cheaply second-hand. If you have the Wii game disc you can play it on Wii U. If you have a DS game cartridge you can play it on the 3DS or 2DS. You can play many Xbox 360 game discs on the Xbox One.

Some new systems offer a digital-only option. For example, the Xbox One S All-Digital Edition can only play downloaded games as it doesn't support discs. This is a cheaper option than the standard Xbox One S and works well if you are intending to access games via its subscription service or buy new games digitally, but it does rule out buying cheap second-hand games on disc.

As with anything bought used, there is a risk in terms of warranty and lifespan, but many high street second-hand shops offer a guarantee to cover this.

Online Gaming

Online gaming is an increasingly important part of the gaming experience for children. These are games that enable multiple players to collaborate and compete when not sat in the same room. These range from football and car racing with a few other players, to online war games involving hundreds of other players from around the globe.

Online gaming requires the latest version of the game, a good internet connection and reasonably new console, smartphone, tablet or gaming computer. While some games allow players from different consoles to play together, it's worth checking which system your child's friends have, as this guarantees they can play together online and makes finding each other easier.

Part of the enjoyment children get from online gaming is chatting to friends as they play – both to socialise and to communicate game strategies. Unless you disable these features, they can exchange messages with other players and chat via a headset. The language and maturity (or immaturity) of this talk falls outside the PEGI and ESRB ratings, which means a child may hear swear words from other players, even in younger-rated games.

When children are older they may want to use a headset with a built-in microphone to enhance this communication. Dedicated headphones improve the quality of the game audio, but most systems come with basic headphones that will do the job. In fact, any pair of headphones with a microphone on the cable will work.

As we discussed in Chapter 4, it's important that you understand who your children are talking to and that you use the parental controls on the system to limit who they can friend and what information can be shared. Do this from a young age in conjunction with your child. Aim to create an open conversation so you understand the impacts of these boundaries and that they know what to do if anything happens online that upsets them.

Playing online games usually requires a monthly subscription to the online gaming service related to the console or system you are using. Xbox Live Gold, PlayStation Plus and Nintendo Switch Online are required to play most online games. There are exceptions to this, with some free-to-play games like *Fortnite* offering online play on these systems without subscriptions. Although online gaming services represent an additional cost, they also provide access to a small catalogue of games you can download each month and extend online functionality of your system to include features such as backing up game progress to the cloud.

In addition to online gaming services you can access more games by subscribing to ready-made game libraries for your particular system. Once subscribed you can download a digital copy of the included games and play straight away.

- On the Xbox you can expand the library of games substantially with an Xbox Game Pass subscription that provides 100 top-tier titles.
- On iPhone, iPad, iPod Touch and Apple TV, an Apple Arcade subscription provides access to over 100 games with no adverts or in-app purchases. It offers many exclusive games from developers it supports, not available elsewhere for a period of time.
- On Amazon Fire tablets the Fire for Kids Unlimited subscription provides a library of games (and movies, books and TV shows).
- On Android devices, Google Play Pass subscription (only in the US at time of writing) offers hundreds of games with no ads or in-app purchases.

- On PC, the Humble Choice subscription offers hand-picked games each month with 5% of the fee going to charity.

These game library services are an affordable way to access a large number of games provided in a ready-made digital library. The games have been carefully selected for the service and, although there will be a wide range of age ratings, the high quality of the selections and absence of in-app purchases or adverts (on Apple Arcade and Google Play Pass) makes them a good option for families. It's a great way to ensure your video game spending is predictable, and it can also help you discover new games as they are added to the service.

Online streaming services like PlayStation Now, Google Stadia and xCloud on Xbox are another up-and-coming way to access games. Rather than purchasing high-end hardware, you subscribe to access games that are streamed to your screen in a similar way to services like Netflix or iPlayer, only here you are also controlling the action with a gamepad. This two-way communication needs a fast internet connection and can be less responsive than playing on a console

running the game in your own home, but it grants access to hundreds of games without having to own dedicated gaming technology.

For example, a PlayStation Now subscription currently enables you to play 700 PlayStation games on your Windows PC (or PlayStation 4).* It also includes the option to download 300 PlayStation 4 games and play them on your console in the normal way. xCloud is the Xbox equivalent (in preview at the time of writing) and enables you to play Xbox games on a compatible Android device.†

 MASTER NOTIFICATIONS

As with any modern technology, notifications that pop up on smartphones, tablets and other mobile devices are a key driver of behaviour. There's a reason that Facebook, iMessage and WhatsApp are battling for control of these messages: this is the frontline of attracting our attention.

Borrow your child's smartphone or tablet for an evening to see how prevalent this is for them. Gaming apps will send pop-up reminders to come and play. Console apps deliver messages from other players and notify youngsters when their friends are online. Game chat and streaming apps like Discord and Twitch remind players when friends or new content are available.

Spend time with your child going through the 'Notifications' settings of their mobile device. This enables you to set times when they aren't pestered in this way. You can also mute certain notifications that aren't useful to them. Switch from 'Push' notifications that pop up like a text message to 'Pull' notifications that silently wait for them to be ready to check in.

Taking time to get this set up appropriately, along with parental controls that specify times of day when their device is offline, ensures your child has the space to make their own decisions about when to play without being pestered. This is good for healthy gaming habits and a healthy digital future.

---

* 'PlayStation Now', PlayStation.com, available at www.playstation.com/en-gb/explore/playstation-now

† 'Project xCloud', xbox.com, available at www.xbox.com/en-GB/xbox-game-streaming/project-xcloud

Device Cruising

Hybrid consoles like the Nintendo Switch, handheld gaming devices like the Nintendo 2DS or 3DS and game streaming services on smartphones and tablets enable games to be played anywhere. There are real benefits to this flexibility, both in reducing competition for use of the main screen in the house and being able to continue playing on journeys or when away. It democratises access to video games.

However, this cruising of technology to play games makes it harder for both the child and parents to know how long they actually play each day. Happily, there is some super simple and powerful technology to enable parents and carers to manage this. On consoles and smartphones, you can set individual time limits for weekdays and weekends. Once these have run out, the game pauses until you put in a password. A step further are services like Circle that enable you to specify how long a child can access specific activities across all their devices. It enables you to set different time limits for YouTube, *Minecraft*, *Fortnite*, *Roblox* and Netflix along with a general bedtime.

When I tell parents about this, they breathe a sigh of relief. Children are initially less enthusiastic about the prospect. Either way, the real power of these tools is the context they create for

well-informed discussions between parents or carers and children. It starts as a conversation about how long is too long but soon becomes a deeper discussion of what value children get from gaming and what the costs are.

Still, nothing beats keeping the best and biggest games in shared family spaces. This not only ensures that you can see what and how long children are playing, but it also means you're more likely to have good conversations about the games. It also creates natural breaks as family members compete for use of the television. And, of course, the tech is ready and waiting for you to try out games when the kids are in bed.

Understanding Game Ratings

The world of video games can seem like uncharted territory when you first start engaging with it. Happily, though, there are excellent organisations set up specifically to help parents navigate their way through it.

Pan European Game Information (PEGI) ratings in Europe and the Entertainment Software Rating Board (ESRB) ratings in America offer consistent, detailed and clear information about the content of every video game sold in stores. These age ratings are displayed on the front of game boxes, with more detail on the back. They are also displayed in online storefronts.

In Europe, legislation for a standardised PEGI age rating of all physical boxed games has ensured that parents have access to a reliable reference point. This has been voluntarily extended by game console makers to all games sold on their online game stores.

Google has joined Xbox, PlayStation and Nintendo in adopting PEGI or ESRB ratings for all online game sales. The Epic and Steam game stores provide PEGI or ESRB where they are available but include many games not rated. The Apple app store has its own ratings. This means a little more investigation is warranted when purchasing games on iPhones, iPads via the App Store, or via the Epic and Steam online store for PCs and Macs.

INDUSTRY RESOURCE:

PEGI VIDEO GAME RATINGS

The VSC Rating Board is an administrator of the PEGI age rating system which is used in over 30 countries throughout Europe. In 2012 the PEGI system was incorporated into UK law and the VSC was appointed as the statutory body responsible for the age rating of video games in the UK using the PEGI system. In the UK, PEGI 12, 16 and 18 rated games are legally enforceable and cannot be sold to anyone under those respective ages.

 PEGI 3 games are suitable for all age groups. The game won't contain any sounds or pictures that are likely to frighten young children. A very mild form of violence (in a comical context or a childlike setting) is acceptable.

 PEGI 7 games may contain scenes or sounds that may possibly frighten younger children. Mild forms of violence (implied, non-detailed, or non-realistic violence) are acceptable for this age rating.

 PEGI 12 games may show violence that is more detailed. Realistic violence towards fantasy characters is permitted but violence towards humans must be unrealistic. Sexual innuendo or sexual posturing can be present, but any offensive language in this category must be mild.

 PEGI 16 games may depict realistic violence to human characters or more graphic violence to fantasy characters. Sexual activity and nudity are permitted as long as there's no visible genitalia. The use of bad language may be more explicit. A PEGI 16-rated game may also contain prominent use of illegal drugs, tobacco or alcohol.

 PEGI 18 games are for adults only. This rating allows depictions of graphic violence, apparently motiveless killing, and violence towards defenceless characters. The encouragement of the use of illegal drugs, tobacco and alcohol, and explicit sexual activity would also fall into this age category. Simulated casino-style gambling can also be present (e.g. virtual blackjack or poker).

Along with the age rating on the front of the box, there are descriptors on the back that define why the game got its rating (violence, sex, drugs, bad language). The PEGI app is an excellent way to get further information, as you can search for a game, see its rating and read the examiner's report in full.

Content descriptors appear on the game's box or on the online store to show you why a game received a particular age rating. These include the following:

 Fear/Horror

 Bad language

 Sex

 Discrimination

 Violence

 Drugs

 Gambling

 In-game purchases*

* This descriptor is for information only and does not affect the age rating of a game. This also states 'Includes Random Items', where players don't know exactly what they are getting prior to the purchase, as is the case with 'loot boxes'.

Games rated PEGI 3 and PEGI 7 are examined by NICAM – the Netherlands Institute for the Classification of Audio-Visual Media. PEGI 3 and PEGI 7 ratings are advisory only and exempt from UK law. The VSC Rating Board has responsibility for games rated 12, 16 and 18.

ESRB VIDEO GAME RATINGS

The Entertainment Software Rating Board (ESRB) was founded in 1994 by the Entertainment Software Association (ESA) as part of its role representing the US video game industry, along with conducting research, providing regulatory analysis, and owning and operating E3, a large and long-running video game event where the latest video games are revealed. Its ESA Foundation also provides grants and scholarships to encourage the next generation of video game developers. For families, its yearly Essential Facts report provides a useful window onto the industry as a possible career as well as how game-playing is evolving from generation to generation.

The ESRB is the non-profit, self-regulatory body for the United States video game industry, assigning ratings for video games and apps to help parents make informed choices. The rating system is voluntary; however, all console manufacturers, all national US retailers, and certain mobile or online storefronts require ESRB ratings for the games or apps they offer.

Boxed games sold in stores display a rating in the lower front corner of the game's packaging. Additional rating information, including the 'Rating Category', 'Content Descriptors' and 'Interactive Elements', appear in the lower back corner of the packaging. Ratings for physical games can also be found by searching on esrb.org or using ESRB's free app. Here you can also read 'Rating Summaries', which provide a more detailed explanation.

Ratings assigned to digital games and apps are displayed on the online store.

EVERYONE

Content is generally suitable for all ages. May contain minimal cartoon, fantasy or mild violence and/or infrequent use of mild language.

EVERYONE 10+

Content is generally suitable for ages 10 and up. May contain more cartoon, fantasy or mild violence, mild language and/or minimal suggestive themes.

TEEN
Content is generally suitable for ages 13 and up. May contain violence, suggestive themes, crude humour, minimal blood, simulated gambling and/or infrequent use of strong language.

MATURE
Content is generally suitable for ages 17 and up. May contain intense violence, blood and gore, sexual content and/or strong language.

ADULTS ONLY
Content suitable only for adults ages 18 and up. May include prolonged scenes of intense violence, graphic sexual content and/or gambling with real currency.

RATING PENDING
Not yet assigned a final ESRB rating. Appears only in advertising, marketing and promotional materials related to a physical (e.g. boxed) video game that is expected to carry an ESRB rating, and should be replaced by a game's rating once it has been assigned.

Content Descriptors indicate content that may have triggered a particular rating and/or may be of interest or concern. There are more than 30 Content Descriptors, including:

- Violence
- Suggestive Themes
- Nudity
- Blood and Gore
- Language
- Substances
- Gambling

Among the remaining descriptors, 'Interactive Elements' highlights the interactive or online features of a product; others indicate users' ability to interact with each other ('Users Interact'), the sharing of users' locations with other users ('Shares Location'), whether the purchase of digital goods or services is offered ('In-Game Purchases') and/or whether unrestricted internet access is provided ('Unrestricted Internet').

It's worth noting that video game ratings, like film ratings, are cultural decisions. The appropriate age for a person to access a certain type of content will differ from country to country. This is the reason a particular game may have different age ratings in different territories (as is the case for some of the entries in the Gaming Recipes in this book).

The ratings do not take into account the context of the content. Violence, for example, is rated according to what occurs on the screen, without consideration of the surrounding story or why the violence is happening. In-app purchases, user-created content or user interactions are noted in the ratings but do not affect the specified age of a game.

It's also important to note that these ratings are about the content of the game, rather than how hard it is to play. Plenty of games with very low age ratings are too complex for youngsters to enjoy.

Age ratings are a useful tool to help parents to make informed decisions about games rather than make ethical decisions for them. For this reason, it is not illegal for a parent to let a child play a game that is rated for older children. Equally, parents and carers shouldn't see a low age rating as meaning they don't need to play their usual guiding and educating role.

 AUTOMATIC AGE RESTRICTIONS

You can set up your console, gaming computer, tablet or smartphone to limit access to games of a certain PEGI or ESRB content rating. Once you have selected the appropriate PEGI or ESRB rating in the device's settings, you can apply a password. This means your child will need to consult you about any older-rated games before they can play them. In this way the age ratings become not only a way to limit access but also provide another opportunity to have a conversation about their gaming and gain an understanding of it.

It's worth applying a little extra caution on smartphones and tablets, and with console games that don't have a physical, boxed version. These PEGI or ESRB ratings of online-only games are often applied via the IARC (International Age Rating Coalition) self-certified questionnaire by the developer rather than an expert examiner.

Along with the peace of mind that comes with automatically restricting access to older-rated games, the broader information available on the ratings providers' websites enables you to have a conversation with your child before they play a particular game. This is more important where free games can be downloaded without a financial transaction that might otherwise trigger such a discussion.

Before You Wrap the Box

If you're giving a new game console, smartphone, tablet or portable gaming device as a gift to a child, it's important that you set things up yourself before wrapping that big present.

Unpack the box completely and plug the console into the television. If it's portable plug the device in to top up its charge level. If it's new it will take you through a set-up process that will require an internet connection and an email address. If it's second-hand, reset factory settings that will start this process for you. Make sure you put in an email address you regularly check as this will be used for purchase receipts.

The first time you connect the console or put in a new game, it is likely to need to download updates or install files onto the system. This is to ensure you are on the latest version of the operating system, with all the best protection and controls. The download can take a number of hours to complete – and on Christmas Day, when everyone is doing it, it can take a lot longer.

The controllers that come with the system will need to be synced so they can communicate with the console. This is usually achieved by temporarily plugging them into the console with the cable provided and pressing a button as instructed. The same cable is also used to charge the controller, so this is a chance to ensure that the controllers are fully charged.

Once you have the basics set up, it's important to configure accounts for the different family members. Creating specific child accounts not only lets you apply limits and controls, but provides information on what games they have been playing. Set up the appropriate ratings, online interactions and passwords for purchases on each account. Finally, set a password for the main account so your children can't adjust these settings without asking you.

This all sounds more complicated than it is. Most consoles, tablets and smartphones are designed to lead you through this

process with a series of simple questions. The PEGI app, ESRB app and askaboutgames.com website also provide easy access to further family settings guidance. Along with the advice here, this should enable you to get everything working how you want it. All that remains is to pack it all away and wrap it up.

Levelling the Playing Field

Once you have the technology sorted it's important that everyone in the family is part of this journey. There's no point integrating gaming as a positive part of life if particular siblings or parents struggle to keep up or take part.

Playing a wide range of games helps ensure that children and parents with different tastes and abilities are engaged in the fun. Taking turns to pick what to play and spending the time to find games that may pique interest of children and parents is important.

Games where you can specify different difficulty settings for each player are useful. Some of the games I suggest in the back of the book let you jump to any level, which can be helpful if you get stuck. But equally, don't feel that looking up tips and advice in online forums or videos is a failure – this is actually a big part of how the wider gaming community enjoys and shares these experiences.

For really young or new players, simple controls can help. A recent version of *Mario Kart*, *Mario Kart 8*, is a good example: as well as being able to set the difficulty level for young racers, you can help prevent them from ploughing into the sides of the track by switching to motion controls that don't need precise motor skills and assist modes that keep them in roughly the right direction.

Taking turns on a controller is a nice way for new players to dip in and try a game without being overwhelmed. Some systems offer ways to play games in pairs. The Xbox One's Copilot option enables two controllers to be used to control a single-player game. This works really well in families where a child is teaching a parent about one of their favourite games. But it's also good for very young players, who can get help from an adult without losing the sense of control and ownership of what is happening on the screen.

Where children have a specific disability there is a range of ways to make games accessible. It is no trivial thing for a disabled child if their brother or sister is playing *FIFA* or *Minecraft* and they can't have a turn themselves. Charities like SpecialEffect offer support, guidance and, in some instances, equipment to enable children with all manner of disabilities to access the same games as other players.

This inclusion in the virtual worlds that games let you visit is an empowering experience. In fact, once well set up, gaming can be one of the most level playing fields that families of varying abilities and disabilities can share.

INDUSTRY RESOURCE:

XBOX ADAPTIVE CONTROLLER AND COPILOT CONTROLS

Microsoft has taken a lead on accessibility by developing a special adaptive controller for its Xbox One console. Either independently, or with the help of charities like SpecialEffect, this enables players to control games using all manner of switches, large buttons and gestures.

'The Xbox Adaptive Controller came out of Matt Hite's idea,' said Chris Kujawski, Principal Designer for the Xbox Adaptive Controller. 'With others on the team, he came up with a prototype to prove the idea that you could take a standard controller and externalise the buttons. The following year we picked it up at the hackathon and it really started to gain steam.'[*]

Mark Saville, Communications Officer at SpecialEffect, a UK charity that helps disabled gamers access video games, highlighted how the Xbox Adaptive Controller complements the Copilot feature already available on the Xbox. 'We really like the way this product continues the work done with Copilot, the feature on Xbox which allows you to combine controllers to control one player in-game. Now there are more ways it can be used, such as adding accessibility switches to your controller.'

The Adaptive Controller and Copilot features bring this kind of accessibility into the mainstream. Not only does the controller inherit high-end Xbox product design but it addresses a spectrum of accessibility needs. In the family, this might be a parent who is dyslexic or has low dexterity and can benefit from a copilot. Or it may be a physical disability that would previously have been a severe barrier but can be mitigated with adaptive controls.

'The stigmatisation that happens with accessibility technology can make children feel like they are not part of the pack,' says Kujawski. 'So designing a product that allows them to play as equals and peers is really important. But then making it look like an Xbox product, it is important that it looks like a cool device that isn't going to stigmatise them.'

This isn't just about accessing entertainment. Any parent or carer who has seen how much children get from the games they play knows that it's crucial that no child is unable to get involved. As SpecialEffect puts it, this work is essential for 'inclusion and independence, confidence and creativity'.

---

[*] Andy Robertson, 'Xbox's adaptive controller packaging is an unsung innovation other products will adopt', *Forbes*, 11 February 2019, available at www.forbes.com/sites/andyrobertson/2019/02/11/xbox-adaptive-controllers-packaging-is-an-unsung-innovation-other-products-will-adopt

Getting Ready for Game Culture

Getting ready for video games isn't just about the games themselves. Games have many related activities: videos to watch, forums on which to ask questions, webpages to consult, books to read, apparel to wear and groups to join – to name a few.

As children get into gaming, particularly as they get older, these things become part and parcel of what it means to play a game: community, identity, learning and prestige. My kids have spent hours researching the physics of momentum and collision to improve their *Rocket League* play. I hear them in fits of laughter watching fan-made animations of the *Halo* characters. Then there are the notebooks full of ideas and diagrams about their next *Minecraft* or *Terraria* castle.

Googling whatever game your children are playing along with terms like 'Wiki', 'Let's play', 'Tips', 'Fan Art' or 'Fan Fiction' enables you to dip a toe into this wider community. These may be aspects of gaming children have already found, but you may uncover new ways to extend the gaming experience in different directions.

Big game franchises often have their own array of books and audiobooks. These range from guides and reference books on how to progress, to official novels that flesh out the backstory of the game, or even spin-off fiction set in the game world but written by independent authors. These can be a good way to get children reading as well as creating natural breaks away from the screen.

While the reading and research side of these wider gaming worlds is a familiar way to consume media for parents, watching videos of other people playing is relatively new. On YouTube, Twitch and Facebook, 'streamers' share pre-recorded and live videos of themselves gaming and commentating on their play. Be aware that there is a wide variety in tone, language, dress and personality of the player-hosts, as well as the game content they're playing in their videos. Adverts are often displayed by streaming platforms before, during and after these videos, and popular videos often include paid-for use of brand's products as well as a place to sell the host's own merchandise. Once a video has finished, another one will be suggested to watch, often based on the topic rather than appropriateness for the age of the audience. It's a firehose of content with the focus often on volume rather than quality.

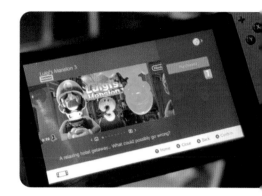

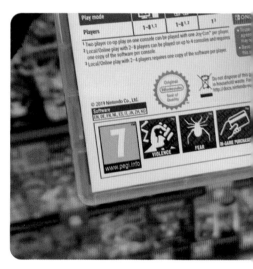

For both gaming videos and general videos aimed at children, using a child-focused app to access video content is a good idea. As the main YouTube site and app is not designed for children under 13, the YouTube Kids app is a better choice. It uses automated checks to filter out inappropriate content. You can also select which channels your child can watch from a curated list provided by the app, as well as how long they can watch each day. Perhaps most crucially, you can disable the search

facility to keep kids on the videos from the lists you selected. Bear in mind, however, that it still includes advertising, unless you pay for YouTube Premium.

There are other apps that provide videos for children that have been vetted by real people rather than an algorithm. The Jellies and kiddZtube apps are good examples, with the latter having a focus on education. Away from YouTube content, apps like Nick Jr., Netflix and Disney+ offer produced content, although this usually comes with a subscription or viewing fee.

TURN CONSUMERS INTO CREATORS

One of the most exciting things about streaming services like YouTube is that you can publish your own videos. Unlike traditional broadcasting, children can become contributors as well as consumers of content. This sounds like it will be complicated and long-winded, but with a smartphone you have everything you need to create imaginative and creative content.

If your child wants to do this, get them to plan on paper what their video will be. Then help them create the different shots they need using a smartphone. iMovie on iOS and Vizmato on Android are examples of apps that enable you to edit videos and add text and effects before uploading. Or to begin with you can just upload your content without editing it.

It's important that children are careful with personal information, and that the content they share is appropriate for others to watch. Create a family account on the video service to upload videos rather than a child doing this themselves. This ensures you are in control of the content being uploaded and see comments and interactions if you decide to have these enabled.

There's an empowering excitement when a child first makes their own video. This not only changes how they see YouTube but starts them on a journey using skills of self-expression that might also lead to a future career. Being proactive in this area can steer them from just wanting to be the next big 'influencer' or 'streamer' to recognising the wider skills creating videos requires. You can encourage this further with video creators clubs, like the fast-growing Tubers Academy for video creators.

As with playing games, the simplest way to keep track of what children are watching is to keep their viewing in shared family spaces and regularly check in with your child to ask what they're watching. Take some time to watch videos yourself and skip through to see how they develop. Although it can be irritating, it's worth getting children to watch videos without headphones so you can hear what's happening on their screen.

When my children were younger and just starting to watch YouTube, we had a ground rule that they could watch certain creators when they wanted but would ask before watching someone new. They would also ask if they wanted to start watching an older-rating game on YouTube, even if it was a YouTube creator we knew.

Even as children get older and start to use the main YouTube site, set an age on the account and turn on 'Restricted Mode' in the settings. It's also worth turning on the history tracking so you can see what videos they've been watching. You can also stop the next video starting automatically by clicking the 'Auto Play' slider on the right of the current video.

Away You Go

Playing games yourself; playing games with your child; guiding your child towards a wider diet of experiences; setting things up so they are safe; commiserating with their gaming failures; celebrating their success; paying for it all; sharing your family TV with them. I know all this might sound like a lot of hard work. But like with the rest of parenting and caring for children, you can work this out as you go. Start while your children are young and learn together as they grow older and the complexity of their gaming increases. Using the Gaming Recipes that follow, you can be one step ahead, as you are in other areas.

Take time to find games you enjoy yourself and have fun playing. It may not always seem like it, but each small step you take – each question you ask about their game, each answer you listen to without completely understanding, that 30 minutes you spend playing with them, each time you find a great game they haven't heard of – is making a real difference to how your children relate to video games and to the health of their digital future.

You know your children better than anyone. Your family has its own unique values and traditions. Don't change that, but go into parenting this area of life equipped with a first-hand understanding of what games are and what they can be for you and your children.

'The best time to plant a tree is 20 years ago,' says the old proverb, 'the second-best time is now.' Whatever age your children are, the best thing you can do for their video game health is to get started on your video game journey with them.

During my childhood I had two favourite moments in the television show *We Are the Champions*: the funny faces and thumbs-up expressions each young competitor would pull at the start, and the moment all the kids were released from the rigours of competition to dive into the pool at the end. So far in this book I expect I've got you pulling strange faces of your own in surprise, disbelief or incredulity as I've stretched your understanding of video games. But now the inflatables are in the water, you're standing on the edge of the pool and it's time to jump in, get wet and have some fun. As presenter Ron Pickering always shouted before the titles rolled: 'Away you go!'

10. GAMING RECIPES

If you've got this far, I'm hoping you feel better equipped to engage with your child and the games they play. So now comes the most enjoyable and powerful part of the book: the Gaming Recipes.

Each of the games here is presented as a recipe that tells you what it will be like to play, the age ratings for Europe (PEGI) and the USA (ESRB), how many players it needs, how long it takes to play and what equipment you'll need to play it (the 'Ingredients'). 'Serving Suggestions' are examples of how other families have enjoyed playing the game. Then, if you find a game you love, the 'To Follow' section points to what you can play next. With this information to hand, you can be a video game expert overnight.

Each game has been hand-picked after trying it out with families I've worked with over the past 15 years. Like film or book recommendations, you may not like all of my choices, but they provide a starting point from which to dive in and develop your own likes and dislikes.

The first section focuses on games for people who've never played before. Then there are categories for children in infant or junior school before going into specific themes, for older children: facing tough decisions, having fun laughing together, waking up your emotions, solving a mystery, inhabiting another world, stepping into someone else's shoes, working together to survive or just enjoying some good old-fashioned matinee-movie-style fisticuffs and shoot-outs.

These recipes are written specifically for parents and carers. Because of this I go into considerable depth about the games' stories, characters and endings. This means my recipes may include spoilers, because it's important to explain why these games are worth investing time in.

It's worth remembering that variance in ratings from PEGI in Europe and ESRB in the USA derives from different cultural sensitivities. Bear in mind too that all user-created games, maps and interactions as well as in-app purchases fall outside the domain of PEGI and ESRB, so they are not reflected in the age of the rating apart from the inclusion of the Users Interact or In-App Purchases descriptor text.

While many of these games are suggestions for parents and carers to enjoy with the whole family, I've included some with adult age ratings. These are important examples of games adults can enjoy playing on their own, and illustrate the full sweep of themes, topics and interactions that games have to offer. As teenagers approach adulthood, these games can also be good for parents and their children to play together. Building this first-hand breadth of understanding is what helped me to continue to engage in my children's gaming as they matured into adults.

GAMES FOR NON-GAMING GROWN-UPS

These games are perfect if you've never played one before. They open the door to the gaming world for non-gaming parents and carers. They are short, straightforward and easy to understand, so you don't need to commit hours to learn to play them, and they are played on technology you probably already have in your pocket or in your home. They address mature themes such as love, hope, power, homelessness and even traffic planning by inviting you to interact and play a part in these worlds and stories.

THIS SECTION INCLUDES THE FOLLOWING GAMES

Mini Metro
Alto's Adventure
That Dragon, Cancer
Reigns
Bury Me, My Love
Thomas Was Alone

MINI METRO

Create an ordered, efficient underground train system. It sounds like hard work, but the simple Tube-map visuals, calm music and streamlined interactions make this relaxing, like sudoku. Dip your toe in this strategy challenge and keep the system running smoothly as the number of passengers increases.

The simple premise and uncluttered interface make this a strategy game perfectly laid bare for beginners. Daily challenges and different cities gently increase the challenge.

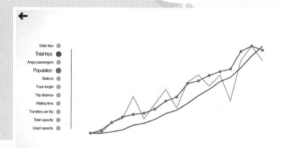

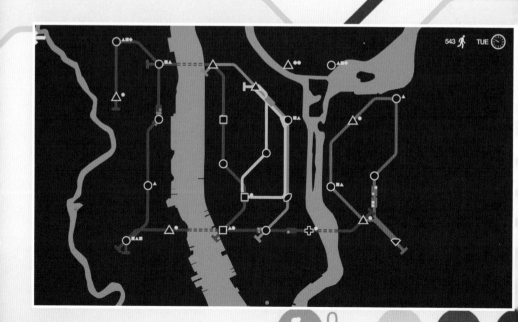

Rating:
PEGI: 3
ESRB: EVERYONE

Player(s): 1

Duration: Each round can last up to 20 minutes, depending on how well you progress. Daily challenges set targets that are usually a little more difficult and shorter.

Ingredients:

- PC, Mac, PlayStation 4, Nintendo Switch, Android or iOS.
- The game itself.

Serving Suggestions:
As your family plays the game on separate devices, come together to talk about which strategies work best. Do you create circular lines or crisscrossing webs? Do you choose to expand your resources with more trains, carriages or underground lines? The daily challenges are a good way to see who can get the highest score and to try out different strategies because the stations and passengers appear identically each time you play.

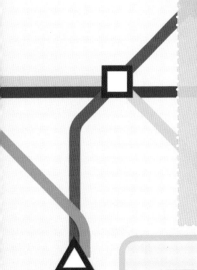

To Follow:

Mini Motorways (iOS Apple Arcade, PC or Mac) is by the same developer as *Mini Metro* but tasks you with planning a road network rather than subway. You lay down roads, traffic lights and motorways to ensure enough cars can get to the buildings that pop up in your city as time passes. It's slightly more complex than *Mini Metro* but with the same simple aesthetic and moreish gameplay.

In *Wilmot's Warehouse* (PC, Mac or Nintendo Switch) you organise hundreds of items of stock. These identical square boxes are labelled with rudimentary icons. On your own or with another player, you must decipher what each icon depicts and invent ways to categorise them. Customers then appear wanting specific combinations of products and you have limited time to find and deliver them.

A Dark Room (iOS or Android) is an adventure where you try and survive in the wild. It has a similarly simple start — a single option to stoke a fire — but also evolves into an incrementally complex system of resource management as a larger story unfolds.

ALTO'S ADVENTURE

Descend beautiful mountains, dunes and canyons on a snowboarding journey full of serenity and secrets. All you have to worry about is tapping to jump to avoid chasms, rockfall and other hazards. It's simple and moreish due to the stunning landscapes and to a feeling of flow as you charge down the mountain, but there's real skill to doing it well. *Alto's Adventure* is a good first sports game because it's simple to control but requires a deep understanding to master.

Rating:
PEGI: 3 with in-game purchases
ESRB: EVERYONE with in-game purchases

Player(s): 1

Duration: A single play of *Alto's Adventure* can take from 2 to 20 minutes depending on how long you are able to survive. To unlock the various characters in the game will take a considerable number of hours.

Ingredients:
- Mac, PC, iOS, Android, PlayStation 4, Xbox One, Nintendo Switch or Kindle Fire.
- The game itself.

Serving Suggestions:
Once you have unlocked the different characters, set each other challenges to get the highest score with each one. See who can chain together the most tricks on one run; find ways to keep the chain going, such as bouncing on rocks or campfires; see who can be first to pull off expert tricks like a proximity backflip or proximity wingsuit by flying close to the ground; or thread the needle by flying through an arch.

To Follow:
Alto's Odyssey (iOS or Android) is the follow-up that extends gameplay challenges with balloons to jump on and new achievements to chase.

Gris (PC, Mac or Nintendo Switch) offers a similar-feeling (and aesthetically beautiful) game with swooping jumps and slides, while adding in more traditional running and jumping platforming elements and a stronger narrative.

THAT DRAGON, CANCER

A game about a family with a young son who has terminal brain cancer. It sounds off-putting and morbid but this living biography invites you to join the family and find hope, faith and love in the face of an insurmountable challenge. It's a unique collage of poetry, phone calls, diagnosis rooms and home movies full of raw emotion. In game form, lightness combines with weight and sadness to create a unique perspective on cancer and losing a child.

The mature theme and simple click-to-move interface make it an ideal first game. If you get stuck, you can simply move to the next scene, which is always unlocked.

Rating:
PEGI: 3
ESRB: EVERYONE

Player(s): 1

Duration: The game is divided into chapters that in total take about 2 hours to complete. Revisiting scenes and experiencing every aspect of the game, like the messages and art displayed in the hospital level from real-world cancer patients, will take considerably longer for those who wish to linger.

Ingredients:

- PC, Mac, Android or iOS.
- The game itself.

Serving Suggestions:
You can play the game on your own or with your family, if they are mature enough for the topic, by taking turns to play a particular level while the others offer suggestions on how to progress or which parts of the game to investigate next. The emotive material and intimate engagement with this family's story make it important to take time to discuss the game. After playing, you can engage further in the story with a documentary, *Thank You for Playing*, about the family behind the game.*

---

* David Osit and Malika Zouhali-Worral,
  Thank You For Playing, 2017,
  www.thankyouforplayingfilm.com

To Follow:
Eastshade (PC, Mac, PlayStation 4 or Xbox One) is another game you explore by walking around. Here, though, you play a travelling artist capturing the grand flora and fauna on canvas as you go. It's another game that places you with purpose and responsibility in the world so that you feel part of it.

Firewatch (PC, Mac, PlayStation 4, Xbox One or Nintendo Switch) is an explorative adventure where you play a fire lookout in the USA's Shoshone National Forest. You slowly uncover a story about loneliness, mental health and catharsis in a grand, sun-drenched landscape.

REIGNS

Take charge of a kingdom, one decision at a time. Each choice is presented to you as a playing card with some advice or a question from one of the thirty-eight different characters. Swipe left or right to make a decision that will impact the church, people, military and wealth of your domain. You have to make choices about complex issues without knowing all the consequences. As you do, a string of intriguing story-threads emerges that will influence your strategy.

It's a good first role-playing game because it boils things down to simple decisions while raising themes about the complexity of politics.

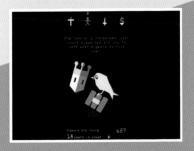

Rating:
PEGI: 7 with implied violence
ESRB: TEEN with violence and blood

Player(s): 1

Duration: A single round of *Reigns* may only last 10 minutes, but to complete the game and unravel the various aspects of the story you need to play it many times, and this can take several hours in total. To find all the extras and the complete achievements will add many hours to that.

Ingredients:
- PC, Mac, iOS, Android or Nintendo Switch.
- The game itself.
- A pen and paper for making notes on characters and who to trust.

Serving Suggestions:
As a family you can each play the game separately then pool your knowledge to work out what's going on in the kingdom. Making and comparing notes on the characters you meet, and playing through the game multiple times, soon makes it the topic of conversation over dinner.

To Follow:
Reigns: Her Majesty (PC, Mac, iOS, Android or Nintendo Switch) extends the game to a new kingdom with power in a woman's hands. New characters and a fresh story add to the intrigue about correct choices.

Reigns: Game of Thrones (PC, Mac, iOS, Android or Nintendo Switch) draws on the popular TV series and books for characters and plot. If you're a fan of the series, this can be a good game to start with.

Professor Layton (iOS, Android, Nintendo DS, Nintendo 3DS or Nintendo Switch) is a puzzle-game series. In different locations you must solve brainteasers with maths, logic, maze-solving and lateral-thinking skills to move the story on.

BURY ME, MY LOVE

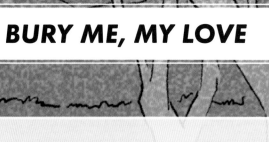

Don't be put off by the name and theme of this intriguing game, an adventure played by choosing responses in what looks like a messaging app. You take the role of the husband of a Syrian migrant travelling to Europe. As the game unfolds in real time, her messages pop up on your phone throughout the day. Choosing the different answers to her questions influences the decisions she makes and the path of her journey. Each play-through results in a different journey and one of twenty different endings.

The mature theme, easy progression and low time-commitment make this an excellent first game for adults to try. Experience the life of a Syrian migrant in a unique and moving way.

Nour
Online

Oh, look !
09:36 AM

09:36 AM

Ruins!
09:36 AM

Answer...

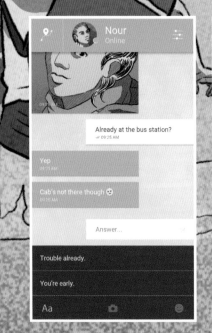

Nour
Online

Already at the bus station?
09:25 AM

Yep
09:25 AM

Cab's not there though 😣
09:25 AM

Answer...

Trouble already.

You're early.

Aa

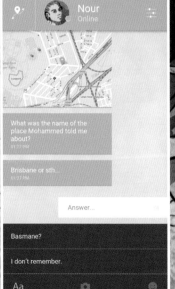

Nour
Online

What was the name of the place Mohammed told me about?
01:27 PM

Brisbane or sth...
01:27 PM

Answer...

Basmane?

I don't remember.

Aa

Rating:
PEGI: 7 with mild violence and implied violence
ESRB: EVERYONE 10+ with mild violence

Player(s): 1

Duration:
Play for a few minutes a day and you'll complete the game in a week or so. The game world proceeds in real time, so if the character is travelling or sleeping, there will often be considerable time before the next interaction. This slow pace is part of the charm and immersion, but there's a setting to speed it up if you want to complete the game faster.

Ingredients:
- PC, iOS, Android or Nintendo Switch.
- The game itself.
- You can try the game's prologue for free in any web browser via burymemylove.arte.tv/prologue

Serving Suggestions:
I played this game on my mobile device at the same time as my daughter and my wife each played it on theirs. In our separate games we inevitably made different choices, and this led to very different journeys. We got our phones out during our evening meal to compare our progress and talk about the decisions we'd made. It led to conversations about taking risks, trusting strangers and how it felt to be powerless. Once you've finished the game, it's interesting to replay and make different decisions.

To Follow:
My Child Lebensborn (PC, iOS or Android) is a game about caring for a child after the Second World War who faces a hostile community having been born to parents of both occupied and occupying forces.

80 Days (PC, Mac, iOS, Android or Nintendo Switch) is a travel and culture discovery game set in 1872, where decisions about your journey around the world impact the course of the story and characters.

Florence (iOS or Android) is a simple interactive story about falling in love. You don't change the story but are instead drawn in with beautiful storybook drawings and everyday tasks.

THOMAS WAS ALONE

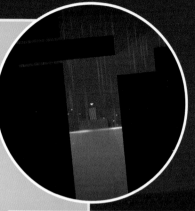

Control different-coloured rectangles in this simple running, jumping and puzzle-solving platform game. It sounds boring and derivative but each of the distinctly coloured shapes comes to life in the game as a character embroiled in this escape story about friendship, curiosity and sacrifice. Like any platform game, you jump, run and use special abilities to complete levels. As you do so, you get to know each shape's personality through the storytelling of the quipping narrator.

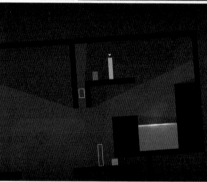

The simplicity of design makes this an ideal first platform game, while the novel narration makes it a good introduction to how games make you care deeply about even the simplest of characters.

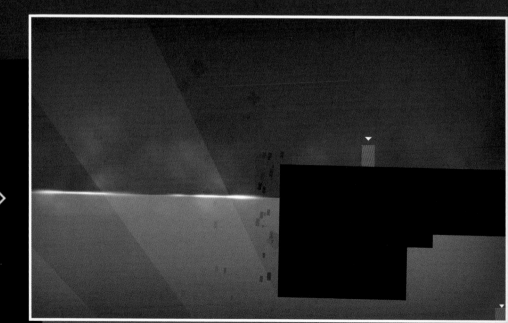

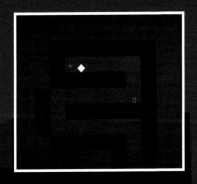

Rating:
PEGI: 12 with bad language
ESRB: EVERYONE with mild fantasy, violence, mild language

Player(s): 1

Duration: To complete all the puzzles and finish the main story of the game can take up to 6 hours, although proficient players can complete it in less than 4 hours. Finding every collectable in the game will extend duration with multiple play-throughs.

Ingredients:

- PC, Mac, iOS, Android, PlayStation 3, PlayStation 4, PlayStation Vita, Xbox One or Nintendo Wii U.
- The game itself.

Serving Suggestions:
Members of the family can play through the game separately then compare how you related to the different shapes. Was there a favourite character and what were they like? Did you trust the narrator? What did you make of the epitaphs introducing each level? Would you spend as much time with other forms of abstract art?

To Follow:
Monument Valley and *Monument Valley 2* (iOS or Android) are puzzle mazes made from optical illusions. You interact with each level to change the pathway and get your character to the exit. Its striking, calm visual theme is used to build atmosphere and slowly reveal a moving story about parenting, independence, getting lost and the bittersweet inevitability of children growing up.

Mutazione (PC, Mac, iOS Apple Arcade or PlayStation 4) pits you as a 15-year-old girl visiting her grandfather on a faraway island inhabited by friendly but mutated villagers. By finding seeds, tending to gardens and talking to people, you uncover a tightly knit web of characters with unrequited love, hidden trauma and difficult memories. By tending to the people as well as the gardens, you nudge the island towards processing its losses.

NURTURE CHILD-LIKE IMAGINATION

These games are for children under seven years old, who will, with some help, discover activities they want to try that will expand their imaginations while establishing the role of your guidance and engagement as part of the gaming world as they grow up. The more-open imagination of young children lends itself to games that offer an open world. Rather than forcing the player in a particular direction, open-world games let players explore wherever they want and at their own pace. The games here offer unusual and age-appropriate experiences that are often educational but keep the emphasis on the sheer joy of interactive play rather than hard learning.

THIS SECTION INCLUDES THE FOLLOWING GAMES

Go Vacation
Toca Life: Town
Fruit Ninja
Vignettes
Metamorphabet

GO VACATION

This is a resort exploration game where 50 mini-games can be discovered and played. The mini-golf, skating, surfing, volleyball, car racing, tennis and other games use the Wii and Switch motion-sensitive controllers and are simple fun for youngsters. But the real excitement is exploring the resorts and collecting treasure: 'Marine', 'City', 'Snow' and 'Mountain'. Each requires different ways to get around, including horseback, motorbike and kayak. Up to four players can explore at the same time, catching fish and collecting photographs of the animals they find. This is a great game for younger children because it's simple to control and enables them to explore where they want and at their own pace in a detailed cartoon world with lots to do.

65"56

52

Rating:
PEGI: 3
ESRB: EVERYONE with mild cartoon violence

Player(s): 1–4

Duration: You can complete the main elements of the story and collecting in around 20 hours, but to see everything will take players hundreds of hours spread over many months of play.

Ingredients:
- Nintendo Switch or Nintendo Wii.
- The game itself.
- One controller per player.
  - On Nintendo Wii, one Wii remote and one Nunchuck per player. You can also use the Wii Balance Board to add more fun.
  - On Switch, one Joy-Con per player.

Serving Suggestions:
Young players enjoy getting around the island on the different modes of transport, and particularly novel is the public transport system that you can challenge them to use to get to a destination. With multiple players exploring together, youngsters love it when their paths cross. Children often make up their own races and challenges in the different resorts. Who can get to the top of the mountain first?

To Follow:
The Legend of Zelda: Breath of the Wild (Nintendo Switch) offers a much-expanded and more detailed open world to explore. Although rated for older children, the world exploration side of the game is great for youngsters playing with a parent. Climbing mountains, riding horses, swimming in lakes and climbing trees are a fun side of the game you can access without the fighting.

Lego City Undercover (PC, PlayStation 4, Xbox One, Nintendo 3DS, Nintendo Switch or Nintendo Wii U) offers an open world to explore. While most *Lego* games have an open-world element in at least some areas, this one keeps play open throughout so that children can enjoy exploring at their own pace. On PlayStation 4, Xbox One and Nintendo Switch you can do this with two players.

In *A Short Hike* (PC or Mac) you play penguin-like character Claire, who needs to climb a mountain in a beautiful national park to receive an important phone call. Presented in cute pixel graphics, the game invites you to explore the park, help other animals, and find seashells and even buried treasure. In return you're given greater stamina and tools with special powers so you can make it to the top of the mountain. And that's just the start.

TOCA LIFE: TOWN

The *Toca* series of games comprises what are essentially toys in electronic form. Recreating interactive everyday things like shopping, hospital, vacation or pets, children can create imaginative play scenarios with no right or wrong way to do things. The games encourage children to explore, experiment and discover with a depth of character and interaction not often found in other games aimed at younger children. This complements other forms of play while enabling unique digital interactions to spark the imagination.

Rating:
PEGI: 3
ESRB: EVERYONE with
comic mischief

Player(s): 1

Duration: The open-ended and
unstructured play means that
sessions can vary in length from a
few minutes to half an hour. It does
take some time to work out how
the different locations and items
interrelate and interact. Children will
continue discovering new aspects of
the game for many hours.

Ingredients:
- PC, iOS, Android or Kindle Fire.
- The game itself.

Serving Suggestions:
Sitting together and exploring the
town lets parents prompt children
to investigate different locations.
Some parents and carers enjoy
setting their child tasks to do in the
game, like buying some groceries
for lunch or making a particular
type of meal in the kitchen. It can
also be fun to make up and act out
different stories together, like Cops
and Robbers, Shop Worker or
Camping Trip.

To Follow:
Other *Toca Life* apps (iOS or Android) for *City*, *Vacation*, *School* and *Farm*
are a good way to expand play into new locations and meet new characters.
Toca Hair Salon 3, *Toca Cars*, *Toca Kitchen* and *Toca Pet Doctor* are other
examples of games in the series that take play in different directions. These
are not only a lot of fun but a good way to try different styles of play.

Sizzle & Stew (iOS or Android) is a cooking game where you don't have to
follow the rules. It's a lot of fun and works well in the two-player split-screen
mode. Experiment as you explore all the kitchen gadgets to make a meal, or
just see what happens when you put a doughnut in a washing machine!

FRUIT NINJA

An array of brightly coloured fruit flies into the screen area and you need to slice each piece in two before it falls to the floor. The technicolour action combines with simple interactive taps and swipes to make it accessible to all ages. Particularly good for pre-schoolers is the Xbox Kinect version, which uses a camera to display an outline of the person's body on the screen. This allows the child to use arm and leg movements to slice the fruit. For children aged 12 and over there is a PlayStation VR version that extends the experience into a virtual world, encouraging more movement and interactions.

Rating:
PEGI: 3 with in-game purchases
ESRB: EVERYONE with in-game purchases

Player(s): 1–2

Duration: The levels of *Fruit Ninja* are mostly timed to last just a few minutes, but progressing to collect all the challenges and improve scores will take considerable time. The PlayStation VR and Xbox Kinect versions of the game take a bit more time to set up before you start playing.

Ingredients:
- PC, iOS, Android, PlayStation 4, PlayStation Vita, PlayStation VR, Xbox 360 Kinect or Xbox One with Kinect camera.
- The game itself.
- To play Xbox Kinect version: Xbox 360 Kinect camera or Xbox One Kinect camera.
- To play PlayStation VR version: PlayStation 4, VR headset and 2 Move motion controllers.

Serving Suggestions:
Try out *Fruit Ninja* on a tablet or smartphone to see if you like it, then try the Xbox Kinect version, which creates a more exuberant and energetic challenge to get children moving. What's particularly good on the Kinect version for families is that it allows multiple players at once. For expert, older players, the PlayStation VR version offers a more complex challenge with greater depth and skill.

To Follow:
Donut County (PC, Mac, iOS, Android, PlayStation 4, Xbox One or Nintendo Switch) offers a similarly simple style of play. You drag a hole around the screen; the more things you can make fall in, the bigger the hole gets. You start with bricks, road cones and bushes, but eventually you're swallowing whole houses.

Like *Fruit Ninja*, *Prune* (iOS or Android) involves slicing, but here you must carefully cut off tree branches to encourage the tree to grow in a particular direction. It starts simply but turns into a challenge for parents and young children to work on together.

Child of Eden (Xbox 360) is another Xbox Kinect camera game where you use your body to shoot and move. Rather than fruit, however, here it's beautiful firework-style visuals and music that are the challenge.

VIGNETTES

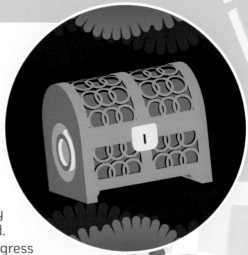

Explore shapes that change into different objects as you spin them around with your fingers. What starts as a novelty evolves into a collecting challenge where interacting with one item leads to another. Rescue a stray cat, awaken an ancient snake-spirit, re-enact a moon landing or travel back in time. Each object has a story to tell as you push and pull it around. You don't win or lose, but you do progress through the series of different objects.

Infant-school children will enjoy the simple object recognition and how one thing magically transforms into another with their careful interactions.

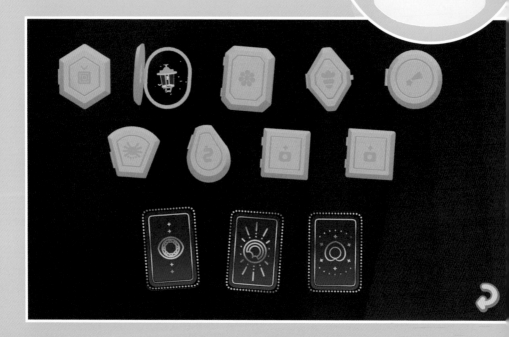

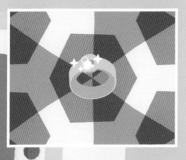

Rating:
PEGI: 3
ESRB: EVERYONE

Player(s): 1

Duration: While you could find every object in about an hour, the time to discover and explore each of the objects makes this a game that will last for many hours for young players.

Ingredients:
- PC, Mac, iOS or Android.
- The game itself.

Serving Suggestions:
Let your child explore the app by themselves and discover some of the objects. Then play with them to work through some of the transformations they've not managed yet, using more interactions to uncover different items, like tapping the rubbish bin to reveal the eyes that turn into the car, rather than going straight to the moon.

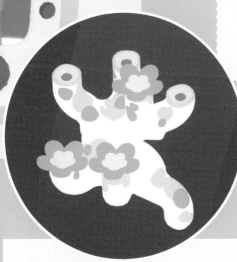

To Follow:
Marching Orders (iOS or Android) puts you in charge of a disorderly animal marching band. Listen to each animal's requests to get them in the right order.

Dragon Box (iOS or Android) offers a simple matching challenge that starts with fruit but builds to understanding proper mathematical concepts. It sounds educational, which it is, but it's also a lot of fun and doesn't feel like learning.

METAMORPHABET

Explore the alphabet by pushing and pulling the letters around to create different things beginning with that letter. It's simply presented with sound effects and voiced words for each object. It excels at making each letter and object feel tactile and responsive to each touch. Not only does it introduce the alphabet, it also encourages young fingers to ambitiously explore screens.

This is a good game for infant-school children because it feels more playful than educational, more like a toy than a textbook.

Mouth

Parade

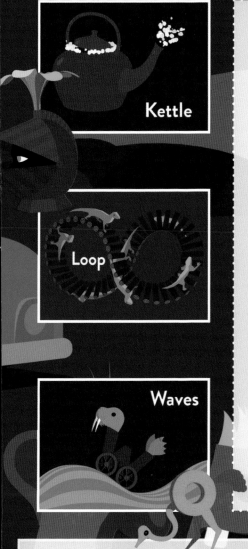

Kettle

Loop

Waves

Rating:
PEGI: 3
ESRB: EVERYONE

Player(s): 1

Duration: To work through the alphabet without stopping takes about 20 minutes, but children will enjoy interacting with each object and character so they're likely to take longer. Although the list of objects for each letter doesn't change, repeated play-throughs are still enjoyable because of the varied possible interactions.

Ingredients:
- PC, Mac, iOS or Android.
- The game itself.

Serving Suggestions:
Playing through the game with your child for the first time means you can race each other to guess what each object is before it's revealed. Like reading a familiar bedtime story, as children become familiar with the game they enjoy the predictable repetition while at the same time learning the letters of the alphabet.

To Follow:
Hidden Folks (PC, Mac, iOS, Android or Nintendo Switch) tasks you with exploring hand-drawn worlds to find particular people. It's simple enough for youngsters to control but complex enough to keep parents and carers involved too.

Kids (iOS) is an unusual game where you tap to interact with groups of monochrome cartoon children. Seeing the little kids run around and respond to each other creates a playful and intriguing game than only lasts half an hour but will be played many times.

One Person Story (iOS, PC, Mac or Nintendo Switch), called *One Life Story* on Android, is a puzzle game about life's challenges. You use a single button to open and close gates in simple mazes to get your bouncing ball to progress. Each puzzle is designed as an allegory about life's opportunities and challenges. Played with a child, it's a gentle way to consider questions of civility, friendship, hurt and courage.

NOURISH YOUTHFUL AMBITION

As children get older, they develop stronger ideas of what they want to play. Friends at school and YouTube stars create popular gaming fads for the latest titles. These are a lot of fun, but children's choices can end up being narrowed down to big-budget or on-trend games. The games suggested here go beyond the usual suspects. While offering age-appropriate alternatives to older-rated games, they are still exuberant and intriguing, and create raucous gaming fun that fires the imagination of children aged 7 to 13 years old.

THIS SECTION INCLUDES THE FOLLOWING GAMES

Roblox
Minecraft
MovieStarPlanet
Splatoon 2
Dreams
Kingdom: Two Crowns
Tearaway Unfolded

ROBLOX

In this game, amateur game-makers create simple online games that often mimic real-world grown-up scenarios, like working in a pizza restaurant, surviving natural disasters, escaping prison, scuba diving or playing hide-and-seek. The library of games is fast-changing, and specific games mimic the evolving rules of playground games. Playing with other children and the novelty of familiar topics make this game hugely popular. It also offers children a safe way to experience a huge variety of make-believe scenarios online.

Rating:
PEGI: 7 with mild violence, fear, users interact and in-game purchases
ESRB: EVERYONE with fantasy violence, users interact and in-game purchases

Player(s): 1 per screen, typically interacting with up to 100 players in online games.

Duration: Due to the different games varying in style, their duration varies considerably, but the majority of games are conducted in rounds that last no more than 10 minutes.

Ingredients:

- PC, Mac, iOS, Android or Xbox One.
- The game itself.
- Internet connection.
- Roblox account on the Roblox.com website:
  - In 'Security Settings': specify an account PIN and set Restrictions to 'On'.
  - In 'Privacy' settings: you can turn off in-game chat.
  - Link this account to the game on the device it will be played.

Serving Suggestions:
Parents and children can play different *Roblox* games to talk about and discover which types of games they enjoy playing. It's not only a lot of fun but helps parents develop gaming literacy and understand first-hand how their children respond to different games. It's a safe and free way to encourage children to be more ambitious about the range of games they choose and to try some games outside their comfort zone. Also, because many of the games are made by other youngsters, a bit of research will enable you to help your child understand how to use *Roblox* to make games as well as play them.

Roblox games like *Speed Run*, *Scuba Diving at Quill Lake* and *Work at a Pizza Place* are a good place to start. Older children may also enjoy more hectic and involved games like *Jailbreak*, *Natural Disaster Survival*, *Super Bomb Survival* and *Shark Bite*.

To Follow:
Super Mario Maker (Nintendo 3DS, Nintendo Switch or Nintendo Wii U) is a game-making system. As well as making your own running and jumping platform games, you can play hundreds of games that other amateur game-makers have created.

Super Lucky's Tale (Xbox One or PC) and *New Super Lucky's Tale* (Nintendo Switch, Xbox One or PlayStation 4) are platform games where you play a fox on a quest to recover pages from a magical book that will save his world. This takes the puzzles, running and jumping found in many *Roblox* games and uses it to create a larger experience with a story of its own.

MINECRAFT

Although *Minecraft* — where players place blocks to build structures, sculpt the landscape and create adventures — is the best-selling game of all time, some of the best aspects of it are little known. Along with the exploration, building and survival-play, children can use complex 'Red Stone' circuitry to automate their creations and make interactive spaces. The game is constantly evolving, with updates adding new blocks, enemies, capabilities, characters and interactions. Upcoming extensions of the *Minecraft* experience include *Minecraft Dungeons*, which offers an action-adventure challenge for up to four players on any standard gaming platform. The stand-alone *Minecraft: Story Mode* games also offer character and choice-driven adventures. *Minecraft Earth* enables players to build structures that look like they are in the real world with a new AR (augmented reality) app. There's also an array of online 'server games' where children can compete against others online in different battles.

This is a great way for children to experiment with ambitious building projects, as well as learn the principles of programming to make their creations come alive.

Rating:
PEGI: 7 with mild violence, fear, users interact and in-game purchases
ESRB: EVERYONE 10+ with fantasy violence, users interact and in-game purchases

Player(s): 4 per system on console, PC or Mac; 1 person per device on tablet or smartphone. Interaction with multiple players in online games.

Duration: The way you play *Minecraft* affects how long a play session will last. The open world offers a stream of new things to do. Children will happily play for hours and return to work on their creations week after week. The online multiplayer server games are usually over in a matter of minutes as they are competitive and played in rounds.

Ingredients:
- PC, Mac, iOS, Android, PlayStation 3, PlayStation 4, PlayStation Vita, Xbox One, Xbox 360, Nintendo 3DS, Nintendo Switch or Nintendo Wii U.
- The game itself.
- One controller for each player.
- Xbox Live Gold subscription to play online with other players on PC, Android iOS or Xbox One.
- Nintendo Switch online subscription to play online with other players on Nintendo Switch.
- PlayStation Plus subscription to play online with other players on PlayStation.
- To play online on PC, Xbox One, Nintendo Switch and tablets you need a Microsoft account.

Serving Suggestions:
The two-player cooperative play suits parents and children working together. This, combined with the visual style, gives the game the feel of a Saturday-morning cartoon show. Taking charge of either Nessa or Demelza and exploring the island on their bike is an entertaining and well-observed recreation of backwater holiday destinations.

To Follow:
Eco (PC or Mac) extends the resource-collecting and building of *Minecraft* by introducing environmental implications to your actions. Using resources like trees will erode the soil; mining might pollute the river; and each animal depends on another.

Terraria (PC, Mac, Android, iOS, PlayStation 3, PlayStation 4, PlayStation Vita, Xbox One, Xbox 360, Nintendo 3DS or Nintendo Wii U) looks like a 2D version of *Minecraft*. To the world-crafting and survival it adds hundreds of items to collect, characters to defeat and bosses to battle.

Starbound (PC or Mac) is a newer version of the *Minecraft* idea from the same developer that takes the game into space and to other planets.

Lego Worlds (PC, PlayStation 4, Xbox One or Nintendo Switch) takes virtual building back to the classic bricks with familiar figures, buildings and challenges from other Lego video games in an open world where your imagination can go wild in a bottomless bucket of bricks.

MOVIESTARPLANET

There are lots of games offering social interaction for children and teenagers, but *MovieStarPlanet* and its follow-up *MovieStarPlanet 2* stand out for keeping interactions open and feisty while also being safely moderated. It's a movie-themed, fully fledged social playground where children can try out online interactions and relationships. Along with styling and dressing their avatar, they can create animated movies, art books and outfits, and share other content.

Children and teenagers can chat in the game with automatic filtering and behaviour analysis that are reviewed by its trained moderators. The play feels fun and light, but along the way children have a chance to learn online etiquette and respect.

Rating:
PEGI: 3
ESRB: EVERYONE

Player(s): 1 per device on web, tablet or phone. The user has the possibility to interact with multiple players.

Duration: *MovieStarPlanet* is an open-ended game, although play sessions are likely to last 20 to 30 minutes. As players get more into the game, this time will naturally increase.

Ingredients:
- PC, iOS, Android tablet or smartphone.
- An account set up by parents for players under 13 years old; opt in for online interactions and viewing YouTube content.
- In-app purchases expand the interaction and clothing options, though most play the game for free.

Serving Suggestions:
This social networking game is a good way for parents, carers and children to step into online interactions in a safe and fun way. The game is backed by both staff and resources to help flesh out parental understanding. Links, suggestive vocabulary and images are automatically filtered and moderated by staff.

Working on outfits, decorating their room, and making movies and art books together lead naturally into sharing these things with the game community. Chat, accepting and choosing friends, and playing games with other children and teenagers expand the experience without overwhelming it.

As with any online community, the behaviour, attitude and age of other players will vary. Play this with your child to offer them an exuberant and realistic taste of online spaces. It's a context that will raise all manner of pertinent scenarios to teach them how to thrive online in the open waters of other social networks when they are older.

To Follow:
The Sims (PC, Mac, iOS, Android, PlayStation 3, PlayStation 4, Xbox One, Xbox 360 or Nintendo Wii) puts you in charge of a world of characters living normal lives. Your task is to make them happy by providing a home, a job, leisure, friendships and even love interests in this open-ended game.

Dreams (PlayStation 4) is a game where you create and share your own games, music and movies. The tools to create scenes, characters and music offer even young players a way into understanding how interactive spaces are constructed. Once you've made something, you can easily share it with the community online.

SPLATOON 2

Shoot ink rather than bullets in this deeply skilled combat game. As well as taking out opponents, teams work together to cover the arena with their colour of ink. This not only decides who wins but enables them to rapidly traverse areas in their colour. Weapons are both varied and imaginative, ranging from paint rollers to buckets of paint and water-cannon-style shotguns.

For juniors, this is a good alternative to more violent shooting games like *Fortnite*, but every bit as skilful and exciting.

Rating:
PEGI: 7 with violence
ESRB: EVERYONE 10+ with cartoon violence and users interact

Player(s): 1 per Nintendo Switch. Up to 8 friends can compete in the same room if they share a console, or a total of 8 players can play online.

Duration: Battles last around 3 minutes each, but players will want to play multiple battles in a session. Unlocking weapons and upgrades requires a greater time investment, as does becoming proficient at the controls.

Ingredients:
- Nintendo Switch console. (You can play the original *Splatoon* on the Wii U.)
- The game itself.
- Nintendo Switch online subscription.
- Optional extras:
  - Nintendo Switch Pro Controller (for extra precision).
  - Nintendo amiibo figures (to unlock outfits and character enhancements).

Serving Suggestions:
If you've not played a game like this before, it's a good idea to start with the offline single-player story. In 'Hero Mode' you can meet the enemies and try out the weapons. From there, the multiplayer online 'Salmon Run' mode is a good step. Work with other players to fend off waves of enemies. Then, as your prowess improves, take part in an online Splatfest event, where you join one of two teams over a weekend and try to win points for your side in each battle and earn unique clothing.

To Follow:
Plants vs Zombies: Garden Warfare 2 (PC, PlayStation 4 or Xbox One) is a high-skill shooting game that keeps the violence low by having plants and zombies battling each other rather than real people.

Overwatch (PC, PlayStation 4, Xbox One or Nintendo Switch) is for children 12 and older, but still has a focus on teamwork and skill rather than violence. Along with games like *Rocket League* it has professional e-sports competitions where players compete for prizes.

Screencheat (PC, Mac, PlayStation 4, Xbox One or Nintendo Switch) pits four players against each other in a shooting battle on one system but keeps the violence low by making the players invisible. You win by peeking at other players' portion of the screen to figure out where they are as you hunt them down.

DREAMS

Anyone can learn how to create their own video games, music, animations and art in *Dreams*. Everything is controlled with accessible menus and interactions via the PlayStation 4 controller. This makes it easy to dive in and create something simple. Then, as skill and imagination grow over time players can take their creativity in any direction they wish to make highly detailed and nuanced experiences: quirky art, professional-looking games, original music, detailed sculptures. These can then be shared online or just kept for the family.

Dreams comes with a game made by the developer along with the thousands of unique experiences shared by the community of players. Browsing these creations, you'll uncover a treasure trove of things to play, listen to or watch. Players can rate and recommend them to friends or take inspiration for their own designs.

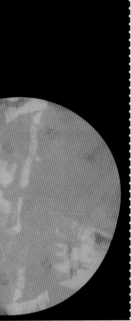

Rating:
PEGI: 12 with bad language and violence
ESRB: TEEN with fantasy violence and language

Player(s): 1–4 players can collaborate to create and play in *Dreams*.

Duration: While you can complete the developer's sample creation in *Dreams* in a few hours, there is an endless supply of community-created content that will keep you occupied for as long as you want. Making your own games can absorb many hours of creativity.

Ingredients:
- PlayStation 4.
- The game itself.
- Online subscription to PlayStation Network.

Serving Suggestions:
Although *Dreams* is a game creation tool, many families enjoy browsing and playing the games that other people have made. While these often look as good as professional games, because they are made by amateur creators using the *Dreams* tool, children can use them as inspiration for their own designs.

Working together on a project in *Dreams* enables a family to take different roles depending on their skills. One person can make the music, another the background art and another the characters. Because the tools make it easy to collaborate and put these things together, you can start to have something to show for your effort relatively quickly.

To Follow:
Super Mario Maker (Nintendo 3DS, Nintendo Switch or Nintendo Wii U) is another game-making system. It's simpler than *Dreams* but still offers a huge array of ways to create running and jumping platform games that can then be shared online. You can play hundreds of games that other people have created.

No Man's Sky (PC, PlayStation 4 or Xbox One) invites you to take your spaceship to explore and colonise a universe rich with diverse planets, creatures and fauna. It's a huge space where you need to craft your own story and find a way to survive. Like *Dreams*, it offers a beautiful virtual universe to explore and be surprised by.

KINGDOM: TWO CROWNS

In this retro-look strategy game, you must
defend your town from the nightly attack
of zombies as you develop your technology
and civilisation day by day. But unlike other
tower-defence games — where you set up
defences and fend off waves of attacking
forces — there's no access to any statistics
so you must discover the best strategy
by trial and error. As you incrementally
advance, you discover new technology and eventually
sail to safety on the next island.

Junior players will enjoy the compelling jeopardy
of each night and the thrill of discovering new
weapons and defences. The simplicity of the game's
trial-and-error strategy makes it accessible to a
wide range of ages. Playing with a sibling or parent
expands the enjoyment and defensive options.

Rating:
PEGI: 7 with mild violence
ESRB: EVERYONE 10+ with fantasy violence

Player(s): 1–2 (single-player *Kingdom: New Lands* also available on iOS, Android or Nintendo Switch)

Duration: To complete the game can take 50 hours. This unfolds slowly and requires a considerable amount of trial and error. Games can be paused at any time.

Ingredients:
- PC, Mac, PlayStation 4, Xbox One or Nintendo Switch.
- The game itself.
- One controller per player.

Serving Suggestions:
Playing for the first time in single-player mode helps you gain some understanding, but this is a game about making decisions without all the information you might want. Children enjoy making notes about the effects of different expansion options and plotting their next move. Then, moving to two-player mode, you can work efficiently together to develop your civilisation. Talk and communicate about each decision and use the extra pair of hands to get things done more quickly as the game progresses.

To Follow:
Stardew Valley (PC, Mac, iOS, Android, PlayStation 4, PlayStation Vita, Xbox One or Nintendo Switch) looks like a farming simulator. That's partly what it is, but you must also develop relationships with the other townsfolk and delve deep into the mines. Its quirky, labyrinthine attention to detail is inviting for young players to try their ambition on.

Bad North (PC, Mac, iOS, Android, PlayStation 4, Xbox One or Nintendo Switch) is another stylised strategy game. You control an army defending an island and must train and develop your forces efficiently. The simple visuals and knife-edge Viking combat along with the jeopardy of losing precious troops make this a lot of fun.

TEARAWAY UNFOLDED

A world created entirely from paper is the setting for this fantastical adventure. It's beautiful and funny, and offers a running, jumping exploration challenge. Drawing on Algonquian North American native folklore, it creates a story about identity and bravery against the odds in a quest to reach the source of life. Whether played on the portable PlayStation Vita or PlayStation 4, it uses unusual motion, camera and touch controls to draw the player into the action.

Junior-school children will enjoy the adventurous challenge, and parents will appreciate the way the game rewards progress with physical cardboard cut-out models of the game's characters ready to colour, stick and fold.

Rating:

PEGI: 7 with fear

ESRB: EVERYONE with mild cartoon violence and users interact

Player(s): 1 with another assisting on a tablet

Duration: The main story takes around 10 hours to complete but collecting everything in the game can take 20 hours.

Ingredients:

- PlayStation 4 or PlayStation Vita.
- The game itself.
- One controller if played on PlayStation 4.
- For two-player collaboration on PlayStation 4:
  o iOS or Android tablet.
  o PlayStation app.
  o Sony Entertainment Network account.
- For the papercraft:
  o Account on https://tearaway.me
  o Printer.
  o Paper, pens and glue.

Serving Suggestions:

Families can enjoy playing the game together on a weekend morning, then spend the afternoon downloading, printing and creating the paper versions of the characters that they won in the game. You can extend the creativity using the PlayStation app to let a second player customise the world while you play, as well as help with solving particular puzzles. This is also a good way to track which papercraft models you need to find on each level.

To Follow:

Nintendo Labo (Nintendo Switch) is another game themed around physical folding, colouring and cutting. Here, though, you get a cardboard pack with the game that folds up to make objects into which you slot the screen and controllers. Whether it's cardboard steering wheels, fishing rods, robot suits or pianos, each item is then put to good use in specific interactive games.

Tori (iOS or Android) combines physical and virtual play. The game comes with toys that you place on a play surface to control the game's spaceships and catapults. Children can also create and colour their own cardboard versions of the toys and use them to control the game.

LAUGH AT SILLINESS

Video games have their roots in fun and play. This makes them an excellent way to forget the worries of the day and dive into some silly fun together. Particularly in multiplayer games, where parents, carers and children take on bizarre or precarious challenges, the play often descends into giggling and laughter. The games in this section have been selected because they get players doing absurd activities and chuckling together. It's tongue-in-cheek entertainment with challenges that don't take themselves too seriously — not seriously at all, in fact.

THIS SECTION INCLUDES THE FOLLOWING GAMES

WarioWare Gold
Octodad: Dadliest Catch
Super Pole Riders
Untitled Goose Game
Worms W.M.D.
Just Dance

WARIOWARE GOLD

Games don't get any sillier than the *WarioWare* series. Each of its mini-games presents a basic yet peculiar challenge for the player. A simple scene appears on the screen with a one-word clue about what to do. In the few seconds of the countdown you have to figure out what the task is then press the appropriate button. From picking your nose or shaving a chin to stomping on enemy mushrooms or popping bubble wrap, you can play each crazy mini-challenge multiple times to get better at it.

WarioWare: Gold incorporates the best of the mini-games from the other games in the *WarioWare* series for a total of 300 challenges that are bound to make you laugh.

Rating:
PEGI: 7 with violence
ESRB: EVERYONE 10+ with cartoon violence and crude humor

Player(s): 1

Duration: The game is played in rounds that collect mini-games into 5-minute challenges. To complete them all will take up to 16 hours.

Ingredients:
- Nintendo 2DS or 3DS.
- The game itself.
- *WarioWare* on other systems:
    - Gameboy Advance: *WarioWare, Inc.: Mega Microgames!* and *WarioWare: Twisted!*
    - Nintendo DS: *WarioWare: Touched!*
    - Nintendo Gamecube: *WarioWare, Inc.: Mega Party Games$!*
    - Wii: *WarioWare: Smooth Moves*
    - Nintendo Wii U: *Game & Wario*

Serving Suggestions:
Although most of the *WarioWare* mini-game challenges are single-player, there are modes where different family members can compete against each other. Taking turns on a particular challenge is also a lot of fun.

To Follow:
What the Golf? (PC, iOS Apple Arcade or Nintendo Switch) is a golf game as bonkers as *WarioWare*. Each golf course has an unexpected twist, such as hitting yourself into the hole rather than the ball. It's a brilliant parody that's as much about making you laugh as getting a hole in one.

Baba Is You (PC, Mac or Nintendo Switch) requires some lateral thinking. Each level is controlled by rules written on the screen, such as 'Lava Is Hot', 'Wall Is Stop' and 'Flag Is Move'. By moving the words around with your pixilated character, you subvert the level's logic to your advantage.

PaRappa the Rapper (PlayStation, PlayStation 4 or PlayStation Portable) is a bizarre rhythm game where you play a paper-thin rapping dog trying to win the heart of a flower-faced girl. You do this by pressing buttons to rap in time with the music to impress her. It creates a silly yet endearing game about rhythm, true love and cooking.

OCTODAD: DADLIEST CATCH

Most games design their controls to be easy and accessible. *Octodad: Dadliest Catch* takes a different approach. Using a combination of sticks and buttons, it creates an awkward, stomach-churning feeling of having too many limbs that you can't directly control. Traversing the simplest of rooms and completing simple tasks like opening a cupboard become brain-achingly tricky. It's the kind of peculiar difficulty that quickly results in a heady mix of frustration and hilarity as you blunder your way through each level, limbs flailing and sending furniture flying, to the gleeful screams of others in the room.

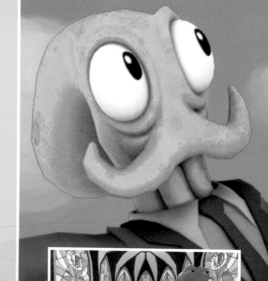

Rating:
PEGI: 7 with violence
ESRB: EVERYONE 10+ with cartoon violence and crude humor

Player(s): 1–2

Duration: To complete the single-player story will take around 7 hours and then another 10 or so to collect everything.

Ingredients:
- PC, Mac, iOS, Android, PlayStation 4, PlayStation Vita, Xbox One, Nintendo Switch or Nintendo Wii U.
- The game itself.

Serving Suggestions:
Octodad: Dadliest Catch is particularly fun to play with people who think they're good at video games. The peculiar controls and premise will have them struggling to walk in a straight line as much as anyone else. Once you've mastered the game as single players, you can opt for a cooperative mode where each player can choose which legs and arms they control. This makes the game a bit harder as you have to coordinate how to walk and hold things. It also makes it even funnier to watch and play.

To Follow:
Human: Fall Flat (PC, Mac, iOS, Android, PlayStation 4, Xbox One or Nintendo Switch) takes the idea of rag-doll characters and movement in the direction of a platform game. You run, jump and solve puzzles with your elastic character, either on your own or with another player. Get it wrong and you fall flat on your face, often with comedic timing.

I Am Bread (PC, Mac, iOS, Android, PlayStation 4 or Xbox One) takes the malleable, real-world physics gameplay and applies it to a slice of bread. By controlling each corner with a different stick or button, you make your way around the kitchen and other rooms of the house. Playing a slice of bread is funny in its own right, but it gets really silly as you become covered in all sorts of household detritus.

SUPER POLE RIDERS

A cross between the high jump, jousting and basketball, *Super Pole Riders* is a simple game where four players must get a ball hanging from a wire to the opponent's goal using long poles. It's the controls that make this game so much of a giggle to play. One of the controller joysticks operates the pole while the other moves your character. This enables you to pull off batting, jumping, hurdling and whacking moves in various fashions.

The rounds start calmly, with players edging around to get the upper hand, but it usually ends in frantic shouting and hitting of buttons as they wrestle to get the characters to do what they need them to do. It's deeply silly and a lot of fun for all ages.

Rating:
PEGI: 7 with violence
ESRB: EVERYONE 10+ with fantasy violence and crude humor

Player(s): 1–4

Duration: The rounds each last a few minutes, but players will want 'just one more go' for long sessions.

Ingredients:
- PC, Mac, PlayStation 3 or PlayStation 4.
- One controller per player.
- *Super Pole Riders* is part of the *Sportsfriends* pack which, when purchased, gives access to this and three other unusual games.

Serving Suggestions:
When you first try this game, the unusual controls can be a bit confusing. Giving players some time to learn how to move the player and the ball-on-a-wire avoids frustration. Once everyone has got a hang of the controls you can start a competitive match.

With four players, the fun and laughter are amplified as teammates must try to work together to win. Own goals and clattering each other mistakenly with the pole are common. The more you play, the more skill is involved, but there continue to be moments where chance and fortuitous interactions win the day and make it all the funnier.

To Follow:
Cricket Through the Ages (iOS Apple Arcade) is a competitive sport game themed around cricket but with little to do with the rules of that game. Players face off and aim for each other as much as wickets. Controls work by holding or tapping the screen to spin limbs and release the ball (or whatever you are holding). It's all very silly, in a quintessentially English way.

Heave Ho (PC, Mac or Nintendo Switch) is a team game where you have unusually long limbs with which you hang on to platform levels and other players. Up to four people cooperate and coordinate their hanging-on and letting-go to traverse through a series of challenges. Flinging, falling, hanging and spinning have never been so funny.

REKT! High Octane Stunts (PC, Mac, iOS, Android or Nintendo Switch) is a stunt racing game for up to four players on one system. Players compete to chain tricks, nail landings, drift corners and unlock more cars. The multiplayer game is where things really heat up, as players attack each other and score points to claim the crown.

UNTITLED GOOSE GAME

This is another silly and funny game but with a dastardly vibe. You play a mean goose who is intent on ruining the day of the inhabitants of a sleeping English village. By stealing items, squawking and otherwise making a nuisance of yourself, you slowly discover why the goose is so angry. The absurdity of playing as a goose is matched by how much fun it is to pull silly pranks on the unsuspecting villagers.

Rating:
PEGI: 3
ESRB: EVERYONE

Player(s): 1

Duration: It takes about 6 hours to complete the game although possible to rush through it more quickly.

Ingredients:
- PC, Mac, PlayStation 4, Xbox One or Nintendo Switch.
- The game itself.

Serving Suggestions:
This is a game you need to be in the right mood to play. In a group, with one person taking charge of the goose, you can figure out together what to do next. The trick here is to work through a chain of events that lead to the outcome you desire.

From stealing the gardener's keys and dropping them in the pond to filling the fountain with soap or taking a child's glasses so they can't see and fall over, it's all stuff children will enjoy because they would be told off for it in real life. Here, though, the silly mischief of it all makes you laugh as well as feel a bit mean.

To Follow:
West of Loathing (Mac, PC, iOS or Nintendo Switch) is another comedy adventure, although here you role-play as a stick-man cowboy. The quipping characters and intricate puzzles work better with teenagers, but the slapstick comedy will make anyone laugh. Traverse snake-infested gorges, punch skeletons wearing cowboy hats, grapple with demon cows and investigate a wide variety of disgusting spittoons.

Goat Simulator (PC, PlayStation 3, PlayStation 4, Xbox One, Xbox 360 or Nintendo Switch) takes the animal avatar in a cloven-hoofed direction. It's an open-world third-person action game where you steer your goat to do as much damage as possible. What started as a joke prototype turned into this extremely silly game with a cult following.

WORMS W.M.D

This is a long-standing multiplayer fighting game. The twist is that all the players are worms. With bizarre attacks on opponents that range from exploding sheep to self-deploying ninja rope, the battle is on the far end of crazy. Players take turns choosing an attack for each of their worms to make, although once chosen they have a limited time to target and fire. The worm characters have become embellished with hats and funny voices over the years, so this now looks and sounds like an episode of *Monty Python*.

It works as a silly game because it not only makes you laugh and shout but is a well-balanced tactical battle that requires real skill.

Rating:
PEGI: 12 with bad language and violence
ESRB: EVERYONE 10+ with cartoon violence, crude humor and language

Player(s): 1–5

Duration: It takes about 15 hours to complete the single-player game, but the real longevity is in the endless multiplayer fun. Each battle can last up to an hour.

Ingredients:
- PC, PlayStation 4, Xbox One or Nintendo Switch.
- Previous versions of *Worms* are available on other platforms:
  - *Worms 4* (iOS or Android)
  - *Worms 3* (iOS, Android or Mac)
  - *Worms Battlegrounds* (PlayStation 4 or Xbox One)
  - *Worms Clan Wars* (PC or Mac)
  - *Worms Revolution* (PC, Mac, PlayStation 3, PlayStation Vita or Xbox 360)
  - *Worms Battle Islands* (PlayStation Portable or Nintendo Wii)

Serving Suggestions:
It's worth playing the single-player campaign battles before diving into the multiplayer. This ensures you get a good grip of how the main weapons work. Each one has a different way to deploy and trigger and mistakes can be costly.

First attempts at the multiplayer game are relatively chaotic, and who wins is often down to chance. But help younger players push through the frustration and it soon becomes a highly enjoyable, and often bonkers, family battle as each of the worms under your command puts its bizarre arsenal of weapons to effective use.

To Follow:
Cannon Brawl (PC, PlayStation 4 or Xbox) is a two-player battle where you collect resources and build weapons and defences, all in real time. It's shout-out-loud fun where one wrong shot can let your opponent get the upper hand. Each battle is as frantic as it is silly. To win requires real skill.

The *Burnout* series (PC, PlayStation 2, PlayStation 3, PlayStation 4, PlayStation Portable, Xbox, Xbox One, Xbox 360 or Nintendo GameCube) is an over-the-top racing game where you're encouraged to crash, bash and ram other cars. Throughout the series (*Burnout, Burnout 2: Point of Impact, Burnout 3: Takedown, Burnout Revenge, Burnout Paradise*) the bravado and crashing increases, but they all have the same silly core gameplay. From *Burnout 2: Point of Impact* onwards the game includes an over-the-top 'Crash' mode part-game where you have to cause the biggest wreck to win. *Burnout Paradise* adds an open world to explore and destroy.

JUST DANCE

Dancing in front of each other isn't something we often do in families. *Just Dance* is released with new songs and features each year. It gets parents, carers, children and even grandparents off the couch and dancing along with the on-screen moves. Players hold a motion-sensitive controller or stand in front of a camera (PlayStation Camera, Xbox Kinect camera) that tracks how well they are pulling off each dance move. It's super-simple, with on-screen dancers who demonstrate each move and a prompt of what's next at the bottom.

With themed dancers depicted in silhouette and bright visuals, it doesn't take itself or the competitive dancing too seriously. Giggling because you can't get the moves right, or at parents strutting their stuff, *Just Dance* is a unique way to bring the family together to get fit and have a laugh.

Rating:

Rating for *Just Dance 2020*:

PEGI: 3 with in-game purchases

ESRB: EVERYONE 10+ with mild lyrics, mild suggestive themes, in-game purchases and users interact

Player(s): 1–4 on PlayStation 3 and PlayStation 4, Xbox 360, Wii and Wii U, and 1–6 on Xbox One with Kinect camera and Nintendo Switch.

Duration: Each of the songs takes a few minutes to dance to. There are 40 songs included with the game and 500 more available via paid subscription.

Ingredients:

- PlayStation 3, PlayStation 4, Xbox One with Kinect camera, Xbox 360 with Kinect camera, Nintendo Switch, Nintendo Wii or Nintendo Wii U.
  - On PlayStation, the addition of PlayStation Camera improves tracking.
  - On Xbox, you need the Xbox Kinect camera to play.
  - You can use a smartphone *Just Dance* app to select the next song more easily.
- The game itself.
- A controller for each player, apart from the Xbox Kinect version, where players don't hold a controller.
- On PlayStation 4, Xbox One and Nintendo Switch you can purchase an additional 'Unlimited Pass' subscription to access all 400 songs.

Serving Suggestions:

Although the *Just Dance* games have developed over the years, you may want to pick one based on the songs they include. Like yearly greatest-hits albums, *Just Dance* picks popular songs from the year to dance to. There are also special editions focusing on Abba, Disney, hip-hop and show tunes that can be a good option if you have fans of those genres.

Although the game is rated for children, it's worth noting that the nature of some songs is more mature. *Just Dance 2020* includes lyrics about alcohol and sex. There's a 'Kids Mode' in recent versions of the game that provides dances tailored towards younger players and specially selected kid-friendly songs. There is also a *Just Dance Kids* series of the game with songs for even younger dancers.

To Follow:

Just Dance Now (iOS, Android, web browser, Apple TV or Chromecast) offers the *Just Dance* formula without the need for a console and lots of controllers. You load the Justdancenow.com page on your computer or television, then connect your smartphone app to play. The phone is your controller and you can play with as many people as you want, locally or online. After the free trial you can purchase a VIP pass for a specified duration to access more of the 500 songs available.

INHABIT ANOTHER WORLD

Whether it's a simple puzzle grid, a battlefield or a universe of planets to visit, all games create virtual spaces in which to play. Some of these are simply the background to a campaign — the game's unfolding drama, missions or challenge. But others invite you to invest in the worlds they create, move in, tend to and inhabit in fantastical ways.

The games in this section invite you to spend time in spaces that have a sense of place, life and character. Worlds that hold history and lore in their landscapes, flora, fauna and inhabitants; environments that respond to your presence and invite you to restore them to their former glory.

THIS SECTION INCLUDES THE FOLLOWING GAMES
The Legend of Zelda: Breath of the Wild
Flower
Forza Horizon 4
Tunic
Animal Crossing
Fe
Subnautica
Hollow Knight

THE LEGEND OF ZELDA: BREATH OF THE WILD

This game departs from the previous *Zelda* formula with the scale and depth of its world. You walk, fly, ride and climb your way through a landscape that varies in climate, terrain, inhabitants and vegetation. Weather and the passage of the sun and moon extend the deep encounter with the fantastical world, but it's the sense of history in the dilapidated buildings and long-untouched wilds that draw you in. You must work with the land, foraging for food, scaling snow-covered mountains and searching for shade in scalding deserts to continue your quest to uncover its history and restore balance.

This is a magical world that exists not only as a backdrop for adventure but as a living, breathing environment that must be negotiated as intelligently and carefully as any monster you fight.

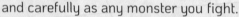

Rating:
PEGI: 12 with violence
ESRB: EVERYONE with fantasy violence, suggestive themes and use of alcohol

Player(s): 1

Duration: Varies greatly depending on approach and ability. Most will be able to complete the main threads in 50 hours. But to do everything in the game is a huge challenge, taking over 200 hours over many months.

Ingredients:

- Nintendo Switch or Nintendo Wii U.
- The game itself.
- Optional amiibo figures to unlock additional equipment.
- Optional add-on purchases that offer new quests and equipment.

Serving Suggestions:
The family can share this *Zelda* adventure by taking responsibility for different roles. Younger members of the family can play the cooking element of the game to make older siblings useful meals for their next adventure. More experienced players can take on the four beasts and progress the main story, while others can set themselves to exploring every corner of the land.

To Follow:
In *The Witcher 3: Wild Hunt* (PC, PlayStation 4 or Xbox One) you play monster-hunter Geralt in a vast open world as he searches for his missing adopted daughter. The game responds to your actions and has dynamic environments, weather and day—night cycles that affect the creatures you hunt. It's a fantasy world of humans, elves, dwarves and monsters but with a substantial sense of place. Lakes, cities, forests, rivers and castles dot the landscape and invite you not only to conquer the game but to explore the furthest reaches of the beautiful lands.

No Man's Sky (PC, PlayStation 4 or Xbox One) invites you to take your spaceship to explore and colonise a universe rich with diverse planets, creatures and fauna. Facing so vast a space is daunting at first, but a rhythm of survival, combat and trading draws you into a space drama of your own making. Choose a home planet and join other players to subdue the wilds of this breathtaking universe.

FLOWER

Control the breeze blowing across fields of grass and blow petals into other flowers to make them bloom. *Flower* is simple and single-purpose in evoking the feeling of the wind. What starts as an awkward struggle to control the breeze soon turns into a flowing race, skimming the tops of grass blades as you master the motion- or touch-controls. Your task is to collect more petals. As you circle and loop through these spaces, the rain might fall or night arrive, but it's the ongoing reaction of the landscape that makes it a place to linger and play. It's a magical world that not only responds to but is transformed by your presence. A transformation that leads from the countryside to the city and back again.

Rating:
PEGI: 3
ESRB: EVERYONE

Player(s): 1

Duration:
You can finish the game in under 3 hours, but to find every flower and secret can take up to 7 hours. It's also a game that warrants repeated play.

Ingredients:
- PC, iOS, PlayStation 3, PlayStation 4 or PlayStation Vita.
- The game itself.

Serving Suggestions:
Families enjoy playing this game together and working to find all the hidden green flowers. When you have found these for any particular level, you get more leaves falling into the pot at the end and unlock a special trophy. Others have used the game as part of a daily relaxation, picking a level and then silently playing through it on their own, letting the music and visuals wash over them before they start the day.

To Follow:
Feather (PC or Nintendo Switch) brings you, as a bird, to a beautiful island. You can explore freely, collecting items and soaring on the breeze. Often, other players will join you to create a flock of birds flying together, making music on the wind.

LocoRoco (PlayStation 4 or PlayStation Portable) creates a world of plants and creatures to investigate. The novelty, besides the character's singing and cute aesthetic, is that you control the game with just two buttons, tilting and bumping your characters through each level.

FORZA HORIZON 4

This is a thrilling racing game where you race all manner of vehicles across a wide range of landscapes. This fourth iteration is set in the United Kingdom, with Edinburgh's narrow streets, the Lake District's hills and rainfall and the Cotswolds' historic villages. There may be 420 cars to earn and race against other players, but it's the world you race through that stands out. Seasons change, leaves fall, lakes freeze or the summer heat shines off the tarmac. Each day the sun rises and sets, and different weather blows in to complete the sense of immersion.

This isn't just a world to race in but one to freely explore. Uniquely in racing games, this is distracting enough to make players pull over and just watch the view changing in front of them.

Rating:
PEGI: 3
ESRB: EVERYONE with users interact and in-game purchases

Player(s): Single-player with Xbox Gold Live online multiplayer for 2–12 people and Xbox Gold Live co-op for 2–6 people

Duration: The main story development can take up to 16 hours, but with so much to do in the open world of the game, seeing and completing everything will take more than 60 hours.

Ingredients:

- PC or Xbox One.
- The game itself.
- Internet connection for online play.
- Xbox Gold Live for online multiplayer.

Serving Suggestions:
Challenging family members to set the fastest times on particular challenges and races is a popular way to enjoy the game together. Finding the right place to break, or the racing line that saves seconds, parents and children egg each other on to improve their times and get a genuine understanding of driving and racing mechanics along the way.

With its changing weather, day–night cycle and beautiful British landscape, there's also considerable enjoyment to be had from finding the best views and sharing them with each other. Then there's a *Forza Horizon 4 Lego Speed Champions* purchasable add-on that turns the cars and landscape into Lego. Families and younger drivers enjoy exploring the Lego valley and collecting bricks for items in their Lego house and garage.

To Follow:
Forza Motorsport 7 (PC or Xbox One) is the pure racing equivalent of *Forza Horizon*'s open experience. The focus is on the cars and super-accurate racing mechanics. This is the world of the racing professional fantasy and to excel you need to learn real driving skills.

Burnout Paradise (PC, PlayStation 3, remastered on PlayStation 4, Xbox One or Xbox 360) uses its huge world as a playground for exhilarating and sometimes destructive driving. Crashing is part of the fun as you earn points for near misses as well as winning.

Gran Turismo (PlayStation 4) is a driving simulator that focuses on a photo-realistic driving experience. Players race real-world cars where bodywork and interiors are perfectly modelled. Whether hatchbacks or super cars, this game lets you step into the world of the automobile fanatic.

TUNIC

You wake up on an island as a small fox, with no memory of how you got there. From a fixed overhead perspective, you push through trees, pick up weapons and learn new moves to discover an expanse of forests, caves and landscapes. Choose your own way forward and decide how and when to take on new areas and enemies. Many routes and secrets are hidden in plain sight for the more inquisitive player.

With hand-drawn-style visuals and an eerie soundscape, *Tunic* tells a story about overcoming loneliness. As a stranger in a strange land, you push on to discover if you are the only one here. Cryptic runes and flashbacks hint at your memory of the place, but it remains unfamiliar. Venture too far too soon and it becomes clear that this is not a world inviting your presence. There are terrible things out there, and this tiny fox is going to dig deep to find out why.

Rating:
PEGI: Rating pending game release
ESRB: Rating pending game release

Player(s): 1

Duration: Given that players can explore the areas around them in any order, duration varies considerably. It's likely to take around 8 hours or so the first time you play. Repeated play-throughs may be quicker, though, as you can take advantage of the knowledge you have already learned about the game's world.

Ingredients:

- PC, Mac, Xbox One or Xbox Series X.
- The game itself.
- Pen and paper.

Serving Suggestions:
Parents enjoy playing *Tunic* with children, taking turns at the controls. Equally it's fun to let one player have the gamepad while the other helps with navigation and strategy by writing down the different runes and messages to decode the language and secrets of the wider world.

The art style appears simple and childlike but there is considerable depth to *Tunic*. You can choose your own path through the game, and nothing is locked off at the start — if you know where to look.

To Follow:
Ori and the Blind Forest (PC, Xbox One or Nintendo Switch) is a platform game where you play Ori to restore life to the forest. It's a common premise, but this game creates a deep and beautiful land to explore. From the roots and lava underground to hilltop sunrises, it's a breathtaking ride backed by an orchestral score. The jumping and shooting challenge is substantial, rewarded with a world you will want to spend time in.

Hollow Knight (PC, Mac, PlayStation 4, Xbox One or Nintendo Switch) is a more action-oriented platform game, with a more challenging complexity that offers intricate and intriguing details about the world in which you play.

ANIMAL CROSSING

You live on a small island teeming with life. Insects, fish, trees, vegetation and fossils are represented with cute cartoon visuals. Rather than the scale or grandeur of other game worlds, it's the interconnected minutiae of this diorama that makes it fascinating. This interconnection comprises not only how you impact the world but how you relate to the other inhabitants and how the island changes with real-world time. Along with special events such as the Christmas and Easter festivals, you need to play in different seasons and times of day to collect particular insects and fish.

This is a controllable fantasy escape but one that's still intimately connected to the ticking of the real-world clock. It's a place to visit for short bursts each day over the course of a full year.

Rating:
PEGI: 3
ESRB: EVERYONE

Player(s): 1 but other players can visit your island if you let them

Duration: This is a game played in short bursts each day through the whole year. It changes with real-world time, seasons and festivals, so it takes hundreds of hours to complete.

Ingredients:

- *Animal Crossing* is played on Nintendo Gamecube.
- *Animal Crossing: Wild World* is played on Nintendo DS.
- *Animal Crossing: City Folk* is played on Nintendo Wii
- *Animal Crossing: New Leaf* is played on Nintendo 3DS
- *Animal Crossing: New Hozizons* is played on Nintendo Switch.
- Spin-off games that offer a reduced experience in the *Animal Crossing* world:
  - *Animal Crossing: Happy Home Designer* is played on Nintendo 3DS.
  - *Animal Crossing: Amiibo Festival* is played on Nintendo Wii U.
  - *Animal Crossing: Pocket Camp* is played on iOS or Android.
- The game itself.
- amiibo figures can be purchased to unlock content in the Nintendo 3DS, Nintendo Wii U and Nintendo Switch versions of the game.

Serving Suggestions:

This is a great game for families to enjoy sharing at different times of the day. The kids will play for 20 minutes after school, running errands in the game, catching fish and increasing their collections of furniture. Older siblings can take a turn later in the evening to catch insects that appear at sundown. Then parents can play later at night to catch the creatures only out after dark. You need to agree some family goals for the island and the home you're building, to avoid someone selling a hard-won piece of furniture or pulling up the flower beds you were working on. Another alternative is to have a character each, living on the same island.

To Follow:

Viva Piñata (Xbox 360, Microsoft Windows, Nintendo DS or Xbox One via Rare Replay) is a fantasy garden-simulation game where your tending and care encourages one of sixty different piñata animals to make it their home. You use gardening tools to plough, sow seeds, create ponds and sculpt the land. Do this well and more animals will appear, who in turn need nurturing to be happy and to procreate.

Sim City (PC, DS, iOS, Android or Wii) and *Cities: Skylines* (PC, Mac, Xbox One, PlayStation 4 or Nintendo Switch) greatly expand the transport-management challenge to every aspect of a modern city. This game moves away from the elegant, meditative style of *Mini Metro* but has a similarly expanding scope of challenges.

FE

You play a fox in a magical fairy-tale forest. The world extends in front of you in stylised form, with trees, mountains and streams glistening with sparkles of life. You run, jump, climb and dip your paws in every aspect of the world. But it's the plants and other creatures, and how they respond to you, that really draw you in. Looking deeply into these creatures' eyes, you share a song and learn new abilities from them. You progress by embracing this interrelated ecosystem and finding your place at the heart of the world.

Fe's world comes into its own after completing the few hours of challenge, when you can explore to your heart's content. The space that initially seemed alien and otherworldly has been restored to harmony and becomes a place to coexist in.

Rating:
PEGI: 7 with violence and fear
ESRB: EVERYONE with mild fantasy violence

Player(s): 1

Duration: You can finish the main game in 7 hours. However, there are many other things to discover and collect that will take upwards of 15 hours.

Ingredients:
- Nintendo Switch, PlayStation 4 or Xbox One.
- The game itself.

Serving Suggestions:
Although there may be slight confusion at first, you'll soon discover how to move around, climb trees, dip in rivers and communicate with other animals. *Fe* lets you explore its world at your pace. Take your time enjoying the environment and experiencing what it's like to be a tiny creature setting out into a world.

To Follow:
Proteus (PC, Mac, PlayStation 3 or PlayStation Vita) takes you to a pixelated island. As you explore you discover that your presence changes the seasons and time of day. Delving deeper, there are rudimentary interactions with the creatures that inhabit the land, and rain clouds that blow in from the sea.

The Endless Forest (PC) is a whimsical online multiplayer game where you play deer in a peaceful forest. You freely explore ruins and ponds, and meet other players, communicating in symbols. The world is like a moving painting, but one that players have a strong sense of ownership over. An avid community of players have contributed to the game's evolution, and a new version is in development.

SUBNAUTICA

Dive into an underwater ocean on an alien planet and collect the resources you need to establish a base and survive. There's an open and immersive watery world to discover as you construct tools, bases and submersibles, and interact with wildlife. Construction is predictably challenging, with air pressure and resources a battle to keep balanced. These housekeeping concerns are as occupying as the daunting, enigmatic and mysterious depths of *Subnautica*'s world. Although set in the future, *Subnautica* draws back a curtain on the real underwater worlds we know but can't explore in a prolonged way.

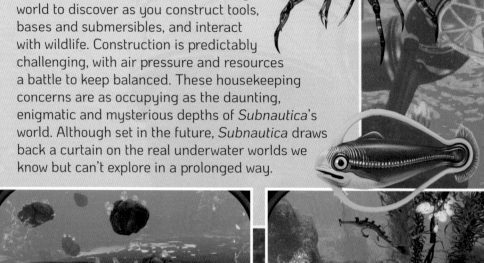

Rating:
PEGI: 7 with violence and fear
ESRB: EVERYONE 10+ with fantasy
violence, mild language and users interact

Player(s): 1

Duration: The main story can be completed in about 32 hours, depending on ability and how much you focus on progressing. To see everything and completely build out your base can absorb many hundreds of hours.

Ingredients:
- PC, PlayStation 4 or Xbox One.
- The game itself.

Serving Suggestions:
Enjoy the lessons of *Subnautica* by playing it with your children. Together you need to decide how deeply you will investigate the ocean before heading home. This bravery feels very real in moments of underwater panic if things go wrong. Water pressure isn't just a factor to limit your progress; it must be managed and worked with as you build your base.

Along with the science lesson, the game offers insights into the beauty and benefits to be found in this underwater alien world. Unlike the real world, where oceans are polluted, and unlike other games, *Subnautica* intentionally denies players any means of domination. There are no guns, for example. This world is one to be explored and studied rather than subjugated.

To Follow:
Endless Ocean (Wii) and its sequel *Endless Ocean 2: Adventures of the Deep* are versions of a diving adventure game where you explore the Manaurai Sea to identify different fish and recover artefacts. As experience is gained you can encounter dolphins, huge whales, underwater wrecks and deep-sea trenches.

ABZÛ (PC, PlayStation 4, Xbox One or Switch) is an adventure in a lush underwater world. You descend into the heart of the ocean to find ancient secrets and encounter majestic creatures. This combines the beautiful weightlessness of diving with an ancient story of meaning and place in the world.

HOLLOW KNIGHT

Run, jump and battle your way through
the underground kingdom of Hallownest.
It's not uncommon for platform games
to invest in the environments through
which you pass, but the haunting depths
in this game contain more than a veneer
of ancient mysteries. Rendered in simple
2D visuals, the world bristles with lore and
backstory to the point that this becomes as much
as a driver for exploration as powering-up your
abilities or defeating enemies. This simplicity
also enables *Hollow Knight* to create a huge
labyrinth of interconnected spaces, each
with their own enemies, hazards and history.

This over-delivery of world-building is
more than any platform game requires,
but it transforms the experience from a
power fantasy to an investigation into this
otherworldly civilisation and alien history.

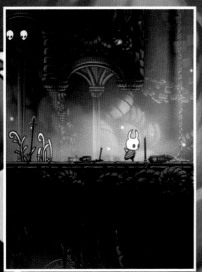

Rating:
PEGI: 7 with mild violence and fear
ESRB: EVERYONE 10+ with fantasy violence and mild blood

Player(s): 1

Duration: You can finish the main campaign of the game in 20 hours, but more than other games, this varies depending on ability and how focused you are. Many people play the game for over 70 hours before they are finished.

Ingredients:
- PC, Mac, PlayStation 4, Xbox One or Nintendo Switch.
- The game itself.

Serving Suggestions:
Hollow Knight's rich ecosystem, characters and gameplay can be enjoyed in all sorts of ways. Some patience and persistence are needed to push past the first couple of difficult hours, but the effort is rewarded with a unique and expansive world.

For children who have a fascination with insects, there are arthropods aplenty in this game: a firefly shopkeeper, a rhino beetle blacksmith, a mystic moth and even a charm-selling mollusc.

To Follow:
Okami (PC, PlayStation 2, PlayStation 3, PlayStation 4, Xbox One, Nintendo Switch, Nintendo Wii or Nintendo DS as *Okamiden*) has a unique visual style and invites you to inhabit its painted world with brushstrokes of your own. Whether you're in combat or bringing new life to the flora and fauna, *Okami* is an epic saga built around a unique location that needs to be painted back to the multicoloured world it once was.

Bioshock (PC, Mac, iOS, PlayStation 3, PlayStation 4, Xbox One or Xbox 360) is a shooting game set in 1960 in an underwater dystopian city called Rapture. It's an alternative world built to escape the government and religions of the surface, but one that has spiralled into chaos. Although you do a lot of shooting, the real appeal is the believable and detailed world that unfolds as you explore. Architecture, audio diaries and inhabitants invite you to play a role in saving or destroying this great project.

COMPETE ON THE COUCH

Raucous, unbounded, exuberant, all-age, competitive fun is something video games are known for. Find the right games for your family and you can create important and healthy ways to let off steam, excel and persevere as you sit next to each other on the sofa. These games can play a big part in raising children to be magnanimous in victory and generous in defeat. Kids love competing online, but the games here focus on battling in the same room. Played with multiple controllers and a shared screen, they offer challenges that require real skill and give everyone a chance to rise to the top of the family pile.

THIS SECTION INCLUDES THE FOLLOWING GAMES

TowerFall
Nintendo Land
Horizon Chase Turbo
Wordhunters
Tricky Towers
Joust Mania
Hidden in Plain Sight
Super Bomberman R

TOWERFALL

Each player selects a pixelated knight and fights to eliminate opponents by shooting them with arrows or jumping on their heads. The arena is a single shared screen. What makes it so competitive is the limited resource of arrows and the ability to dodge and catch them if you get the timing right. It's frantic and requires a lot of shouting and screaming from participants. It's a great family battle because of the simple action, short rounds and ability to extensively customise power-ups, teams, weapons and ways to claim victory.

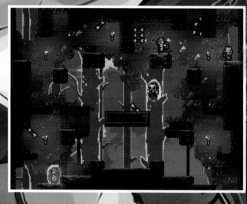

Rating:
PEGI: 7 with mild violence

ESRB: EVERYONE 10+ with violence and blood

Player(s): 4 on most systems, 6 players on the Nintendo Switch version

Duration: Each round lasts just a few minutes. Multiplayer matches are a race to a certain number of wins, which can make them last up to 30 minutes depending on the settings.

Ingredients:
- PC, Mac, PlayStation 4, PlayStation Vita, Xbox One, Nintendo Switch or Ouya.
- One controller for each player. On the Nintendo Switch, each Joy-Con pair can be split between two players.
- The game itself.
- Additional levels, weapons and characters can be purchased via the *TowerFall Dark World Expansion*. This is included in the Nintendo Switch version for free.

Serving Suggestions:
When playing in a family of mixed experience and ability, you can set up teams for a level playing field. There are also tens of settings that change the gameplay in subtle or substantial ways. Some settings, such as being encumbered when you have lots of arrows, can be applied to specific players as a handicap.

The single-screen battles can seem bewildering at first, but their simplicity and slightly chaotic nature make it possible for players of all abilities to win a round or two.

To Follow:
Nidhogg (PC, Mac, PlayStation 4 or PlayStation Vita) is a fast two-player duelling game whose simple visuals belie the skill required to defeat your opponent. The novelty is that upon death you reappear in the next screen. The player to advance through the most screens wins. *Nidhogg II* extends the fighting options but includes frequent arcade-style violence.

Videoball (PC, PlayStation 4 or Xbox One) is a minimalist sports game for up to six players. The aim is to get one of the balls into the opponent's goal by shooting it with triangles. It's highly skilled, frantic and works brilliantly in a competitive family setting.

NINTENDO LAND

This collection of Nintendo games was created for the Nintendo Wii U launch. It uses the console's tablet screen to create specific roles for different players. In *Mario Chase*, the hiding player uses the tablet controller screen while the four seekers use the TV to try and find them. It means the hider can keep their location secret because no one else can see their screen. In *Metroid Blast*, one player uses the tablet to pilot a spaceship while the others fight on the ground using the TV. In *Ghost Mansion*, one player uses the tablet to secretly control the ghosts while the others on the TV try to escape.

The games would be impossible without the Wii U hardware and tablet controller and offer a unique, exuberant and high-quality way to battle, particularly with younger children in the family.

Rating:
PEGI: 7 with violence and fear
ESRB: EVERYONE 10+ with cartoon violence and crude humour

Player(s): 1–5, although this varies depending on the selected game

Duration: The compendium of games results in different durations, although most of the games can be played in 30-minute sessions. You may complete the single-player aspects in 10 hours, but multiplayer modes will offer hundreds of hours of entertainment.

Ingredients:
- Nintendo Wii U.
- The game itself.
- One Wii remote controller for each player (the same ones as for the original Wii), in addition to the player using the Wii U tablet controller.

Serving Suggestions:
Grandparents have enjoyed playing this with grandchildren. Teaming up to find where Granny or Grandad are hiding in *Mario Chase* is a chance for older family members to outsmart the youngsters. Similarly, teaming up to hunt down ghosts in *Luigi's Mansion* works brilliantly across wide age-gaps. The simplicity of aiming with the Wii U tablet controller in *The Legend of Zelda: Battle Quest* enables novice players to quickly learn the ropes. Finally, *Yoshi's Fruit Cart* rewards mature observation and memory rather than youthful reactions and button-mashing.

To Follow:
Wii Sports Resort (Nintendo Wii or Wii U) offers motion-controlled sports, with hidden gems like table tennis and archery being both super-competitive and accessible.

Wii Party (Nintendo Wii) and *Wii Party U* (Nintendo Wii U) are games where up to four players compete to score the most points on a series of novel mini-games. Whether you're trying to press buttons as fast as you can, count apples, race horses, do chin-ups or chop vegetables, it's great fun everyone can share. The Wii U game adds games that use the Wii U tablet screen in novel ways.

HORIZON CHASE TURBO

This is an arcade racing game with the focus on competitive fun rather than realism; its graphics make it look like it was plucked from the nineties' arcades, with a nod to *Outrun* and *Lotus Turbo Challenge*. It balances modern affordances with retro visuals to create a brilliant way for families to race each other. Four players can race each other on one system as they battle to learn each track's twists and turns, to manage turbo and collect fuel. The single-player, 100-tracks campaign mode is excellent, with the added challenge of finding every blue token and perfectly managing your fuel.

The blistering pace, simple steering and rudimentary collision detection are part of the fun and level the playing field for all ages more than the nuanced controls of games like *Mario Kart*. This is a great place to start your video game racing journey.

Rating:
PEGI: 3
ESRB: EVERYONE with in-game purchases

Player(s): 1–4

Duration: It will take 30 hours or so to complete the single-player races, but much longer to collect everything and enjoy the multiplayer modes.

Ingredients:

- PC, PlayStation 4, Xbox One or Nintendo Switch.
- *Horizon Chase – World Tour* is a simpler single-player version on iOS and Android.
- The game itself.
  - *Rookie Series* downloadable content is free and adds modes for novice players.
  - *Turbo Summer Vibes* downloadable content can be purchased separately to add new cars, redesigned circuits and locations with a summertime theme.
- One controller for each player.

Serving Suggestions:

Along with racing four players at a time, it's also a fun game for competing for time trials and circuit scores. Who can get the fastest lap time and finish time, collect the most tokens and have the most fuel left? You can extend this competition to friends and family outside the home with the online 'Ghost Mode', where you see opponents as a ghost car that you must beat.

The 'Playground Mode' is available after accruing 700 points and offers a challenge that changes every two weeks. Players can also battle to get the best score on remixed circuits with extreme or unusual aspects (night, wind, harder computer opponents) to make them more difficult. Scores are ranked with other players online and the winners are published at the end of the two weeks.

For younger players in the family there is the free downloadable 'Rookie Series' that tailors the game for beginners: twenty-four selected races with easier, computer-controlled cars and without the need to collect fuel. This also enables you to unlock each track just by finishing. It's a great way to extend the game to include everyone on the sofa.

To Follow:

Trials Rising (PC, PlayStation 4, Xbox One or Nintendo Switch) is a four-player side-on motorbike racing game controlled by pressing 'accelerate' or 'brake' and using the stick to shift the weight of their riders' bodies. The game emulates real-world physics, so you have to balance your motorbike's speed, trajectory and camber. Like previous games in the series — *Trials Evolution* (Xbox 360), *Trials Fusion* (PC, PlayStation 4, Xbox One or Xbox 360), it's nail-biting competition as you wrestle to get your bike through each outlandish course ahead of other competitors.

WORDHUNTERS

This is a world-travelling word game you play on the PlayStation using a smartphone or tablet rather than controller. The smartphone and tablet screens make picking letters easy for all ages, and the camera on these devices is used to put each player's photo in the game. If you score the highest in a round, you can choose two letters from the name of the current geographical location to complete your special four-letter word. This adds real tactics to choosing the next destination, particularly as you see other players progress with their word as they board the plane.

Rating:
PEGI: 3
ESRB: EVERYONE

Player(s): 1–6

Duration: It's played in a series of rounds in different locations that together take around 30–45 minutes to complete.

Ingredients:

- PlayStation 4.
- The game itself.
- One PlayStation 4 controller.
- A tablet, smartphone or iPod Touch for each player, each loaded with the *Wordhunters* app.

Serving Suggestions:
Wordhunters works well in larger families as you don't need to buy expensive controllers for each player — you just use the devices you already have. The focus on word challenges makes it simple to understand, while the secret word you are collecting letters for makes the choice of countries tactical. Players can join and leave the game whenever they want. You can even play in a different language (French, Italian, German, Castilian Spanish or Latin American Spanish) to help build a foreign vocabulary.

To Follow:
That's You! (PlayStation 4) is another PlayStation game played with smartphones. This one is a family quiz where you are tested on your knowledge of each other to score points. It makes clever use of the smartphone interface, getting players to take selfies, draw things and tap the screen to select answers.

The Jackbox Party series (PC, Mac, Android, PlayStation 3, PlayStation 4, Xbox One, Xbox 360, Nintendo Switch or Apple TV) offers similar party games using the smartphone and TV combination but can be played on most devices.

TRICKY TOWERS

This battle puzzle uses shapes, but instead of creating lines, you must balance them in towers that mustn't fall over. Real-world physics apply, along with wind and attacks from other players to make your stack topple. Up to four players can race to build a tower of a certain height or the one that survives the longest without toppling over.

The simplicity of this challenge works for all ages. Older players may have nostalgic memories of playing *Tetris* in their youth, while others will connect with the Jenga-like stacking gameplay.

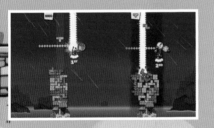

Rating:
PEGI: 3 with in-game purchases
ESRB: EVERYONE with users interact

Player(s): 1–4

Duration: You play a single battle round in a few minutes, but it's a game that increases in fun as you repeat this in a selection of tournament modes that will take around 30 minutes, depending on the number of rounds you select.

Ingredients:

- PC, Mac, PlayStation 4, Xbox One or Nintendo Switch.
- One controller for each player.

Serving Suggestions:
Tetris block-stacking is a premise the whole family can relate to. Family members often find themselves practising to improve in the next showdown. The more novel modes, like 'Puzzle', where you have to stack a set number of blocks as neatly as you can, or 'Race', where you need to be the quickest to create the tallest tower, provide more variety once you've got used to the stacking challenge.

To Follow:
Tetris 99 (Nintendo Switch) is a game where 100 people battle each other to be the last man standing as in *Fortnite*, but here you have to stack shapes tidily and quickly to win rather than shoot opponents.

Tetris Effect (PlayStation 4 VR) is a version of the game on PlayStation 4 that combines play with music for a relaxing experience that also works on PlayStation VR.

JOUST MANIA

This movement-sensitive game of tag is played in the real world, holding PlayStation Move motion controllers. First appearing as one of the games in the *Sportsfriends* pack, and then evolving as *Joust Mania* with more modes and up to 16 players, it's an active video game that doesn't require the screen. Players must jostle each other to move opponents' controllers by pushing, shoving or other reasonable contact while at the same time keeping their controller still. The controller light goes out when you have died. You can play as teams, add vulnerable king players that must be protected or traitors who try and get their teammates out. While this is going on, music plays, the speed of which determines how sensitive the controllers are and how easy it is to be out.

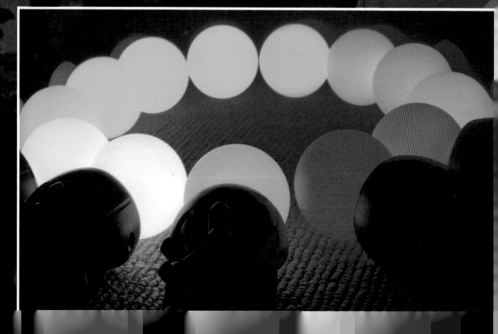

Rating:
Not rated by official bodies as this is a non-commercial, community-made game.

Player(s): 1–16, depending on the system you're running the game on.

Duration: Each round lasts a few minutes but players need multiple attempts to understand what's happening and to develop team strategies. When I run the game at arts festivals or community groups, 2 hours is a good duration, although during that time 100 different people may play.

Ingredients:

- *Joust Mania* for up to 16 players.
  - 1 PC, Mac or Raspberry Pi.
  - 1 USB Bluetooth adapter for 6 players.
  - The *Joust Mania* game itself.
  - A PlayStation Move controller for each player.
- *Joust* in the *Sportsfriends* pack.
  - PlayStation 3 for up to 7 players, PlayStation 4 for up to 4 players, PC or Mac for up to 7 players
  - 1 PlayStation Move controller for each player.
  - The *Sportsfriends* game itself.

Serving Suggestions:
This is a game that is fun to play in larger rooms at home or in the garden. The physical movement is a novelty that players of all ages can enjoy, and it works well at parties. Families have also set this up for community groups and schools where it can be played in large halls or outside. Connecting a loudspeaker is useful so the music can be heard in larger spaces. By adding multiple Bluetooth adaptors you can play the game with up to 16 players at a time.

More novel game modes that move from electronic tag towards tactical team games are harder to understand initially but worth the effort to practise. In 'Zombies', each player starts as a villager and has to avoid infection. In 'Werewolves', certain players are secretly designated to attack villagers without getting discovered. In 'Fight Club', players take it in turns to battle each other one-on-one.

To Follow:
Bounden (iOS or Android) is a smartphone dance game that gets players to use their bodies. Two people hold opposite ends of one smartphone then move together to keep a cursor over the ball.

Mekamon (iOS or Android) is a physical mechanical robot that moves like a spider. The lifelike motion is used in a range of games and play-patterns including an augmented-reality battle that combines the player's physical movements with virtual enemies.

HIDDEN IN PLAIN SIGHT

This unique battle requires keen observation rather than quick reflexes. Up to four players fight to protect or assassinate the king, catch a thief or race across the screen without being stopped. The twist is that you each have numerous computer-controlled doppelgängers. You have to pay careful attention to how each one moves and behaves to try to spot (and then stop) the human players. Not only does this create knife-edge battles fraught with excitement, it requires very different skills from other competitive video games.

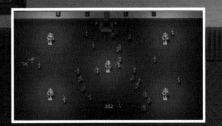

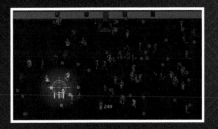

Rating:
PEGI: 7 with mild violence
ESRB: EVERYONE 10+ with fantasy violence

Player(s): 2–4

Duration: Each round lasts a few minutes, but perfecting strategies against other players requires longer attention and repeated play.

Ingredients:
- PC, Mac, Xbox One or Ouya.
- A controller for each player.
- The game itself.

Serving Suggestions:
Like family-favourite board games, setting aside an hour or two to play this together is not only a lot of fun but an enjoyable way to relax. The quick rounds allow for time to catch up with each other and pass around the snacks. Repeatedly playing the same mode leads to the development of more subtle tactics. The simple premise of each of the five games leads to surprising depths as players try to outsmart each other.

To Follow:
Spy Party (PC or Mac) is a game about observing behaviour. One player is a spy at a party among many computer-controlled guests, with a list of missions. The other player is a sniper who must spot the human-controlled spy by watching the way they are moving and interacting.

Thief Town (PC, Mac or PlayStation 4) is a 2–4 player game where you play in a crowd of identical characters and must identify both yourself and other players to then attack them. Get it wrong and all you do is reveal yourself. The game offers other modes like 'Spy Town', where you can trick and trap other players, and the 1-vs-3 'Drunk Town', where you have limited use of your pistol sights to spot the players.

SUPER BOMBERMAN R

This is the spiritual ancestor to last-player-standing battles like *Fortnite* and *Apex Legends*, but here you all play on the same screen and have the same bomb weapon. There are lots of versions, but in all of them you battle with up to eight players in a variety of modes, power-ups and abilities. As in games like *Fortnite* or *Apex Legends*, everyone fights to be the last player remaining. Here, though, you can see what the other players are doing the whole time because of the shared screen, and it becomes a game of bluff and double-bluff. Also, each round only lasts a few minutes so it's easier to stop when it's dinner time.

Although skilled and competitive, the simplicity of the levels and limited ways to attack make this game accessible for all abilities. It's raucous, explosive fun that fits into family life.

Rating:
PEGI: 7 with violence
ESRB: EVERYONE 10+ with cartoon violence and users interact

Player(s): 1–8 in the same room except on PlayStation 4, which is limited to 4 players. All systems support up to 8 players online.

Duration: Rounds last just a few minutes, but this is a game that can be enjoyed for hours at a time with a group of friends.

Ingredients:
- PlayStation 4, Xbox One, Nintendo Switch.
- A controller for each player.
- The game itself.
- PlayStation 4 requires PlayStation Plus to play people online.
- Xbox One requires Xbox Live Gold to play people online.
- Nintendo Switch requires Nintendo Switch Online to play people online.

Serving Suggestions:
A version of *Bomberman* is available on most systems, although it's worth reading a review of the specific versions before purchasing. For example, there are many versions for the Nintendo DS, but the original *Bomberman* game works best for families as it includes a 'Download Play' option, which allows you to download the game to up to 8 other DS consoles then battle using a local wireless connection.

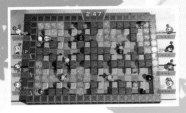

To Follow:
Worms W.M.D (PC, Mac, PlayStation 4, Xbox One or Nintendo Switch) is a multiplayer battle with explosions, like *Bomberman*. Here, though, each player takes turns to attack. This increases the level of tactics involved, although the best-laid plans don't always work.

Super Smash Bros. (Nintendo Switch, Nintendo Gamecube or Wii U) in its various versions offers real-time brawling battles. The tens of characters are drawn from other video games and each has bespoke moves to learn and perfect.

WORK TOGETHER TO THRIVE

Play is more fun when it's shared. This is as true about video games as it is when building a massive sandcastle on the beach or playing hopscotch in the playground. Finding brilliant team games is a great way to involve more people in the fun and share the experience together as a family. More experienced players naturally help novices contribute to the team.

Along with teamwork, the games I've selected here use the fact that players are all sitting next to each other. These are games where players take on different roles in order to complete unusual tasks. The fun is often as much about the conversations (and arguments) that happen in the room as what's happening on the screen.

THIS SECTION INCLUDES THE FOLLOWING GAMES

Affordable Space Adventures
Fru
Spaceteam
Sky: Children of the Light
Beasts of Balance
Knights and Bikes
Keep Talking and Nobody Explodes

AFFORDABLE SPACE ADVENTURES

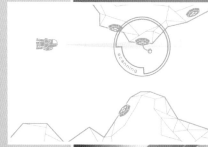

Three people work to pilot a diminutive spacecraft through a hostile environment. One player uses the Nintendo Wii U game tablet to control engines, power and shields, a second player controls lights and weapons, and a third player steers the craft through the world. Players must talk to each other and combine their different roles to solve puzzles and get the small spaceship to the end of each level.

The asymmetric play is a simple premise that blends with the atmospheric music and visuals to create an intriguing exploration of different planets.

Rating:
PEGI: 7 with violence and fear
ESRB: EVERYONE with mild
fantasy violence

Player(s): 1–3

Duration: 7 hours to complete the main story and 10 hours or so to collect everything.

Ingredients:
- Nintendo Wii U.
- The game itself.
- Wii U tablet controller.
- 2 Wii remotes.
- Optional Nunchuck or Pro controllers for more precise control.

Serving Suggestions:
Although it's possible to play the game on your own, families love assigning different roles to three people. In this way, the 'Engineer', 'Pilot' and 'Science Officer' must work closely to plan and execute manoeuvres so the spacecraft can progress. For younger players it can be fun to make your own cardboard space fort beforehand in which to play and to turn the lights down.

To Follow:
Lovers in a Dangerous Spacetime (PC, Mac, PlayStation 4, Xbox One or Nintendo Switch) offers a similar space-survival challenge, but this time y⏷ must collaborate to defend your circular spaceship.

39 Days to Mars (PC, PlayStation 4, Xbox One or Nintendo Switch) is a game where players cooperate to build and fix a nineteenth-century steam powered spaceship en route to Mars. With another player, you play one of two full voice-acted characters and solve puzzles by interacting with switches, levers and pullies.

Hacktag (PC or Mac) is a fast two-player game: one player is the stealth 'Agen⏷ while the other is the virtually infiltrating 'Hacker'. You work with the other player to carry out espionage in different settings and complete each challen⏷

This is a platform game with a twist. One player uses a controller to run and jump around the level; a second player stands in front of the Xbox Kinect camera and appears on the screen in silhouette. This person must use the outline of their body to create platforms and interact with the world to help the character reach the end of each level. This interaction between body and the screen means the player must communicate and time their movements with the controlling player.

This collaboration is a simple idea but is cleverly executed with levels that stretch the partnership — and bodily contortions — to the limit.

Rating:
PEGI: 3
ESRB: EVERYONE

Player(s): 1–2

Duration: 3 hours to get through the levels, but the unusual interactions and additional challenges extend the longevity considerably.

Ingredients:
- Xbox One.
- Xbox Kinect camera.
- Xbox controller.
- The game itself.

Serving Suggestions:
When played together, it's fun to switch roles for each level. One player stands in front of the Xbox Kinect camera while the other has the controller to move the character. Having a box of props to hand (containing scarfs, swords, hats, umbrellas and the like) is a fun way to add novel solutions to each level.

To Follow:
In *Shadow Puppeteer* (PC or Nintendo Wii U) one player controls a shadow and the other player controls the main character. Their task is to help each other progress through a series of platform levels to recover stolen shadows from their hometown.

The Gunstringer (Xbox 360) is an Xbox Kinect camera game where you use your body to control a cowboy puppet and shoot the villains by forming a gun with your fingers. You can play with two people working together, with one player controlling the character's movements and gun while the other gets their own target.

SPACETEAM

Players pilot a spaceship, each with their own control panel on their smartphone or tablet screen. The switches, dials, sliders and levers are labelled with randomly generated peculiar names: 'Astral Synth', 'Gripvent', 'Starmesh', 'Autospoon'. To avoid crashing, the team must follow commands within a few seconds. 'Set the Astral Synth to 5', for example. The twist is that the instructions on one screen may be for switches on another player's control panel. The challenge is to communicate this quickly enough to other players trying to do the same. It's a communication challenge that is not only entertaining but can be used to teach foreign languages.

This game quickly descends into shouting and then the ship crashes. Teams need to come up with ways to communicate in order to avoid this if they are going to do well.

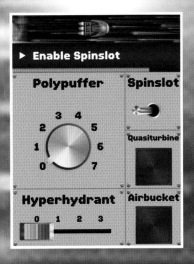

Rating:
PEGI: 3 with in-game purchases
ESRB: EVERYONE with in-game purchases

Player(s): 2–8

Duration: Rounds can last up to 15 minutes or so, as players become proficient. There is a variety of modes and awards to unlock that extend the longevity.

Ingredients:
- One device per player (Android or iOS).
- The game itself on each device.

Serving Suggestions:
This is a game that's fun to play outside because it doesn't need the internet and is played on mobile devices. It works well on car journeys or at the park, with mixed family groups playing it together. The simple challenge of listening and speaking in the group soon descends into raucousness and draws a crowd. It's not long until teams are formed to see who can get to the highest level. Playing the game in a foreign language is a good way to expand vocabulary. *Spaceteam: ESL* is a version of the game designed to teach English as a second language.

To Follow:
Heads Up! (iOS or Android) is a word-guessing game where one person holds the tablet or smartphone on their forehead and guesses the word it displays from clues given by the other players. The others confirm if they got it right or wrong and they flip the smartphone up or down to indicate, whereupon the next word is displayed.

Triple Agent (iOS or Android) is a parlour-style game that uses one device passed between 5–9 players, assigning them either an agent or double-agent role as the game starts. There are tip-offs from the game about other players, discussion around the table with each other and even the chance to secretly switch sides. You then each vote for who are double agents before all is revealed and the winners declared.

SKY: CHILDREN OF THE LIGHT

This is a huge open-world online game designed to create altruism between players. From the developer of *Flower* and *Journey*, it takes you on a social adventure in an ever-expanding world with up to eight other players.

You soar above the clouds to seven dreamlike realms and work together to find buried mysteries and rebuild a fallen kingdom. It's more than just a heart-warming flight simulator, though. As you progress you earn new ways to communicate with and give gifts to other players. Players team up to adventure into darker realms to save spirits and uncover ancient treasures. Like a day at Disneyland, *Sky* is designed to bring families and friends closer together.

Rating:
PEGI: 7 with fear, users interact and in-game purchases
ESRB: EVERYONE

Player(s): 1–8. You can play on your own or with up to 7 others online. The game makes it easy to find friends and family you know and ensures safe chat and permission for those you don't.

Duration: The main story takes 6 to 10 hours for the first play-through, but to discover everything and meet everyone will take many of these trips. Purchasing adventure passes to access new events and characters also extends the longevity of the game, which evolves over time. Players also spend time helping newcomers via the Community hub and earning hearts in appreciation of their efforts.

Ingredients:
- iOS or Android device for each player.
- The game itself on each device.
- Internet connection.
- Game Center account required for each player.
- Optional Apple TV or Chromecast enables you to play the game on a large screen.
- Optional purchase of extra candles, to share with others.

Serving Suggestions:
Because it starts with a basic set of interactions with other players and slowly expands this repertoire, this is a good game to introduce players to online gaming. The game also has an unusual approach to in-app purchases. It's free to start playing, but rather than spending money to unlock items or levels for yourself, you spend money to purchase candles and other items that are used as gifts to help your friends playing the game.

Families enjoy playing this together and helping each other progress in this fantastical world.

You can lead your child to a new discovery, or perhaps they will lead you around to experience something new.

To Follow:
Animal Crossing (Nintendo DS, Nintendo 3DS, Nintendo Switch, Nintendo Wii or Nintendo Gamecube) is more of a solitary experience, although you can visit other players either online or in the same room on a separate system. It offers intricate virtual relationships with the animal inhabitants that encourage care and generosity (and hard work) in return for progression through the game.

The Sims (PC, Mac, iOS, Android, PlayStation 3, PlayStation 4, Xbox One, Xbox 360 or Nintendo Wii) puts you in charge of a world of characters living normal lives. By providing a home, a job, leisure, friendships and even love interest, you work to make them happy. It's an open-ended game as well, although the altruism is focused on virtual characters.

BEASTS OF BALANCE

This game comes with beautifully sculpted physical toys that interact with your iPad to create and nurture creatures in a magical land. You place a toy creature on the plinth provided and it appears in the game. Balance another creature on top of the first to join it. Different items can then migrate and evolve animals to score more points. Players work together to get the highest score. If the tower tumbles, you have a limited time to get it balanced again. There's also a competitive mode where players balance animals to battle each other.

The balancing teamwork gets players supporting each other and discussing how to add creatures without bringing the tower down.

18

FINNEGUANODON
shark has crossed with eagle to create

HOGTOPUS
HAS EVOLVED!

RARKTOR
HAS EVOLVED!

Rating:
PEGI: 3
ESRB: EVERYONE

Player(s): 1–8

Duration: A round will last up to 30 minutes, depending on how good you are at stacking the items on the plinth and how much time you spend deliberating over tactics.

Ingredients:

- Android or iOS.
- The game itself downloaded onto the device.
- Physical 'Battle Card' pack to access the competitive mode.
- Table on which to play.

Serving Suggestions:
The collaborative mode is a good way to understand how the different objects interact with each other in the game. But adding the 'Battle Cards' really brings the fun alive. Along with picking the right pieces to play, you can use cards from your hand at any time by tapping them on the plinth. This adds substantially more tactics and even lets you booby-trap particular creatures and items.

To Follow:
Skylanders (iOS, PlayStation 3, PlayStation 4, Xbox One, Xbox 360, Nintendo Wii or Nintendo Wii U) uses toy figures to unlock characters and save progress. It is no longer manufactured but can be found second-hand quite cheaply and is a lot of fun for young players, particularly when played in cooperative two-player mode.

Lego Dimensions (PlayStation 3, PlayStation 4, Xbox One, Xbox 360 or Nintendo Wii U) also combines toys with interactive online play. Although it's not being updated any longer, its interactive cooperative brick format offers a novel way to play.

KNIGHTS AND BIKES

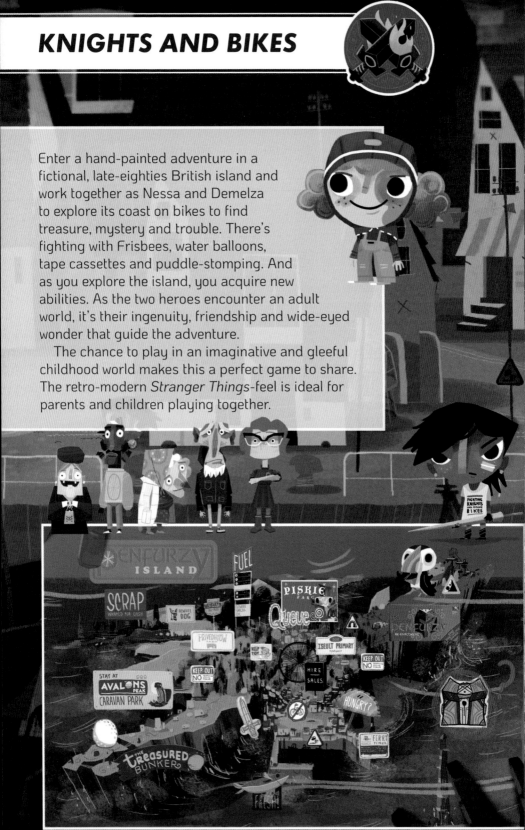

Enter a hand-painted adventure in a fictional, late-eighties British island and work together as Nessa and Demelza to explore its coast on bikes to find treasure, mystery and trouble. There's fighting with Frisbees, water balloons, tape cassettes and puddle-stomping. And as you explore the island, you acquire new abilities. As the two heroes encounter an adult world, it's their ingenuity, friendship and wide-eyed wonder that guide the adventure.

The chance to play in an imaginative and gleeful childhood world makes this a perfect game to share. The retro-modern *Stranger Things*-feel is ideal for parents and children playing together.

Rating:
PEGI: 7 with fear and violence
ESRB: EVERYONE 10+ with
fantasy violence, alcohol reference,
mild language and crude humor

Player(s): 1–2

Duration: The main story of the
game is about 10 hours.

Ingredients:

- PC, PlayStation 4 or Nintendo
  Switch.
- The game itself.
- Two controllers.

Serving Suggestions:
The two-player cooperative play
suits parents and children working
together. This, combined with the
visual style, gives the game the feel
of a Saturday-morning cartoon
show. Taking charge of either Nessa
or Demelza and exploring the island
on their bike is an entertaining
and well-observed recreation of
backwater holiday destinations.

To Follow:
Unravel (PC, PlayStation 4 or Xbox One) and the two-player *Unravel Two*
(PC, PlayStation 4, Xbox One or Nintendo Switch) are a pair of jumping and
swinging platform games where you control a character made out of wool.
As well as making him look super cute, the wool is used to swing around and
interact with objects.

Castle Crashers (PC, Mac, PlayStation 3, PlayStation 4, Xbox One, Xbox
360 or Nintendo Switch) is a side-scrolling brawling game where up to four
players each control a knight. You take on various monsters by tapping
buttons and avoiding getting hit. It's tongue-in-cheek and an excellent
backdrop to an evening in together.

Lego The Incredibles and similar Lego games (PC, PlayStation 4, Xbox One,
Nintendo Switch or Wii U) offer a light, collaborative challenge in narrative
and open-world levels. Themed around Marvel, DC, Harry Potter and other
heroes, they are a brilliant example of irreverent tongue-in-cheek use of film
franchises and characters in aid of fun.

KEEP TALKING AND NOBODY EXPLODES

In this game you're confronted with a bomb on the screen that has to be defused, requiring a series of modules to be disarmed. The bomb-defuser player can see and operate the bomb but the other players, who have the defuse instructions, can't. The bomb defuser must describe the bomb and the other players look up how to defuse it from the bomb manual. If the time runs out, the bomb explodes and you all lose. This simple premise works across different ages and levels of experience because it can quickly be understood by anyone.

THE **DEFUSER**

YOU'RE ALONE IN
A ROOM WITH A BOMB

THE **EXPERTS**

THEY'VE GOT THE MANUAL.
BUT THEY CAN'T SEE THE BOMB

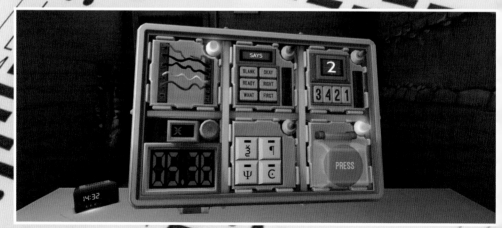

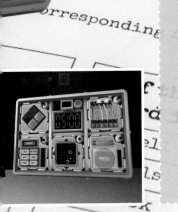

Rating:
PEGI: 3
ESRB: EVERYONE 10+ with mild violence

Player(s): 2 or more

Duration: Rounds last 20 minutes each, depending on how good you are at defusing the bombs together. The whole game takes a good 7 hours to solve.

Ingredients:
- PC, Mac, PlayStation 4, Xbox One or Nintendo Switch.
- The game itself.
- Printed bomb-defusal manual (from the link provided by the game) or device with manual downloaded onto it.
- To play in VR: PlayStation VR, HTC Vive, Oculus Rift.
- To play via mobile VR: Daydream, Gear VR, Oculus Go.

Serving Suggestions:
Played with a parent at the bomb controls and children consulting the manual on how to defuse it, this creates a reversal of power. Suddenly the ones with the knowledge, children must develop ways of communicating the right information clearly. This can start with some frustration, as they want parents to somehow automatically know what to do. But over time they learn to listen carefully to the bomb defuser's description of the bomb and then find the right answers in the manual to help the parent or carer progress.

To Follow:
Overcooked 2 (PC, Mac, PlayStation 4, Xbox One or Nintendo Switch) is a collaborative cooking game for up to four players. You must keep talking to other players to coordinate the various elements of the dishes. It starts simply enough but soon gets more complicated as you prepare food in ever more fantastical locations.

Moving Out (PC, PlayStation 4, Xbox One or Nintendo Switch) is a game of teamwork and communication where you work as removal experts. Getting everything out of the house and into the removals truck requires careful manoeuvring of the different-shaped items. Some items require more than one person to move, which adds to the challenge and the entertaining gameplay.

WALK IN SOMEONE ELSE'S SHOES

While many games include characters to interact with, some are specifically designed to make relationships a central element. Whether this is during the rounds of a puzzle game, amidst a zombie outbreak or as we race cars around a circuit, they can offer a unique way to think deeply about how we relate to each other and to the games people play.

In contrast to films or books, characters and relationships in video games need to be discovered by the player. Some of my favourite relational moments in games happen amidst other action. Often these other actions — whether shooting, puzzle-solving or fetching and carrying — serve to underline the difficult, awkward and snatched nature of interpersonal interactions.

THIS SECTION INCLUDES THE FOLLOWING GAMES

Wandersong
Elite Beat Agents
The Last of Us
A Fold Apart
God of War
Hellblade: Senua's Sacrifice

WANDERSONG

You play a bard on a quest to gather parts of a song. Uniquely, you interact with the environment and inhabitants by singing. Controlled by one of the direction sticks, you can access different notes on the coloured 'Song Wheel'. This unusual way of solving problems and engaging with the world and other characters — townsfolk, grandparents, lumberjacks, doctors and your reluctant, grumpy witch companion, Miriam — builds playful relationships that feel surprisingly deep. As underlined by the singing and some dancing, this is a game about community relationships rather than one heroic individual.

Rating:
PEGI: 7 with fear
ESRB: EVERYONE 10+ with mild fantasy violence

Player(s): 1

Duration:
It will take 10 hours to get through the main story, although those who play more slowly and want to find everything will extend this by a couple of hours.

Ingredients:
- PC, Mac, Nintendo Switch or PlayStation 4.
- The game itself.
- Headphones for an enhanced experience.

Serving Suggestions:
Siblings can enjoy playing this game together, particularly where there is an age gap. The older brother or sister can look after progressing through the story, while the younger one can control the singing sections.

The songs express the hero's mood: when he's sad he sings quietly; when he's happy he belts the songs out — and on PlayStation 4 this is heard through the tiny speaker on the controller. As with any good fairy tale, in young hands these songs become a gentle way to encounter difficult relationships and find the courage to play a part in sorting them out. Children often hum the songs as they go about their day after playing, a sure sign that this is a success.

To Follow:
Paper Mario: Origami King (Nintendo Switch), *Paper Mario: Color Splash* (Nintendo Wii U) and *Paper Mario Sticker Star* (Nintendo 3DS) have a similar visual style and tell stories about cartoon characters subjected to real-life problems. The progression is with battles rather than singing, but still you must work together with the other paper inhabitants to restore the parchment world.

Untitled Goose Game (PC, Mac or Nintendo Switch) requires you to step into a pair of webbed feet, rather than shoes, as you become an apparently malicious goose. This playful way to take on the role of the bad guy in a sleepy English community is not only fun but raises all sorts of questions about the motivations of characters who do bad things.

ELITE BEAT AGENTS

This simple rhythm game requires you to tap the screen in time with the music to advance a story. Each song matches the pictorial narrative that intersperses each verse: getting a pregnant woman to the hospital; materialising a Christmas gift to a daughter whose father has died; helping working mothers who want more quality time with their children. These are complex and potentially disturbing scenarios to step into, but the storytelling and music rhythm implicate our responsibility to these people without this becoming overwhelming.

Although these sketches of complex lives are only a few minutes long, our rhythmic interaction with them creates an unexpectedly deep relational connection.

Rating:
PEGI: 12 with violence
ESRB: EVERYONE 10+ with cartoon violence, crude humour, lyrics and suggestive themes

Player(s): 1

Duration: The main set of songs will take about 5 hours to complete, depending on your sense of rhythm. To see everything takes around 10 hours, and to perfectly complete all the songs will take upwards of 30 hours.

Ingredients:
- Nintendo DS, Nintendo 2DS or Nintendo 3DS.
- The game itself.
- Headphones for an enhanced experience.

Serving Suggestions:
Parents with younger children enjoy taking on different songs, tapping each circle and line in just the right way to get to the end of each related story. Although a few of the stories may want to be saved for when children are older, even the more troubled relationships are addressed with the light touch of a graphic novel and with music. The game is essentially about tapping, but the stories involve the player and often give rise to youngsters' questions and deep consideration of the characters' plights.

   If you want more of this musical storytelling gameplay there are two Japanese versions of the game — *Osu! Tatakae! Ouendan!* and *Moero! Nekketsu Rhythm Damashii Osu! Tatakae! Ouendan 2* — that work on any DS system and offer more stories and songs. However, non-Japanese speakers should note that both the lyrics and narrative are in Japanese.

To Follow:
Rhythm Thief & the Emperor's Treasure (Nintendo 3DS) offers a more substantial story told with cartoons interwoven with rhythm-action challenges. You play an 18-year-old boy with a secret identity as an art-thief. He's searching for his father and, in order to find him, visits various French locations by completing music-rhythm challenges.

Patapon (PlayStation Portable or PlayStation Vita) takes rhythmic button-pressing in a real-time battle direction. You assemble a stylised army and then take your troops to battle by tapping buttons in time with the rhythm.

Sayonara Wild Hearts (iOS Apple Arcade, PlayStation 4 or Nintendo Switch) is a rhythm-action game where you control a running, flying, dancing or motorbike-riding character to collect coins and hearts in time with pop music. The neon visuals and emotively voiced story make this an unusual and compelling way to experience both music and narrative.

THE LAST OF US

You play a father, Joel, whose daughter was killed during the early stages of a deadly fungal outbreak. It's now 20 years later, and he has clearly suffered from the loss. When Joel is given charge of a girl, Ellie, about the same age his daughter was, he is resolute that he won't be the father figure she clearly needs. Equally, the girl is independent, angry and scared, and won't admit her need for his care. As the game proceeds through its 16 or so hours of shooting, exploration and city traversal, you see this dysfunction soften both ways as they slowly gain deep understanding, appreciation and care of each other.

Travelling, shooting and surviving as Joel with Ellie means their relationship builds haphazardly, between and during the action. Even without direct control, you step into the shoes of a father's heartbreak and feel responsible for its resolution.

Rating:
PEGI: 18 with violence and bad language
ESRB: MATURE 17+ with blood and gore, intense violence, sexual themes, strong language and users interact

Player(s): 1

Duration: It's possible to get through the game in 12 hours, but most will need at least 16. Taking your time with the narrative and investigating every area will need upwards of 30 hours.

Ingredients:
- PlayStation 3 or PlayStation 4.
- The game itself:
  - The original on PlayStation 3.
  - Remastered on PlayStation 4.

Serving Suggestions:
Once children are in bed, newcomers to shooting games can play on easy mode and experience the developing relationship between the characters. Although the controls are complex, the game ensures you never lose too much progress when you die. If you find yourself stuck, searching for advice and videos on the chapter you're on can help.

Although this is a game for adults, some parents decide to play this with older teenagers, when they are mature enough, by taking turns at the controls. The relational parent—child theme, reluctance to accept help from strangers, survival at the cost of dignity and evocative end-of-the-world narrative are fertile territory to engage in a range of difficult and complex subjects together.

To Follow:
The Last of Us: Left Behind (PlayStation 3 or PlayStation 4) is extra content that you can purchase once inside the game. Far from a minor addition, these new chapters weave back and forth with the main game's timeline, telling the story of how the fungal outbreak started and Ellie got infected. New relationships take centre stage, and we find another dimension to the parent—child dynamic.

The Last of Us Part II (PlayStation 4) is set five years after the first game, when Ellie and Joel have settled in Wyoming in a relatively stable community of survivors of the fungal outbreak. But when the peace is disturbed, Ellie has to travel once more as she seeks justice and closure. While the first game focused on what love can cause people to endure, this looks at the repercussions of hate.

A FOLD APART

This is a puzzle platform game that explores the emotional rollercoaster of a long-distance relationship — in a world of folding paper. After career choices force them along separate paths, a teacher and an architect vow to make their long-distance relationship work at any cost. Choose the gender of each character and experience both sides of their story as the couple navigates the complexities of (mis)communication and the emotional ups and downs that physical separation brings. By flipping, folding and unfolding the paper puzzles in their handcrafted worlds, you help the couple jump, run and explore their way forward, mirroring the emotional terrain of their relationship and desire to be reunited. With each puzzle solved, you help Alex and Sam navigate their long-distance relationship and share the experience of living apart from someone you love.

Rating:
PEGI: 3
ESRB: EVERYONE

Player(s): 1

Duration: The game takes close to 4 hours to complete, but if you rush through it can be quicker.

Ingredients:

- PC, Mac, iOS (Apple Arcade), PlayStation 4, Xbox One or Nintendo Switch.
- The game itself.

Serving Suggestions:
Although this is a one-player game, the storybook narrative and Pixar-style graphics make this a lovely game to share with a young child. If the child is age six or older, they can likely also take turns solving the puzzles themselves. It leads to some moving moments as players experience the difficulty and emotions of living apart from someone you love. As you select the genders of Alex and Sam, it's also a gentle way for children to consider how gender relates to jobs, appearance and relationships.

To Follow:
Braid (PC, Mac, PlayStation 3, Xbox One or Xbox 360) is another platform game that appears simple but has a twist. The movement of your character is connected to the progression of time in a mind-bending manner. The resulting puzzles are fascinating and connected to a story about relationships and forgiveness.

Old Man's Journey (iOS, Android or Nintendo Switch) is a game about memory and old age. You help a grandfather-figure traverse the countryside by raising and lowering the landscape. Along the way he visits places that evoke the story of his life: a wife, a child and a love of the sea.

Fez (PC, Mac, iOS, PlayStation 3, PlayStation 4, PlayStation Vita or Xbox 360) is also a platform game with a perspective-shifting challenge. By manipulating the world, you collect cubes and cube fragments to restore order to the universe.

GOD OF WAR

You play super-strong Norse fantasy hero Kratos as he takes his son Atreus on a brutal quest in the wake of his mother's death. The exploration, puzzle-solving, climbing and fighting gameplay intertwines with a mythological family drama played out in a dramatic Scandinavian landscape. While Kratos confidently handles all manner of enemies, he struggles to find the strength to connect with his son, who is coming to terms with the loss of his mother. The beauty of the world through which they pass and the singular confidence of Kratos in battle make the unfolding of their relationship both fascinating and at times heartbreaking. This turns the common power-fantasy video game on its head. Atreus needs care and nurturing rather than protection from his father, something which, like the gorgeous world they traverse, takes the whole game to fully navigate.

Rating:
PEGI: 18 with violence and bad language
ESRB: MATURE 17+ with blood and gore, intense violence and strong language

Player(s): 1

Duration: The main story of the game can be completed in 16 hours, but taking it at a steady pace will result in more like 25 hours. To see all of the game takes at least 50 hours.

Ingredients:
- PlayStation 4.
- The game itself.

Serving Suggestions:
Playing this with a son or daughter (of an appropriate age for the violence) is fascinating as you see together how the characters deal with each other. This not only offers a shared experience but a context in which to talk about fathers and sons. More than watching a film together, players are implicated in the broken paternal relationship. The characters are pure fantasy, but the father's gruffness, high expectations and inability to share his emotions are familiar territory.

To Follow:
Rise of the Tomb Raider (PC, Mac, PlayStation 4, Xbox One or Xbox 360) is another recently reinvented series that offers a similar experience but in an open world. Although there isn't the constant father–child presence, hero Lara Croft is motivated by understanding her deceased father. The journey takes her to Siberia and the legendary city of Kitezh.

A Plague Tale: Innocence (PC, PlayStation 4 or Xbox One) follows Amicia and her little brother Hugo as they use stealth to escape soldiers and swarms of rats. Against the stark threat and darkness of the world, the sibling relationship develops as the two learn to trust one another. This plight of the innocent is extended as the pair call on other children to help them on their way.

HELLBLADE: SENUA'S SACRIFICE

This is a dark fantasy adventure, drawing on Norse and Celtic mythology, where you play a young female Pict warrior, Senua. You explore and fight your way to Helheim to rescue the soul of her dead lover. As you play, though, you hear multiple voices in your head and wrestle with a decaying grip on reality. In this way the game aims to represent, and offer a metaphor for, psychosis. You battle difficult enemies and solve puzzles, but often fighting directly or obvious solutions are not the best way forward.

Created in partnership with neuroscientists, mental health specialists and sufferers of mental health conditions, the experience aims to share something of what it's like to live with this kind of illness. The voices, confusion and delusions weave in and out of the action as Senua struggles to come to terms with the trauma and guilt of her past.

Rating:
PEGI: 18 with violence and bad language
ESRB: MATURE 17+ with blood and gore, intense violence and strong language

Player(s): 1

Duration:
The main story of the game can be completed in around 8 hours. Taking your time or playing on a harder difficulty level can extend this challenge to 14 hours.

Ingredients:
- PC, PlayStation 4, Xbox One or Nintendo Switch.
- The game itself.
- Headphones, which is how the voices in the game are designed to be heard.

Serving Suggestions:
For adults, the game can provide a different window into the experience of someone close to them who struggles with mental illness. Some parents have played the game with older children as a way to engage with this difficult subject. The game succeeds by avoiding reducing its rendition to a literal or journalistic recreation. The story of Senua's struggle is as much about resilience, persistence, bravery and dealing with guilt or failure as about any specific medical diagnosis. In this way it offers a deeply relatable experience.

To Follow:
Alan Wake (Xbox One or Xbox 360) takes you on a similarly dark path into a horror game. From the perspective of a writer losing his grip on reality, you must battle dark forces and run to the light to escape.

Mutazione (PC, Mac, iOS, PlayStation 4 or Steam) pits you as a 15-year-old girl visiting her grandfather on a faraway island inhabited by friendly yet mutated villagers. The trauma is largely other people's rather than your own. By finding seeds, tending to gardens and talking to people, you uncover a tightly knit web of characters suffering unrequited love, hidden trauma and difficult memories. By tending to these people as well as the gardens, you nudge the island towards processing its losses.

WAKE UP YOUR EMOTIONS

Video games are known for high-octane, adrenaline-fuelled entertainment, but there are many that address the player's emotions as much as their dexterity. Often overlooked by younger or more competitive players, these experiences can provide a helpful variety in the diet of games your family enjoys.

The games selected for the following section create emotionally rich spaces in which to explore scenarios with feelings rather than facts. In some games this is achieved with beautiful or soothing interactive visuals; others create charged relationships and settings that invite players to take a role in processing these emotions.

THIS SECTION INCLUDES THE FOLLOWING GAMES

My Child Lebensborn
Journey
Concrete Genie
Florence
Celeste

In Norway after the Second World War, you nurture a Lebensborn child who faces a hostile community because they've been born to parents of both occupied and occupying forces. With meagre resources yourself, you must feed, clothe and bathe the child; more importantly, you must help them cope with the heavy inheritance of German soldier genes in a country celebrating its freedom. The child faces not only a challenge of identity and guilt but bullying from teachers as well as classmates.

The demeanour of the child as they cope with the situation requires the player to make good decisions in terms of emotional care and more practical help in matters of food, hygiene and money.

Rating:
PEGI: 12 with mild swearing
ESRB: TEEN with sexual themes

Player(s): 1

Duration: It takes up to 6 hours to complete the game, although this depends on how quickly you interact and how successful you are at looking after your child.

Ingredients:
- iOS or Android.
- The game itself.

Serving Suggestions:
By playing the game once a day with teenagers, this is a unique way to engage with both the civilian fallout from conflicts as well as the difficulty of bullying and prejudice. You can take turns with the day's tasks and decide between you what your Lebensborn child needs. Or played on separate devices you can see how your decisions impact the child's emotional landscape.

To Follow:
The Unfinished Swan (PlayStation 3, PlayStation 4 or PlayStation Vita) invites you to explore a world by splashing paint on it. The tactile experience draws you into a fairy tale about an unfinished painting that leads a child back to his parent.

Valiant Hearts: The Great War (PC, PlayStation 3, PlayStation 4, Xbox 360, Xbox One, iOS, Android or Nintendo Switch) follows four characters through the opening days of the First World War. Solving puzzles by interacting with objects and people is interspersed with real footage and correspondence to offer a window into the human and emotional cost of war.

JOURNEY

This is an adventure in a desert. Exploring the eerie sandscape, you discover a world abandoned by the race that created it. The sense of space and scale evokes feelings of aloneness and being lost. But then the game pairs you with other players, one at a time, who appear on the horizon. You can communicate only using wordless chirps but it's enough to create a camaraderie to take on the wild, vast landscape. This creates a beautiful journey from sand to snow and water that creates an unusual appreciation of help from unknown others.

The game works the emotions successfully and in unexpected ways. While the esoteric journey through the landscape inspires awe, the presence of another anonymous person creates surprising comfort.

Rating:
PEGI: 7 with violence and fear
ESRB: EVERYONE with mild fantasy violence

Player(s): 1, who can be joined, 1 at a time, by other online players.

Duration: It takes around 3 hours to play to the end, depending on proficiency. Discovering all the collectibles and secrets will take around 12 hours. Most players complete the game multiple times.

Ingredients:
- PC, PlayStation 3 or PlayStation 4.
- The game itself.
- Internet connection and a PlayStation Network account for free online play (PlayStation Plus not needed).

Serving Suggestions:
When another online player appears in the game, you can encourage your child to engage with them. The limited interactions lead to more creative communication and often result in players working together. It's a chance to safely and gently introduce interacting with strangers online. You can also encourage children to 'read' other players. Are they experts or novices? Do they need help or are they showing the way? Each line of embroidery on their cloak is for completing the game. The white cloak indicates they have found all the power-up items. The length of the scarf indicates how much flying power they've collected in the current game.

To Follow:
Gris (PC, Mac or Nintendo Switch) is a platform game where you guide a young girl through a crumbling world. Through beautiful metaphoric landscapes and soaring music, the game touches on emotions of loss and longing but doesn't resolve to a firm narrative. Although not hugely varied, its commitment to its aesthetic and painterly development of visuals creates an evocative and meditative game that encapsulates both sadness and hope.

ABZÛ (PC, PlayStation 4 or Xbox One) is a similar adventure, this time underwater. You descend into the heart of the ocean to find ancient secrets and encounter majestic creatures. This combines the beautiful weightlessness of diving with an ancient story of meaning and place in the world.

CONCRETE GENIE

You play a young boy, who is isolated and bullied, in this exploration platform game with a twist. Using motion controls and buttons you can draw beautiful graffiti on the buildings, which come to life. These become the habitat for the creatures you create, who help you progress through the town. It's a sad and dark setting for a small boy, but with the magical drawings you help him find hope, solve puzzles and gain courage.

There's a power in this game. It presents a difficult situation — bullying, sadness, loss — in a gentle way that creates space to be hopeful and allows the emotions to be engaged.

LANDSCAPE

POND · STORM · FIELD · SNOW · MUSHROOM

PAINT
UNDO PREVIOUS
SELECT BRUSH
CONFIRM
EXIT

Rating:
PEGI: 12 with violence
ESRB: EVERYONE 10+ with fantasy violence

Player(s): 1

Duration: The main story will take about 6 hours to complete, although this will be longer for younger players who linger on the painting aspect of the game. To see everything in the game will take about 10 hours.

Ingredients:
- PlayStation 4.
- The game itself.
- For VR modes: PlayStation VR headset, camera and Move controllers.

Serving Suggestions:
Although this is a single-player game, the creative drawing and painting mechanics make it ideal for parents and children to play together. The younger player may be more proficient with the controls, but parents and carers can contribute to designing and deciding what is created.

The bullies in the game develop into fully formed characters as players find compassion for them as well as for the hero. Along the way we find out why the bullies were misbehaving: a difficult home life, parents separating or fathers in prison. The themes of the game — how creativity is used as an ally, and what motivates good and bad behaviour — make a rich context for conversations.

To Follow:
Papo & Yo (PC, Mac or PlayStation) pits you as a young boy exploring a Brazilian city slum. As you solve puzzles and perform well-timed jumps to progress through the city, you must also deal with a monster — both real and metaphorically representing your alcoholic father.

Child of Light (PC, PlayStation 3, PlayStation 4, PlayStation Vita, Xbox One, Xbox 360, Nintendo Switch or Nintendo Wii U) is a platform game presented like a fairy tale, where you play a young girl, Aurora, on a quest to save her kingdom from the darkness. Battle encounters break up the adventure and power up your character. To finally make it home, you must defeat the dark creatures and win back the sun, the moon and the stars.

FLORENCE

This is a little puzzle game that tells the story of a relationship, following the usual stages of loneliness, meeting, dating, falling for and moving in with another person. At first, the puzzle interactions seem trivial and the game doesn't change depending on how well we do. But each puzzle is cleverly designed to reflect the story. Sometimes easy, when the relationship is going well; sometimes almost impossible, when the couple is struggling. These interactions transform the emotional quality of the game and implicate us in what unfolds.

It's hand-drawn and full of whimsy but powerfully clears emotional space to consider the commitments, choices and priorities of relationships in our lives.

Rating:
PEGI: 3
ESRB: EVERYONE

Player(s): 1

Duration: About an hour.

Ingredients:
- iOS or Android tablet or smartphone.
- The game itself.

Serving Suggestions:
Grandparents like to play this game with grandchildren, like sharing a storybook. The simple interactions and picture-book-style storytelling will be familiar. But the game's use of these things to capture what it's like to fall in love is novel and unique.

   If you are new to games, *Florence* is a good choice to try on your own. Some might say it's not a proper game, but the way it builds emotion, not only with narrative and characters but with its interactive demands, is something all good games do.

To Follow:
In *The Stillness of the Wind* (PC, iOS or Nintendo Switch) you are an old woman who looks after a dilapidated farm. Over the course of a few hours, no matter what your efforts, the farm falls apart as you learn about the woman's family and have the chance to ruminate on her loneliness and happy memories.

Sunset (PC or Mac) tasks you with cleaning a large apartment in a fictional 1970s South American city. But outside the apartment there is unrest and rioting. The chaos of the country and the repetitive daily chores grate against one another to create a meditative and unnerving experience. Isolated and helpless, but also cocooned in the opulent apartment, you discover what it feels like to be trapped in an uneasy story.

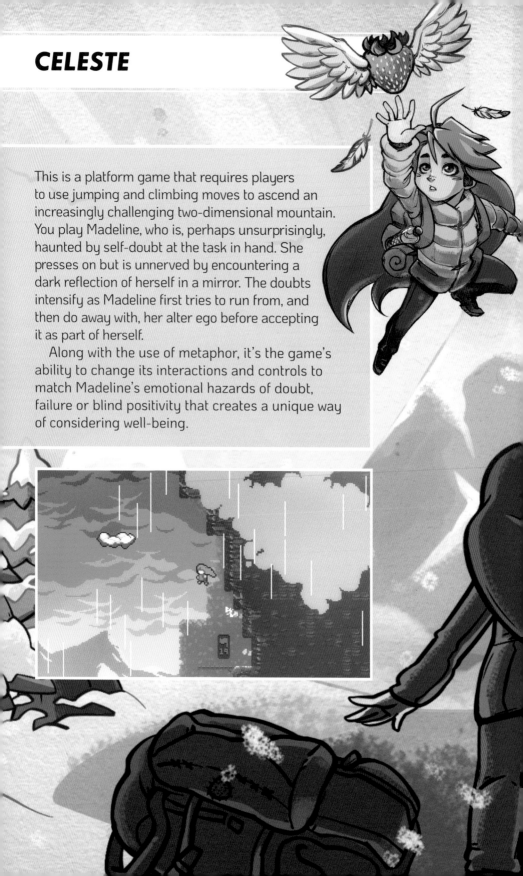

CELESTE

This is a platform game that requires players to use jumping and climbing moves to ascend an increasingly challenging two-dimensional mountain. You play Madeline, who is, perhaps unsurprisingly, haunted by self-doubt at the task in hand. She presses on but is unnerved by encountering a dark reflection of herself in a mirror. The doubts intensify as Madeline first tries to run from, and then do away with, her alter ego before accepting it as part of herself.

Along with the use of metaphor, it's the game's ability to change its interactions and controls to match Madeline's emotional hazards of doubt, failure or blind positivity that creates a unique way of considering well-being.

Rating:
PEGI: 7 with violence
ESRB: EVERYONE 10+ with alcohol reference, fantasy violence and mild language

Player(s): 1

Duration: Expect to need 13 hours for the main story. Seeing and collecting everything will take closer to 36 hours.

Ingredients:

- Mac, PC, PlayStation 4, Xbox One or Nintendo Switch.
- The game itself.

Serving Suggestions:
If you're new to difficult platform games, the 'Assist' mode is a great way to experience this game while also being able to progress when you get stuck. Slowing down the game grants more time for making jumps just right. This enables any player to engage in the subject of emotional well-being in this unusual way.

To Follow:
Brothers: A Tale of Two Sons (PC, iOS, Android, PlayStation 3, PlayStation 4, Xbox One, Xbox 360 or Nintendo Switch) is an action-adventure game where you control two brothers at the same time with a single controller. After their mother passes away, they must find some water from the Tree of Life to save their father. The controls weave into the narrative in powerful ways, making this a unique and moving experience. On the Nintendo Switch you can play cooperatively.

Hellblade: Senua's Sacrifice (PC, Xbox One, PlayStation 4 or Nintendo Switch) is another game that shares the experience of mental health challenges. You wade into a fantasy adventure but soon discover that trauma has left you with psychosis of voices and fractured reality. It's emotionally charged as you try and help Senua survive both the world and her illness.

MATINEE FISTICUFFS AND SHOOT-OUTS

Sometimes you just want to play the hero. These games are violent and include shooting but, as with B-movies and 1980s TV series, it's as much about the quips, characters and fantasy settings as it is about killing. The drama may be peppered with cinematic gunfire but, like those TV series, the real draw is spending time with the heroes every week.

THIS SECTION INCLUDES THE FOLLOWING GAMES

Uncharted: Drake's Fortune
Alan Wake
SteamWorld Heist
Horizon Zero Dawn
Halo 5: Guardians
Limbo

UNCHARTED: DRAKE'S FORTUNE

This is the first game of a five-game series. It starts as an adventure into the jungle for treasure, where an onslaught of fisticuffs and shooting henchmen is punctuated by tongue-in-cheek *A-Team*-style dialogue. One clue inevitably leads to another — along with more henchmen to shoot at and underground caves to explore. You'd be forgiven for dismissing the game as disposable, trashy entertainment, but there's more here than the violence or quips, as Nate meets Elena and a rollercoaster romance threads its way through the action. From the fling in the first game to an unexpected encounter in the second, they are married, separated and reunited before the shooting finishes in the fourth game.

Over five games, we get a window into Nate's obsession with treasure hunting, and the cost of this to the rest of his life. Will he finally hang up his revolver and settle down with Elena?

Rating:
PEGI: 16 with violence and bad language
ESRB: TEEN with blood, language, mild suggestive themes, use of tobacco and violence

Player(s): 1

Duration: To complete the game will take around 14 hours. To find all the treasures will require repeated play-throughs and take upwards of 30 hours.

Ingredients:
- PlayStation 3 or PlayStation 4.
- The game itself:
  - *Uncharted: Drake's Fortune* on PlayStation 3.
  - *Uncharted: Drake's Fortune Remastered* on PlayStation 4.
  - *Uncharted: The Nathan Drake Collection* (includes the first three games in series) on PlayStation 4.

Serving Suggestions:
Although this is a single-player game, the strong story and movie sections mean it works as a shared experience. Parent or carer and child can take turns exploring each level and shooting enemies. Because the action is punctuated with unfolding loyalties and romantic interest between the leading characters, there is plenty more to talk about than which gun to pick or who to shoot next.

To Follow:
The subsequent games in the series continue the matinee quips and fisticuffs but also deeply develop the characters and their relationships. *Uncharted 2: Among Thieves* and *Uncharted 3: Drake's Deception* are on PlayStation 3 and PlayStation 4. *Uncharted: Golden Abyss* is on PlayStation Vita. *Uncharted 4: A Thief's End* and *Uncharted: The Lost Legacy* are only on PlayStation 4.

Enslaved (PlayStation 3) and *Heavenly Sword* (PlayStation 3) both offer a similar mix of heroic storytelling and narrative. Unlike *Uncharted*, they take place in fantasy locations and with a variety of creatures.

Ratchet & Clank (PlayStation 3, PlayStation 4 or PlayStation Vita) looks more cartoony but still offers the B-movie-style action. As Ratchet, you explore planets and space stations, battling enemies with a variety of weapons and gadgets. Sidekick Clank sits on Ratchet's back and offers more abilities, such as diving in water and gliding.

ALAN WAKE

Bright Falls is the sleepy Midwest setting for this *Twilight Zone*-style horror game. The action focuses on surviving attacks from possessed 'Taken' locals. You use flashlights to burn away the possession before dispatching them with firearms. It's violent but the hammy horror script makes the unfolding drama as creepy as the shooting. *Alan Wake* started development as an open-world game before gaining a more focused, linear direction. This grants Bright Falls a substantial geography that adds to the brooding sense of darkness. As the drama unfolds, and you rush from the safety of one well-lit area to the next, you discover you are caught in the pages of the protagonist's novels, and things soon spiral in a surreal *Twin Peaks* direction.

Easily dismissed as just another horror game, *Alan Wake*'s detailed environments and open geography create a world that is both full of foreboding and inviting to investigate.

Rating:
PEGI: 16 with violence
ESRB: TEEN with blood, language, use of alcohol and tobacco, and violence

Player(s): 1

Duration: To complete the game will take towards 16 hours, depending on the difficulty setting and proficiency of the player. To see everything in the game will extend this to at least 35 hours.

Ingredients:
- PC, Xbox One or Xbox 360.
- The game itself.

Serving Suggestions:
This is one to try out before sharing with offspring. Parents who grew up enjoying horror films have found this game a novel way to share that experience with their teenage children. Played together, particularly if late at night, *Alan Wake* not only recreates familiar Stephen King-style scenarios but places you inside them. Surviving the night is an exhilarating experience for those wanting to get their adrenaline pumping.

To Follow:
Inside (PC, iOS, PlayStation 4, Xbox One or Nintendo Switch) offers a similarly dark and creepy setting for a platform game. The follow-up to *Limbo*, its similar black-and-white visuals and young protagonist paint a picture of a disturbing corporation using mind control among its now-ramshackle warehouses.

Control (PC, PlayStation 4 or Xbox One) is an outlandish paranormal fantasy where you are swept into a role as the new director of the Federal Bureau of Control agency of the 'paranatural'. With impressive cinematic visuals and storytelling, your interactions involve exploring, finding cover, shooting, and using new psychic abilities to throw objects and rip apart the fabric of each room. It's far-fetched but well delivered and exhilarating to play, and surprisingly coherent.

STEAMWORLD HEIST

Steam-powered robots fighting for space supremacy sounds like the script for a 1950s B-movie. As in those matinee hits, the point here isn't realism but interesting characters. Like the related games (*SteamWorld Dig* and *SteamWorld Quest*), *SteamWorld Heist* requires you to build a merry band of robots to take on the challenges of space's vast frontier.

The turn-taking gameplay lets newcomers take their time with each shot or movement. For experts, trick shots and optimising progress demand the development of intricate strategies.

This may look like just another shooting game, but play it for a few minutes and you'll discover a joyously irreverent take on space combat that demands both attention and skill.

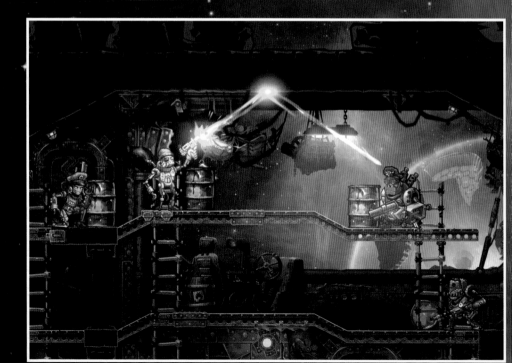

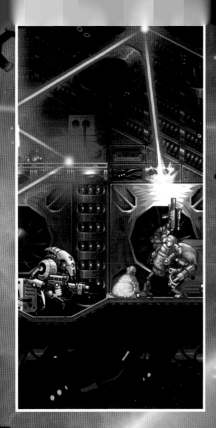

Rating:
PEGI: 7 with mild violence
ESRB: EVERYONE 10+ with
fantasy violence, mild language
and use of tobacco

Player(s): 1

Duration: To complete the main
story-levels will take about 14 hours,
depending on difficulty settings.
To see everything in the game
extends this to over 20 hours.

Ingredients:
- PC, Mac, iOS, PlayStation 4,
  PlayStation Vita, Nintendo 3DS,
  Nintendo Switch or Nintendo
  Wii U.
- The game itself.

Serving Suggestions:
Although it's designed as a single-
player game, it can be played by
families by allotting each player
a character to control; thanks
to it being a turn-based game,
with the action pausing until you
select your move, you can pass
the console to each player in turn.
This not only requires coordination
between the players but is also a
great way to collaborate and to
power-up your chosen character.

To Follow:
SteamWorld Dig 2 (PC, Mac, PlayStation 4, PlayStation Vita, Xbox One,
Nintendo 3DS or Nintendo Switch) is from the same developer but is a more
energetic, fast-action mining game.

SteamWorld Quest (PC, Mac or Nintendo Switch) is also turn-based, but here
you pick card abilities to attack enemies, which moves the strategy from
prioritisation and shooting to combining attack and defence abilities effectively.

HORIZON ZERO DAWN

This game has a post-apocalyptic feel familiar from movies like *Planet of the Apes*. It plunges you into an overgrown landscape with now-crumbling remnants of modern life where animalistic machines have taken over. The exploration and combat don't dwell on the downfall of the world, but there is an interesting undercurrent of self-annihilation that lingers as you play. It's an impressive and enjoyable world to explore that says as much about the downfall of humanity as any direct narrative.

This combination of overblown disaster and sometimes simplistic solutions — such as the discovery of a small group of scientists with a plan to remake the planet — manages not to jar, in a game that doesn't take itself too seriously.

Rating:
PEGI: 16 with violence
ESRB: TEEN with blood, drug reference, language, mild sexual themes and violence

Player(s): 1

Duration: This is a long game, taking a good 25 hours to complete and upwards of 60 hours to see everything.

Ingredients:
- PlayStation 4.
- The game itself.

Serving Suggestions:
The combination of pseudo-dinosaurs — here reimagined as ancient machines — and stepping into a ritualistic tribe of warriors is appealing to older teenagers. The sheer amount to do in the world, along with the central story, makes it a good adventure to share. One person can take charge of the character while the other keeps track of their progress.

To Follow:

Ghost of a Tale (PC, PlayStation 4 or Xbox One) is a swashbuckling adventure where you, as plucky rat Tilo, take on a rich world of evil creatures. It's another game full of lore and backstory, although here it is medieval darkness rather than technological apocalypse. The work of a stand-alone developer, it offers a unique vision of this kind of fantasy and one that is well executed.

Ark: Survival Evolved (PC, Mac, iOS, Android, PlayStation 4 or Xbox One) offers a similar hunting-and-harvesting aspect in a primal setting. Although not as polished or streamlined, this is a more ambitious open world where you can choose your own way to survive. With crafting and building, like *Minecraft* but with realistic visuals, this is a game where you step into your own monster movie.

Arkham Asylum, *Arkham City* and *Arkham Origins* (PC, Mac, PlayStation 3, PlayStation 4, Xbox One or Xbox 360) are a series of games that take the fisticuffs in a vigilante-superhero direction. As you would expect, this is set in the modern-era Gotham City, but the questing and branching missions, along with open-world spaces, give this a similar sense of progression to *Horizon Zero Dawn*.

HALO 5: GUARDIANS

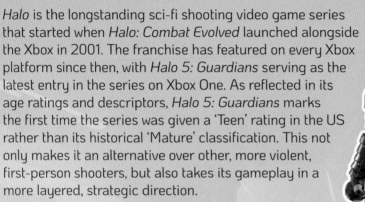

Halo is the longstanding sci-fi shooting video game series that started when *Halo: Combat Evolved* launched alongside the Xbox in 2001. The franchise has featured on every Xbox platform since then, with *Halo 5: Guardians* serving as the latest entry in the series on Xbox One. As reflected in its age ratings and descriptors, *Halo 5: Guardians* marks the first time the series was given a 'Teen' rating in the US rather than its historical 'Mature' classification. This not only makes it an alternative over other, more violent, first-person shooters, but also takes its gameplay in a more layered, strategic direction.

Weapons must be used to deplete opponents' energy shields before being able to damage them, so multiplayer combat encounters are a game of cat and mouse. Add to this the melee of attacks, varied terrain and advanced artificial intelligence of the enemies, and you can see why it takes a long time to master.

The game's futuristic setting, dramatic music, fantastical weapons and diverse enemies make *Halo 5: Guardians* competitive, exuberant and fun, without taking itself too seriously. Whether in its single-player campaign or online multiplayer modes, players revel in the lore, story and heroic characters as much as the necessary quick reactions and headshots.

Rating:
PEGI: 16 with violence
ESRB: TEEN with blood, mild language and violence

Player(s): 1 upwards. The game offers either a single-player story mode featuring online cooperative play or a diverse, multiplayer suite offering online competitive and cooperative play. While *Halo 5: Guardians* doesn't support playing on the same console, the next game in the series, *Halo Infinite*, is expected to reintroduce multiple players on the same console.

Duration: The story mode takes between 8 and 12 hours to complete. The online multiplayer modes can keep players entertained for many years.

Ingredients:
- Xbox One.
- Xbox Live Gold.
- Internet connection for online play.
- The game itself or subscription to Xbox Game Pass, which includes the game.

Serving Suggestions:
Parents and teenagers have enjoyed playing through the campaign together and competing in multiplayer games via online cooperative modes. In addition, *Halo: The Master Chief Collection* (PC, Xbox One or Steam), a compilation of previous games in the series and available with Xbox Game Pass for console, offers an opportunity to play through the series cooperatively, in order, on the same console. While it's worth noting that earlier games in the series had a long time between save points compared to modern games, they still offer an excellent way to establish the narrative and lore of the *Halo* universe, showing how new combat and interactive features were steadily added as the game developed over the years.

Master Chief Collection (Xbox One or Steam) includes *Halo: olved Anniversary*, *Halo 2 Anniversary*, *Halo 3*, *Halo 4*, *Halo* d *Halo: Reach*. Each game has improved graphics and other nts. Players can enjoy the collection with Xbox Game Pass on d on PC, starting with *Halo: Reach*.

e (PC or Xbox One) is the upcoming game in the series that will th the story and ways to play together, both online and on the le.

LIMBO

Control a small boy as he runs, jumps and climbs through a dark, silhouetted forest that clanks and hums with foreboding. As the age rating suggests, he is killed in all manner of gruesome ways. But this is not without reason. Rather than violent indulgence, the repeated downfall of the child builds a protective relationship between the player and their charge. He needs protection, but he also needs meaning. His willing march into the unknown at your command shows great courage and the need to reach his sister.

The wordless interactions with the boy create a powerful parental relationship to get him where he needs to be, whether that's to safety or being reunited with his own family.

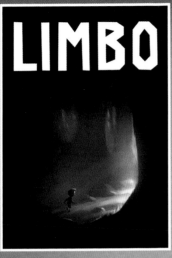

LIMBO

Rating:
PEGI: 16 with strong violence
ESRB: TEEN with mild blood and mild violence

Player(s): 1

Duration: To complete the main story-levels will take about 6 hours, depending on ability. To replay and collect everything in the game extends this to over 15 hours.

Ingredients:

- PC, Mac, iOS, Android, PlayStation 3, PlayStation 4, PlayStation Vita, Xbox One or Nintendo Switch.
- The game itself.

Serving Suggestions:
Some parents have enjoyed playing this so much themselves that they've taken the unusual step of then asking to play it with their teenager. Caution is required with any game that has an older age rating — play it yourself first, talk about the game with the teenager and make it clear that you can stop if it gets too intense — but, with some reassurance and care, *Limbo* can create a powerful experience for parents and children to explore together.

To Follow:
Inside (PC, iOS, Xbox One, PlayStation 4 or Nintendo Switch) is from the same developer. At times it involves more time-based interactions, which can trip up new players, but as a next step it extends the visual storytelling in novel directions.

Deadlight (PC, PlayStation 4, Xbox One or Xbox 360) takes the monochrome running, jumping and shooting action in a more mature direction and with a deeper and more coherent story. It draws on older (and equally excellent) platform games *Another World* (iOS, Android, PlayStation 3, PlayStation 4, Xbox One, Nintendo 3DS or Nintendo Switch) and *Flashback* (iOS, PlayStation 4 or Nintendo Switch). You control Randall Wayne, a single character trying to survive the zombies to get to his family, which he does by running, jumping and solving puzzles.

FACE TOUGH DECISIONS

Games create virtual worlds where you can experience life from other perspectives. This can be entertaining and light-hearted but also presents ethical scenarios that require you to think carefully about consequences.

The games selected here each place you in a challenging situation to give you a first-hand experience of what it's like. It may be nail-biting, heartbreaking or desperate, but often, through all the trials and tribulations, there is still hope. Either way, unlike reading books or watching films about these subjects, here you are emotionally implicated in the choices you are faced with.

THIS SECTION INCLUDES THE FOLLOWING GAMES

One Hour One Life
Papers, Please
This War of Mine
Photographs – Puzzle Stories
Life Is Strange
Detroit: Become Human

ONE HOUR ONE LIFE

This is a civilisation survival game where each player lives a whole life in an hour of play and then passes away. Born as a baby into the care of anonymous other online players, you initially depend on them for food. Quickly growing, you can soon fend for yourself and start contributing to the development of farming, tools and clothing, and to nurturing other players born to you as your own children. At the end of an hour, you die of old age, so any progress benefits those who come after you.

It's challenging because you have to trust and rely on other players, particularly when you start your go, as a baby. It's a game that forces you to choose carefully how you spend your limited life and what to do with the resources and friendships in the game.

Rating:
Taken from the almost identical *You Are Hope* version of this game on Android:
PEGI: 7 with implied violence
ESRB: EVERYONE 10+ with fantasy violence and mild blood

Player(s): 1 on a device, playing with up to 200 others in a game world

Duration: The game lasts exactly 1 hour but it's designed to be played repeatedly as players learn how to better progress and survive, although each go is started from scratch.

Ingredients:
- PC or Mac for original *One Hour One Life*:
  - The game itself.
  - Internet connection.
  - Email address to log in to game server.
- iOS or Android for *You Are Hope* version:
  - Tablet or smartphone.
  - The game itself.
  - Internet connection.

Serving Suggestions:
Plan a session with the game where you take turns just to learn the controls and how to interact with other players. Having the Wikipedia entry about the game available for someone to read is useful and creates more ideas about how to survive. Don't worry if you die a lot at first, but use each go to learn more about the game and what other players are doing. Eventually, you'll have a go where you survive long enough to start deeper interactions with the world and other players.

The game is particularly unusual because the choices you make result in success or failure that then affect the prosperity of other players in your village. You work hard for the good of others and have to hand over everything at the end of each one-hour turn.

To Follow:
Passage (passage.toolness.org) is a super-simple game from the same developer as *One Hour One Life* on the theme of a life well lived. Although just a few minutes long, it offers an unusual interactive metaphor for the different stages of life that can spark deep conversations.

Don't Starve (PC, Mac, iOS, Android, PlayStation 3, PlayStation 4, PlayStation Vita, Xbox One, Nintendo Switch or Nintendo Wii U) is another open-world survival game. Here it's the environment and enemies, rather than other players, that you work with. You need to find and develop food, weapons and shelter to survive. It's enjoyable because it's hard, so repeat-plays to improve performance are common.

PAPERS, PLEASE

You play the role of a border-crossing immigration officer in the fictional dystopian Eastern Bloc-like country of Arstotzka. You review immigrants' and returning citizens' passports and paperwork according to an increasing list of changing rules stemming from a volatile political landscape. Each person, whether legitimate or not, has a story about their journey and the personal impact of not being let in. Your choices not only impact the citizens but your own standing and money for your family. You must also decide whether to uphold the government or work with organisations to establish a new one. You play for 31 days, and depending on your decisions, there are 20 different endings.

These decisions are powerful because of the real stories they tell. There's the jeopardy of acting morally but at risk and cost to your own job and impoverished family.

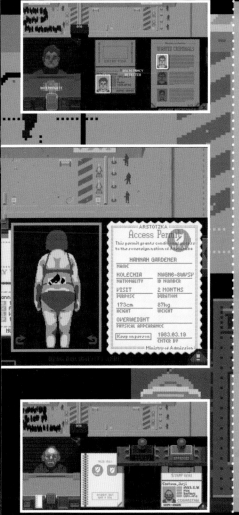

Rating:
PEGI: 16 with bad language
ESRB: MATURE 17+ with blood, drug reference, nudity, sexual themes, strong language and violence

Player(s): 1

Duration:
You can complete the main story in about 8 hours. To see all the endings will take considerably longer, with multiple play-throughs.

Ingredients:
- PC, Mac, iPad or PlayStation Vita.
- The game itself.

Serving Suggestions:
Having played the game yourself to understand the content and theme, this is good to play with older teenagers, together applying different strategies to see how this affects the game. You could decide to make decisions that favour your country, or perhaps you prioritise your family, or maybe you'll work the system to get money for yourself. You could even try to get your family out of the country by stealing passports for them.

To Follow:
Beholder (PC, Mac, PlayStation 4, Xbox One or Nintendo Switch) is a detective game where you spy on tenants in a building, discover their secrets and report violations of laws to the authorities. As the game unfolds and you see more of the controlling totalitarian state, an uneasy tension develops between your conscience and your mission. How the game ends depends on your choices.

Beat Cop (PC, Mac, iOS, Android, PlayStation 4, Xbox One or Nintendo Switch) is a police crime drama where you have been framed for murder. Back on the street you navigate the pixilated 1980s *Miami Vice* world to find out who did it. Your approach and decisions matter. Will you go in with the mafia or stay straight? Your choices determine the narrative and ending.

THIS WAR OF MINE

Inspired by the 1992—96 Siege of Sarajevo, this is a war game where you play the civilian trying to survive during the fighting. You face tough decisions on how to spend time and resources each day to maintain health, hunger and mood levels until a ceasefire is declared. At night you must venture out to gather materials and food. The experience is intensified with *The Little Ones* version, which includes children to look after.

It's a chance to experience the near-impossibility of survival and making the right decisions in these situations, doing the best you can with limited resources.

Rating:
PEGI: 18 with extreme violence and strong language
ESRB: MATURE 17+ with blood, mild sexual themes, strong language, use of alcohol and tobacco, and violence

Player(s): 1

Duration:
The main game takes around 14 hours to complete, although repeated play-throughs are warranted to see different characters and outcomes.

Ingredients:
- PC, Mac, Android, iOS, PlayStation 4, Xbox One or Nintendo Switch.
- The game itself.
- *The Little Ones* optional expansion content, which can be bought with the game or purchased as downloadable content on PC, Mac, iOS and Android.

Serving Suggestions:
Play the game yourself before sharing with older teenagers or other appropriately aged family members. Once you understand the civilian wartime narrative, together you can make choices about how to use your resources and prioritise your time. *The Little Ones* expansion extends these concerns to the needs of children as you have to choose between play, loving contact, sleep, medicine, food and protection for them.

   Discussing which risks are the right ones to take, and how to spend your meagre resources, not only brings home the stark reality of war but can also balance more frivolous use of this setting with other video games like *Fortnite* or *Call of Duty*.

To Follow:
Spec Ops: The Line (PC, Mac, PlayStation 3 or Xbox 360) is unusual in that you still play the powerful soldier, but as the narrative unfolds the impact of war and violence on the soldier's psyche, and the hard choices they must make, is brought home in surprising ways.

Frostpunk (PC, PlayStation 4 or Xbox One) is a city-building survival game set in an alternate 1886 with a devastating winter setting in. You are tasked with running a city by managing resources to ensure the city's survival. Your choices can have negative and positive consequences.

PHOTOGRAPHS – PUZZLE STORIES

Solve different puzzles to advance the lives of five different people: Olympic swimmer, botanist, reporter, settler and time-travelling wizard. Each life evolves as a miniature diorama where you zoom in, search for and photograph clues, and solve puzzles to move things forward. But things don't go to plan, in heartbreaking and sometimes shocking ways. By the end of the game you are deeply connected to each person and have to make a near-impossible decision between which of the tragic endings to change for the better.

The decision you have to make is hard because you've got to know each person's family and life. How do you choose which of your friends to save when you've been a part of their downfall?

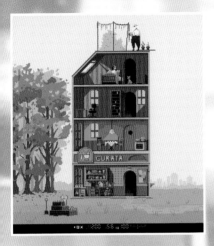

We had a lot of free time, and
we made the most of it

Rating:
PEGI: 18 with extreme violence
ESRB: TEEN with violence and blood

Player(s): 1

Duration: It takes about 45 minutes to play each of the five stories in the game, and 10 minutes to play the epilogue. Total time will vary but most will complete within 4 hours.

Ingredients:

- iOS or Android tablet or smartphone.
- The game itself.

Serving Suggestions:
As the rating suggests, this is a game for adults and older teenagers that shouldn't be taken lightly. However, for a family of the appropriate age and maturity, it's a compelling way to encounter the difficult subjects of suicide and self-harm together. Play this on separate devices and discuss the experience as you progress. Then, in the end, you will inevitably make a different choice about which of the characters to save in the game. The subject matter is violent and it's depicted graphically, but like a mature film, this enables players to reflect and think deeply about hard decisions.

To Follow:
Bioshock (PC, Mac, PlayStation 3, PlayStation 4, Xbox One or Xbox 360) is a first-person shooting game set in a fantastical underwater city. A dark story unfolds about the misuse of surgery and gene therapy. Players must make a decision about whether to save the children they find or harvest their energy for the greater good.

In *FTL: Faster Than Light* (PC, Mac or iOS) you command a spaceship tasked with saving the federation. You make choices about things like how to equip your ship, which crew you send out on missions and how to deal with slave traders. The constant pressure to survive makes each choice fraught with tension.

LIFE IS STRANGE

This is a click/tap-to-move adventure where you play Max, a high-school student in a sleepy American town. Despite the idyllic setting, you have a foreboding premonition of a disastrous storm. Along with this prophetic vision, you discover the ability to rewind time. As the game unfolds through relationships with friends, parents and teachers, you must decide how to treat the people around you. An intriguing mystery develops along with some substantial teen angst, mental health and identity issues.

The choices you make change the story in ways you can see, and, if you so choose, you can rewind and change. At the end of each chapter, you can compare your decisions to other players'.

Rating:
PEGI: 16 with violence, drugs and bad language
ESRB: MATURE 17+ with blood, intense violence, sexual themes, strong language, and use of drugs and alcohol

Player(s): 1

Duration: It takes up to 3 hours to complete each of the 5 episodes, bringing the completion time to 15 hours. To find everything in the game and experiment with alternate choices can take over 25 hours.

Ingredients:
- PC, Mac, Android, iOS, PlayStation 3, PlayStation 4, Xbox One or Xbox 360.
- The game itself.
- On mobile devices, you can download the next chapter ahead of time so you can continue playing on the go.

Serving Suggestions:
Playing the game with a few members of your family, each on different devices, results in a different story for each player. After each chapter you can compare your major and minor progress on the 'Choices' menu. Ask each other what motivated those decisions, and how that affects what sort of character Max is, and who you want her to be.

To Follow:
Walking Dead (PC, Mac, iOS, Android, PlayStation 3, PlayStation 4, PlayStation Vita, Xbox One, Xbox 360 or Nintendo Switch) is a survival adventure game. You explore locations and gather a ragtag group of survivors. How you interact with each of them and make decisions about various dangers results in a branching story where no one is guaranteed to survive.

The Banner Saga (PC, Mac, iOS, Android, Xbox One, PlayStation 4 or Nintendo Switch) is a beautiful fantasy adventure where your strategic choices directly affect your personal story and the world around you.

DETROIT: BECOME HUMAN

A futuristic adventure game played from the intersecting perspectives of three androids, a police investigator, a housekeeper and a caretaker. In different ways, these characters deviate from their programming. To what extent, and how this unfolds, is determined by time-limited decisions made by you. It's even possible for some of the protagonists to die, and the story continues without them.

The combination of a photorealistic video game, a hugely branching narrative and well-observed characterisation makes each choice feel important, with large or small consequences.

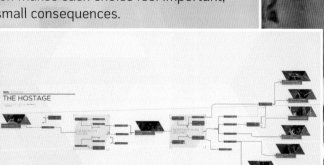

Rating:
PEGI: 18 with violence and bad language

ESRB: MATURE 17+ with blood, intense violence, partial nudity, sexual themes, strong language and use of drugs

Player(s): 1

Duration: It can take 14 hours to finish one play-through of the story. However, to see more endings and every aspect of the game will require multiple plays and up to 30 hours.

Ingredients:
- PC or PlayStation 4.
- The game itself.

Serving Suggestions:
This is a game for adults in the family. Although designed to be single-player, it is an engaging experience to play in small groups. In a group of three, each person can play chapters for a particular main character — either Connor, Kara and Markus. Some decisions are time-bound and will need to be quickly chosen by the player, while others you can discuss. You can view how the story is branching in the timeline and decide to go back and change certain things for a different outcome.

To Follow:
Heavy Rain (PC, PlayStation 3 or PlayStation 4) and *Beyond: Two Souls* (PC, PlayStation 3 or PlayStation 4) are similar games from the same developer as *Detroit: Become Human*. The first focuses on the loss of a child and the price a parent will pay to get them back. The other is about a teenager who discovers she has a supernatural power. Both offer a deep, movie-like narrative that diverges in meaningful ways.

Fable 2 (Xbox One or Xbox 360) is an adventure role-playing game where your interactions with the world and villagers, and decisions about your use of magical power, substantially alter the story and the environment.

SOLVE A MYSTERY

Like a good crime drama or whodunnit novel, solving mysteries and puzzles is a good way to engage in a story. However, rather than just watching these mysteries while someone else does the heavy lifting, these video games place you firmly in the role of the detective. Gathering statements, sifting evidence and making intelligent leaps of deduction require care and attention. These investigations makes these games slower than others, but it's worth the effort each time you find the correct conclusion and move the story on.

These games present you with a mysterious scenario to be solved. Whether with direct puzzles, locations to investigate or crime scenarios to deduce, they offer a unique, first-hand sleuthing challenge.

THIS SECTION INCLUDES THE FOLLOWING GAMES

Return of the Obra Dinn
Her Story
Firewatch
Aviary Attorney
What Remains of Edith Finch
Heaven's Vault
Portal

RETURN OF THE OBRA DINN

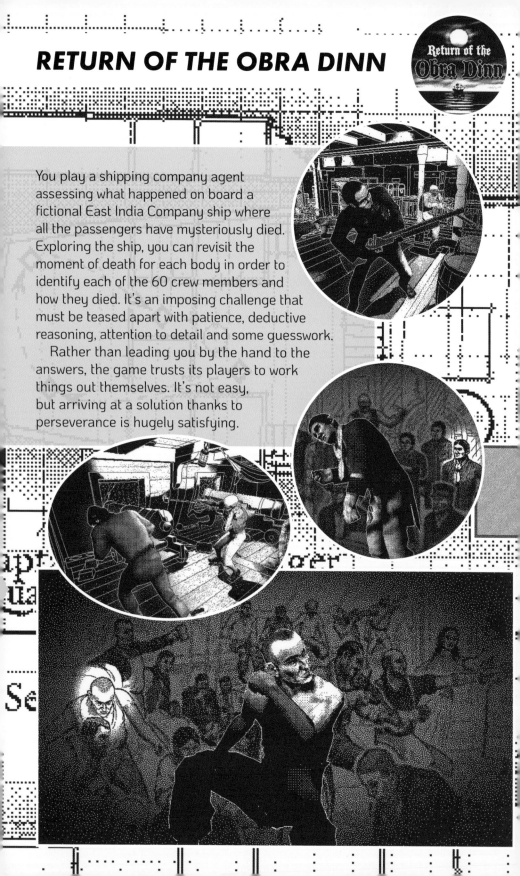

You play a shipping company agent assessing what happened on board a fictional East India Company ship where all the passengers have mysteriously died. Exploring the ship, you can revisit the moment of death for each body in order to identify each of the 60 crew members and how they died. It's an imposing challenge that must be teased apart with patience, deductive reasoning, attention to detail and some guesswork.

Rather than leading you by the hand to the answers, the game trusts its players to work things out themselves. It's not easy, but arriving at a solution thanks to perseverance is hugely satisfying.

Rating:
PEGI: 16 with violence
ESRB: MATURE 17+ with blood, intense violence, language and partial nudity

Player(s): 1

Duration: It's possible to solve the game in 6 hours, although 11 hours is more likely, depending on how good you are at making connections and deducing solutions.

Ingredients:
- PC, Mac, PlayStation 4, Xbox One or Nintendo Switch.
- Pen and paper to take notes.
- The game itself.

Serving Suggestions:
Although there is violence in the game, its black-and-white visuals and static scenes make this more palatable than you'd think. If you have someone in the family who loves solving puzzles or won't stop until the crossword is finished, this is a great game to play with them. Like an Arthur Conan Doyle or Agatha Christie novel, the joy comes from knitting together the clues and making instinctive leaps of deduction.

One family I know played this over one long evening, into the night, treating it like a murder mystery party, complete with themed food and beverages. One of the players took it upon themselves to take notes while together they worked through the evidence of each death to discover what happened on board the ship.

To Follow:
Ghost Trick: Phantom Detective (Nintendo DS or iOS) is a game where you play a ghost that can stop time to solve crimes and save lives. You can inhabit and control objects and possess corpses to alter what happens. The puzzles are mind-bending to solve, but it's the unique way of gaining first-hand insight into the overarching narrative, by living through the eyes of the strong range of characters, that makes this game stand out.

Everybody's Gone to the Rapture (PC or PlayStation 4) lands you in a fictional deserted English village in 1984. As you walk the streets of another era you discover bright human forms who re-enact events like a radio play. Through their eyes you see a web of fear, conspiracy and humdrum disagreements, and piece together the story of the inhabitants' disappearance.

Observation (PC or PlayStation 4) puts you on a space station to solve a power outage and find missing crew. However, here you play the role of the SAM, the System Administration Maintenance artificial intelligence software, rather than human protagonist. Your limited view, due to panning cameras and restricted interactions, makes this both unusual and intentionally creepy.

HER STORY

Solve the 1994 mystery of a murdered man by searching an old police computer archive of interview videos of his wife. The game presents a retro computer interface but the interviews themselves are short films with real actors. Although there are only seven films, they are fragmented into short tapes. Each clip uncovers more events and characters that can be used to search the computer database for further interview segments. It starts as a simple task of observation but becomes a challenge of noticing links and inconsistencies, then figuring out the correct words and phrases to search for specific clips.

The mystery is powerfully compelling because all the information is available if you know what to search for. The forensic search of this historic data is hugely satisfying as the true story finally emerges.

Rating:
PEGI: 16 with strong language
ESRB: MATURE 17+ with sexual themes and strong language

Player(s): 1

Duration: You can solve and complete the main story in about 4 hours, but to see everything in the game will take upwards of 8 hours.

Ingredients:
- Mac, PC, iOS or Android.
- Pen and paper to take notes.
- The game itself.

Serving Suggestions:
Playing this game with another person works well. One of you drives the game, typing in search phrases to find videos, while the other takes notes. Identifying links between the timeline, characters and events that took place requires both players' attention. Playing the investigator — as we frequently see on TV shows — leads to interesting discussions about fact, fiction and how events are remembered, recorded and decoded.

To Follow:

Another Lost Phone (iOS, Android or Nintendo Switch) places a stranger's smartphone in your hands. As you use the phone interface to explore the social life of its young owner, Laura, you piece together messages, pictures and profiles to solve her disappearance. It includes suggestive themes and strong language, and requires maturity and consideration to solve.

Telling Lies (PC, Mac, iOS, PlayStation 4, Xbox One or Nintendo Switch) is another game from the same developer as *Her Story*. The technology is more advanced, along with the number and quality of the acted videos, but the way you solve the mystery is the same.

Black Mirror: Bandersnatch (Netflix) takes the interactive mystery genre a step further towards a traditional TV series. You watch it on your television but make decisions for the characters, which then branches the narrative. With 150 minutes to watch in 250 segments and five main endings, you need to pay attention to what you're doing.

FIREWATCH

You work in Shoshone National Forest, a year after the Yellowstone fires of 1988. Communicating via walkie-talkie, your supervisor, Julia, leads you to investigate the ransacking of your lookout tower, while a shadowy figure appears to be observing you from a distance. As you explore the beautiful Yellowstone forest and guide the conversation with Julia, more loose ends and questions are raised. But your focus is as much on what motivated the characters you've met — escapism, dementia, memory and the need for fresh air — as on what's happened.

The game isn't a tidy puzzle, instead embracing the mess of life and relationships, but the pieces fit together well enough to invite multiple play-throughs.

Rating:
PEGI: 16 with sex and bad
language
ESRB: MATURE 17+ with
suggestive themes, nudity, drug
and alcohol reference, and strong
language

Player(s): 1

Duration: You can complete the
main story in about 5 hours. If
you want to explore further, it will
take you about 10 hours to see
everything.

Ingredients:

- PC, Mac, PlayStation 4, Xbox
  One or Nintendo Switch.
- The game itself.

Serving Suggestions:
This is a game many people choose
to play as a solitary experience.
The vast Shoshone National Forest
lends itself to this, along with the
personal story that unfolds. As with
other exploration games, you need
to embrace the slow pace, from
walking and lingering dialogue.
This makes it better to play over a
couple of evenings rather than rush
through in a single sitting.

To Follow:
Gone Home (PC, Mac, iOS, Xbox One, PlayStation 4 or Nintendo Switch)
places you in the role of Katie, returning from overseas to her family home.
But the house is deserted, and by exploring the rooms, you piece together
what happened to her sister, Sam. It's a mystery to solve, but a common one
of family disagreements, identity and sexual preferences.

Night in the Woods (PC, Mac, iOS, Android, PlayStation 4, Xbox One or
Nintendo Switch) follows college dropout Mae Borowski returning home
to the crumbling former mining town of Possum Springs. But the place
is different now her friends have grown and changed. There's something
suspicious happening in the nearby woods. Investigating reveals not only a
mysterious cult but Mae's broken friendships and dissociation from life.

AVIARY ATTORNEY

Aviary Attorney

A courtroom drama set in nineteenth-century Paris, populated with beautifully drawn animals. Guiding JayJay Falcon, defence attorney, you help investigate each case before each of the four court dates, combing crime scenes, interrogating suspects and gathering evidence ready to pull out during cross-examination. Things get more involved, with limited time to collect everything you need. The writing, animal characters and backing music create a fantasy world that's a joy to explore. The different endings are pleasingly varied and offer a chance for the characters we now know well to reflect on what justice really is.

Solving each mystery and winning the cases is hugely satisfying, but it's the culmination of the four acts into a single story of murder, spying and (of course) revolution that make this really stand out.

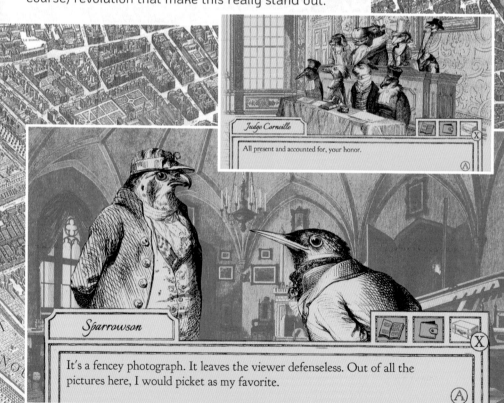

Judge Corneille

All present and accounted for, your honor.

Sparrowson

It's a fencey photograph. It leaves the viewer defenseless. Out of all the pictures here, I would picket as my favorite.

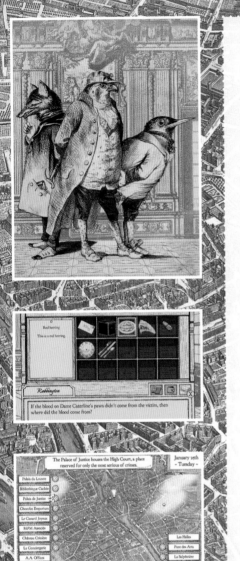

Rating:
PEGI: 12 with mild swearing, moderate violence and simulated gambling
ESRB: TEEN with blood, language, simulated gambling, use of alcohol, tobacco and violence

Player(s): 1

Duration:
You can complete all 4 cases in less than 6 hours. Those who want to explore every avenue of investigation will take this towards the 10-hour mark.

Ingredients:
- PC, Mac or Nintendo Switch.
- The game itself.

Serving Suggestions:
As a game of observation and deduction, this is good to play in a family group. There is a considerable amount of reading to do, and some families have found it helpful for older members to take turns reading out the text of different characters. With this hurdle out of the way, players of all ages can contribute to solving each crime. There is violence in the game, directed towards animal characters rather than humans.

To Follow:
Phoenix Wright: Ace Attorney (PC, iOS, Android, Xbox One, Nintendo DS, Nintendo 3DS, Nintendo Wii or Nintendo Switch) is a courtroom murder mystery series where you piece together clues to challenge testimonies and uncover the truth. It's like a visual novel, although you must interact with characters and evidence to progress.

The Secret of Monkey Island (Mac, PC, iOS, PlayStation 3 or Xbox 360) is a classic tongue-in-cheek pirate adventure game. You click or tap the screen to explore locations, find items and complete puzzles. Playing a young man, Guybrush Threepwood, with a dream of being a pirate, you become embroiled in a kidnap rescue. Using intuition, guesswork and an eye for absurd comedy, you must solve the mystery of the island and save the day.

WHAT REMAINS OF EDITH FINCH

Edith Finch is the surviving member of the Finch family, who seem to have died from a curse. In first-person perspective, you return to the family's coastal home to learn about each relative's final hours by exploring their rooms in turn. Each character's story unfolds uniquely in the style of a fable. Exploring every inch of the intricately detailed, cluttered and lived-in house builds a picture of the family that lived here. Sifting fact from fiction is no easy task as the family's memorialisation of events is often unreliable.

The pieces fit together like a mystery and the house itself holds all this together beautifully, but really the game is a chance to reflect on how families tell their story of home, childhood and parenting. It revels in the glorious peculiarity of life and how we must embrace all of it to be fully alive.

Rating:
PEGI: 16 with strong violence
ESRB: TEEN with violence, blood, drug reference and language

Player(s): 1

Duration: You can complete the story in 3 hours and see everything in about 6 hours.

Ingredients:
- PC, PlayStation 4, Xbox One or Nintendo Switch.
- The game itself.

Serving Suggestions:
Playing the game with older children — particularly those back after leaving home — works well with the game's theme of individuals returning to their childhood home with fresh eyes. As you play you can question who has the right to say what really happened when the children were growing up, and how these stories will be different for each of us.

To Follow:

In *Dear Esther* (PC, Mac, PlayStation 4 or Xbox One) you explore an uninhabited Hebridean island while an old man reads a series of letters to his eponymous deceased wife. Themes of love, loss, guilt and redemption intertwine with the bleak geography and orchestral music. As you explore the derelict remains of buildings, shipwrecks and caves, you find a story that must be interpreted to make sense.

Tacoma (PC, Mac, PlayStation 4 or Xbox One) is set aboard a space station in the year 2088. As you explore and discover how the station's crew lived and worked, using an AR device that lets you review past actions and conversations, you discover clues that unravel a plot of trust, fear and resolve in the face of disaster.

HEAVEN'S VAULT

HEAVEN'S VAULT

In *Heaven's Vault* you play an archaeologist translating an ancient alien language, the decrypting of which weaves through an unfolding drama. While doing real linguistic work you interact with companions and locals. Your choices can open or close vast swathes of investigative opportunities. In turn, this directs the branching narrative in different ways. Intelligent guesswork is required to translate a large number of inscriptions while deciphering the motivations of those around you. An ingenious timeline documents every move, and a brief synopsis each time you start playing keeps things accessible even to infrequent players.

It's a unique and meticulous mystery-solving experience, worth playing not only for a branching story and interactive puzzles, but for how much it trusts and empowers the player to follow (unless they get side-tracked) the complex and mature narrative.

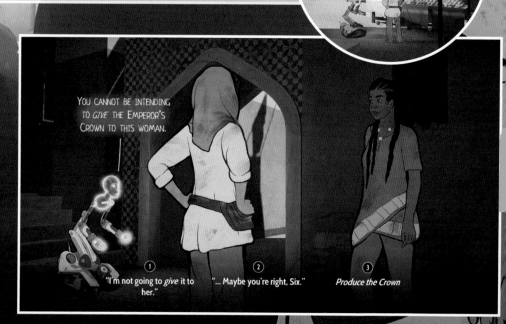

Rating:
PEGI: 12 with suggestive themes
ESRB: TEEN with suggestive themes

Player(s): 1

Duration: The time to finish the game varies greatly because of its diverging nature but is around 18 hours. To linger and see everything, or replay to experience different avenues or missed characters, will take considerably longer.

Ingredients:
- PC, PlayStation 4 or Nintendo Switch.
- The game itself.

Serving Suggestions:
To avid gamers in your household, this game can at first seem slow and laborious. However, spending regular time with the game opens up a deep and mature story about history, religions, memory and language. Families have found this a calming game to play together in the evening. The slow filling of the timeline and detailed work of deciphering words add welcome texture to the more common world-exploration and dialogue decisions. The dialogue and lore make it feel like an epic novel that requires patience and perseverance, but you are rewarded with a unique experience at the forefront of what games can be.

To Follow:
Outer Wilds (PC, Mac or Xbox One) is an exploration space mystery about a solar system trapped in an endless time-loop. After 20 minutes of game time, you must start again — but each time brings a new opportunity to learn how you ended up on the planet and solve the secrets of who built the strange galaxy. As you do so, the world evolves and opens up new secrets.

The Witness (PC, iOS, PlayStation 4, Xbox One or Nvidia Shield) combines maze puzzles in an abandoned world with its own mythology, secrets, themes and story. It's a game with puzzles at the core, but the real mystery is solving what has happened in the world you find yourself in.

You are in a science laboratory where you seem to be being tested. Watched by the artificial intelligence GLaDOS, you have a gun that can create a pair of magic portals on any surface: one is an entrance and the other is an exit. Through a series of increasingly ingenious (and malicious) test chambers, you must use your gun to escape. It's a mind-bending challenge, but the real interest is the darkening tone of GLaDOS, who seems bent on foiling your progress, and the signs of previous test subjects spotted behind the scenes. As GLaDOS's dysfunction turns to straight-up sociopathy, you must take on challenges with her tormenting discouragement ringing in your ears. The isolation is heightened by the introduction of a lifeless companion cube, which mocks your friendless predicament.

Portal is a series of puzzles that you solve with physics and lateral thinking. But behind the puzzles is the bigger mystery of where you are, and what these tests are for.

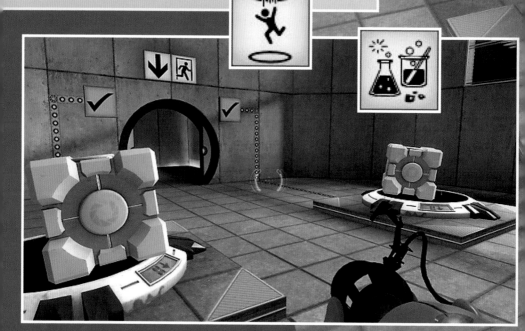

Rating:
PEGI: 12 with violence
ESRB: TEEN with blood and mild violence

Player(s): 1

Duration: To complete the puzzles and get to the end of the game takes around 3 hours, but to see everything requires at least 8 hours.

Ingredients:
- PC, Mac, Android, PlayStation 3, Xbox One or Xbox 360.
- The game itself — either *Portal* or *Portal: Still Alive,* which adds 14 new test chambers.

Serving Suggestions:
Played together as a family, you can take turns on the controls and help each other to solve the mentally stretching physics problems. As the game develops, though, players start to hypothesise on the relationship between the test subject and the corporation. Then in later levels you can stray behind the scenes of the laboratory and discover more about other test subjects. Some care is warranted for youngsters as, although no harm befalls you, it increasingly feels like a horror game with the creepy malevolence of your computer overseer.

To Follow:
Portal 2 (PC, Mac, PlayStation 3, Xbox One or Xbox 360) continues the stories and introduces two-player puzzles. You return to the test chambers and again there is a focus on relationships. This time a floating droid named Wheatley (voiced by Stephen Merchant) guides you through the old test chambers in an attempt to escape, although in so doing accidentally reactivates the dormant GLaDOS.

The three *Luigi's Mansion* games (Nintendo 3DS, Nintendo Gamecube or Nintendo Switch) each challenge you to investigate a haunted mansion. As longstanding Nintendo character Luigi, you play a ghostbuster to capture various mischievous ghouls. The puzzles are beautifully intricate and a satisfying mystery to solve for all ages.

IMAGE CREDITS

A NOTE ON THE AUTHOR

Andy Robertson has been helping families get more from video games for over fifteen years. As a freelance journalist for the *Guardian* and *Forbes*, and broadcaster for the BBC, his pioneering perspective balances the needs of the child and the opportunities of this new medium of video games. Andy's work takes him into homes, schools, theatres, arts festivals and even churches to explore what video games have to offer. He has lived in Exeter with his family of five for the last twenty years.

You can find out more on the website that supports this book. This includes videos, podcasts and a huge, searchable database of video games for your family: www.taminggaming.com

Andy is always keen to hear from parents and carers making the journey into video games. You can contact him via Twitter (@GeekDadGamer) or email at andy@taminggaming.com

Unbound is the world's first crowdfunding publisher, established in 2011.

We believe that wonderful things can happen when you clear a path for people who share a passion. That's why we've built a platform that brings together readers and authors to crowdfund books they believe in – and give fresh ideas that don't fit the traditional mould the chance they deserve.

This book is in your hands because readers made it possible. Everyone who pledged their support is listed below. Join them by visiting unbound.com and supporting a book today.

The Allen Family

Samantha Amos

Lene Amrein

Apricot Centre

Oriana Ascanio

atelier198

Guha Bala

Chris Baldwin

Seth Bandy

Dan Barrett

Ed Barton

Kenza Benchiheb

Nikki Bennett Ms.

Alex Bertie

Ryan Bickham

Ed Bird

Sarah Bird

Paul Booth

Charlotte Buchanan

James Butler

Tom Butterworth

Zach Carpenter

Ann Carrier

Andrea Castello

Gemma Church

Adam Clarke

Steve Comerie

Paul Compernolle

Helen Cordery

Claire Corry

Steve Cosslett

Kevin Craig

Curiscope

Jon Curtis

Mark DeLoura

Drew Dixon

Cariad Eccleston

Henrik Edlund

Amy Ellison

Helen Evans

Dan Fairs

Steven Farrier

Paul Ford

John Forrest

Jane Freeman

Andy Frost

Lee Gallon

Stephen Garner

Rebecca Gentle

Helen Georgallidis

Lucy Gill

Richard Gillin

Andrew Gilmour

Sharon Goble

Mark Goody

Diana Graber

Joe Greenwood

Simon Greenwood

Chris Grieves

Geoff Gunning

Gareth Gwynne

Anne Haas

Daniel Hammond

Joseph Hammond

Jon Hancock

Alex Hansford

Rich Hanson

Russell Harding

Stuart Harrison

Gareth Harwood

Peter Haslehurst

Cole Henley

Monica Hernandez-Alava

Alison Hilborne

Ilaria Hipps

Philip Hirst

Matthew Honeyman

Toby Howden

Anthony Hudson

Ben Hunt

iNet Guardian

Internet Matters

Frances Jaggard

Nickie Jane

Ali Johnston

Alastair Jones

Martin Kelly

Claire Kennedy

Dan Kieran

M Knight

Helene Kreysa

Jacqueline Labrie

Cara LaForge

William Laitinen

Tom Layton

Namhyung Lee

Bex Lewis

James Lloyd

Amy Lockwood

Jordan Loewen

Lucy Lord (James' and
   Michael's Mum)

Adrianne Lowe

Tim M

Alex Mackey

Jessica Magill

Jon Martindale

Jon Mason

Jonathan Massey

Kyle Matthews

Jess McBeath

Caz McCrone

Karen Mcgillion

Tony McNicol

Me and you and a dog named....
   who??

Paul Meager

Carlos Merino Gracia

Veronique Mertes

Karl Meyer

Steven Miller

Matthew Millsap

Bryan Mitchell

John Mitchinson

Fiona Moncur

Adam Moran

Andy Morris

MovieStarPlanet

Matt Mustafic

Carlo Navato

Chi Lang Ngo

Hazel Nicholson

Iain Nisbet

Charlie Nixon

Nici Nixon

Scott Novis

Poppy O'Neill

Chris O'Shea

Ryan Oliver

Jamie Parkes

John Parkinson

Douglas Paterson

Graeme Patfield

Fabrizio Pedrazzini

Piarella Peralta

Toby Pestridge

Vanessa Pestridge

Anna Pickard

Lloyd Pietersen

Justyna Płatek

Justin Pollard

Thayer Prime

Valerie Proctor

Jennifer Protheroe

James Putnam

Robert Quigley

Sarah Race

Nathan Raymond

Bruno Reddy

Simon Rée

Jonathan Reedy

Ben Rees

Ian Rice

Leslie Richards

Alison Ridout

Sarah Ridout

Stacey Riley

Rick and Chantal Robertson

Dan Robinson

Roland Rogers

Adam Rosser

Denisse Rudich

Shahneila Saeed

Lucy Sainsbury

Alison Salm

Marshall Sandoval-Clark

Sam Sayer

Daniel Schmidt

Kevin Schut

Sensible Object

Shout Youth Group –
    Wellington Baptist Church

Jeff Skalski

Brian Smith

Malcolm Smith

Simon Smith

Thomas M. Smith

Ben Sommers

Chris Squire

St Albans Diocesan Youth
    Service

Katie Stanley

Rebecca Stirrup

Karl Straw

Sammy Sturzaker

Julia Sutherland

Stephen Swindley

Erdinc Tarakci

Jay Tholen

Martin Thompson

Pam Thompson

Shelley Thorne

Paul Thorp

Laura Tort

John Tracey

Rob Treacher

Trinity CofE VA Primary and
Nursery School

Madeline Turnipseed

Simon Uden

Brooke Van Dusen

Tye Van Horn

Mark Vent

Video Standards Council (VSC)

Göran Wallgren

Gill Wallis

Sam Watkins

Marieke Westerterp

Nathan Whitbread

Timothy White

Daniel Williams

Mark Wills

Scott Windels

Daniel Wood

Sally Woodhouse

Ido Yehieli

All the wonderful staff at
YMCA Exeter

With grateful thanks to the generous support of the following patrons, without whose major support this book would not have been possible.